3/16

PALE

HORSE

JIMMY BLACKMON

PALE HORSE

HUNTING TERRORISTS AND COMMANDING HEROES WITH THE 101ST AIRBORNE DIVISION

ST. MARTIN'S PRESS
NEW YORK

PALE HORSE. Copyright © 2016 by Jimmy Blackmon. Foreword copyright © 2016 by Stanley A. McChrystal. All rights reserved. Printed in the United States of America. For information, address St. Martin's Press, 175 Fifth Avenue, New York, N.Y. 10010.

www.stmartins.com

Designed by Jonathan Bennett

Map courtesy of the Institute for the Study of War. Photographs by Jimmy Blackmon.

The Library of Congress Cataloging-in-Publication Data is available upon request.

ISBN 978-1-250-07271-9 (hardcover)
ISBN 978-1-4668-8457-1 (e-book)

Our books may be purchased in bulk for promotional, educational, or business use. Please contact your local bookseller or Macmillan Corporate and Premium Sales Department at 1-800-221-7945, extension 5442, or by e-mail at MacmillanSpecialMarkets@macmillan.com.

First Edition: March 2016

10 9 8 7 6 5 4 3 2 1

CONTENTS

AND I LOOKED, AND BEHOLD A
PALE HORSE: AND HIS NAME
THAT SAT ON HIM WAS DEATH,
AND HELL FOLLOWED WITH HIM.

—REVELATION 6:8

FOREWORD

While war is often pictured as the clash of mighty armies with columns of tanks rumbling across vast open spaces, it is often much different. In eastern Afghanistan in 2008–2009, U.S. forces defended small outposts in an effort to bring stability to long-contested border regions within Kunar and Nuristan provinces, home to a dense mix of hard-core Taliban and al Qaeda fighters. American soldiers fought ferocious gun battles from these lonely combat outposts stretched thinly within deep valleys that were often flanked by towering mountain masses. It was not a new kind of war. It was the complex, lethal intersection of politics, terrain, weapons, and humans that has been the burden of warriors for millennia.

In Afghanistan's most recent war, to survive in these brutal conditions, soldiers often looked skyward. The pulsating throb of rotor blades became a comforting sound as the air cavalry warriors of Task Force Pale Horse repeatedly flew into narrow valleys or along rocky hillsides to provide lethal firepower to the soldiers below or to deliver critical supplies and reinforcements. Often they were called into "hot" helicopter landing zones to rescue the wounded and evacuate the dead. Their efforts reflected a deep commitment to support the soldiers on the ground at all costs.

While most histories of warfare describe combat from the perspective of the soldiers on the ground, often recounted many years after the guns fall silent by those who themselves never tasted combat, *Task Force Pale Horse* is unique in the telling. Based on the meticulous journal entries he kept while in command, Jimmy Blackmon paints a stunningly vivid portrait of the rugged beauty that defines

Afghanistan: an incongruous backdrop for the vicious fighting that would come to define the task force's yearlong deployment. Vibrant with the emotions and passions that accompany soldiers in combat, it chronicles the triumphs and personal tragedies of the men and women of Task Force Pale Horse. Viewed through the lens of a combat aviator, it is a story of unhesitating courage and compassion from those who flew and fought from the air to defend those who served on the ground.

The soldiers of Task Force Pale Horse came from every walk of life and every corner of America. The sons and daughters of bankers and farmers, of doctors and deliverymen alike, they were all volunteers, some of whom watched the Twin Towers collapse in New York City on September 11, 2001, and resolved in that instant to leave the lives they had known to join the military. Regardless of their upbringing or station in life, the common denominator among them all was a passion to serve their country in its time of need. Their devotion to each other and to the rough warriors they defended would be tested time and again in places both known and unfamiliar to the average American, places such as outposts Keating and Lowell, Bari Ali and Honaker-Miracle, and valleys made famous by the heroes who fought there, such as the Korengal and Shuryak, the Watapur and Ganjgal.

The soldiers of Task Force Pale Horse were not extraordinary because other men made them so; they were extraordinary by their own actions, often taken at great risk to their own lives. Reinforcing a climate and culture within Task Force Pale Horse of implicit trust in the judgment and decision-making of the pilots on mission, Jimmy Blackmon empowered his soldiers—regardless of rank or position—to find new and innovative solutions to complex problems—exactly the types of problems soldiers encountered every time they flew into the valleys. This approach to leadership unleashed the potential of the most junior soldier and earned Task Force Pale Horse the admiration and respect of the soldiers they served.

In the end, *Pale Horse* is a fascinating window into combat on the most viscerally human level and a moving tribute to the brave men and women who fought. Though their overall mission in Afghanistan served a higher purpose, they ultimately fought and bled for each other and for the soldiers fighting for their lives below. As Jimmy might say, they would do it all over again despite the risks, the personal sacrifices, and the burdens many still carry to this day. This is their story.

—GENERAL (RET.) STANLEY A. MCCHRYSTAL

PREFACE

Suddenly I was awake. The only visible light in my plywood stall was the glowing red numbers on the clock across the room—4:03 A.M. Having just lain down, I wondered how that was possible. I had flown a reconnaissance mission in a helicopter the previous night and as we began to work our way back toward Jalalabad Airfield, just south of the city of Mehtar Lam, the enemy opened fire on us with machine guns. It was a DShK—a big 12.7-mm Soviet antiaircraft gun that the enemy often used against us. We knew when it was a DShk because of the deep thud it made when it fired, versus the crack or pop of smaller-caliber weapons. The sound of that thud sent a surge of adrenaline flooding through our veins and chills down our spines. Our helicopters could absorb a few small-arms rounds, but a DShK could bring us down in seconds.

The bullets cracked in the air as they passed by the aircraft just under the rotors, barely missing us. The event was dismally common; nevertheless, my heart rate increased and my mouth went dry. I was still jittery when I landed back at the airfield, realizing that my life had been spared by mere feet. It had been a night mission, so I didn't get to bed until 1:30 A.M. I lay in bed for what seemed like hours, exhausted yet struggling to fall asleep. Three hours later I lay awake with thoughts of the mission, the deployment, still running through my mind.

I sat up in bed, swung my body around, and placed my feet on the dusty Afghan rug. Head in my hands and elbows on my knees, I thought, might as well go for a run.

I stepped into a moonlit night on the four-mile perimeter road that circled our base. As I ran I wondered what my family, over seven thousand miles away, might be doing at this hour. I had spent three of the previous five years deployed to either Iraq or Afghanistan. It was baseball season at home; I tried to think about something else because it hurt too badly to visualize a double play and an empty seat in the bleachers. In wars past, communication traveled at the speed of the U.S. mail system. With Internet access I was able to see pictures and communicate with emails daily—a constant reminder of what and whom I was missing. We called it a blessing, but it was a painful blessing. I found it strange that something as unnatural as repetitive combat tours could somehow become a way of life that I considered normal. It was absurd, yet true.

Our forward operating base, FOB Fenty, sat just on the eastern side of Jalalabad, which was quiet at that time of the morning. I didn't see a single person during my run, which suited me. The days, and most of the nights, were filled with activity. I was always planning missions, rehearsing missions, or flying missions. As I ran, all alone in the darkness, I felt free of everything else in the world. I was completely alone with my thoughts. It felt good to escape.

I finished my run on the flight line, drenched in sweat. In the east, just above the small, run-down airport terminal, the sky was beginning to grow pink with light. But it would be a while before the sun climbed above the mountains just north of the Khyber Pass.

Suddenly, the morning quiet was pierced by a high-pitched tone: *"Allahu Akbar! Allahu Akbar!"* The *adhan,* or morning call to prayer, emanated from a minaret to the east of the airfield. Within seconds another voice rang out at a mosque to the west. The pitch and tempo of the muezzins' voices varied, giving an otherwise identical call to prayer a refreshing uniqueness. As local Muslims unrolled rugs and prepared themselves for prayer, I headed to my office to read the daily intelligence summary and check emails, trying to remember what day it was.

Days like this were not uncommon. The war had a way of forcing introspection, reminding us of how fragile life is. Close misses were exciting—to find out your number was not yet called was invigorating. But those moments, while usually tucked away in a distant compartment of the mind, almost always returned. Later, when we were alone with our thoughts, each would begin to recall how fortunate we were to have made it through the battle alive, and then the gravity of what we would have left behind, what we would have lost, became a reality.

As I spoke with soldiers about our war experiences, I was amazed at how numerous men in a single battle perceived those same events in vastly different ways. These different perspectives should not have surprised me, as I have studied "the fog of war" in military schools throughout my career, but they certainly did. As I read soldiers' statements, usually written immediately following a battle, I discovered that perceptions varied greatly among those from within the same team, and sometimes between two men in the same helicopter. I concluded that while warfare itself had evolved through the centuries, the fog and friction of combat had endured.

Prior to 2001, the fog and friction of war was nothing more than an academic theory for me; however, after 2001 it was a concept I lived and experienced on a routine basis. No matter how technologically advanced we become, war is, and always will be, a very human endeavor.

War stimulates a broad range of emotions. For the soldier, being so close to death can be shocking, even life-altering, but the fight itself is often thrilling. To pretend that it is not is foolish. Flying into a firefight to support an infantryman in need, machine guns blazing, tracers popping off rocks, and the *whoosh* of a rocket firing out of a pod just three feet from your head is incredibly exhilarating. Ducking, diving, shooting, searching for, and ultimately finding the enemy is an adrenaline rush with which a bungee jump cannot begin to compete. When the mission is over, we watch the infantrymen return to the safety of their outpost. Then as we make one more aerial pass, just to be sure everyone is safely back inside the wire, one of them looks up into the sky and with gratitude waves and gives us a thumbs-up. That feeling, that satisfaction of knowing we made a difference, is worth the risk time and time again. It is impossible to express accurately that feeling, but it is one of the components, if not the chief reason why, we secretly miss combat when we return home. It's intoxicating.

One of my captains, Nathan Longworth, recalled a fight in the Kunar[1] River Valley in which the soldiers on the ground were trapped due to heavy enemy machine gun fire.

Every time we went in for a gun run, the mountainside lit up like a Christmas tree from the enemy firing directly at us. It almost felt like we were invincible. The weather was intense . . . we flew in heavy wind that bounced the helicopter around, clouds covered the surrounding ridgelines, sun setting, and heavy rain to the point I could barely keep an eye on my lead aircraft. Despite the dangerous weather, we felt obligated to stick it out. You felt like brothers to those guys on the ground, a special bond like no other. Hearing gunfire in the background of every radio transmission received from the ground force, you begin to realize that you are the only lifeline to these brothers in arms. Additionally, when you can hear enemy gunshots fired at you, despite the double hearing protection and the rotor noise, it takes the adrenaline to an entirely different level and you begin taking it personal. Breaking station because you are Winchester [out of ammunition] while the ground force is still taking heavy gunfire is gut wrenching. You begin doing things you wouldn't ever think was imaginable (whether it is pushing the limits of weather or firing at the enemy with an assault rifle out the door of the helicopter, etc.). Eventually the enemy fire ceased just prior to sunrise and we headed home. All we could think about was the safety of the ground force until we could make it out there the next day to check on them. That feeling is contagious. Despite the danger, I never felt scared. The army values kick in (duty, loyalty, selfless service, personal courage). We built such a bond with those guys that by Christmas, they created a "Merry Christmas" banner made out of duct tape and an orange signaling panel and held it out for us as we passed by. Of course we landed at the outpost and dropped off some goodies for them on Christmas as well. During their redeployment, they stopped by our troop command post at Jalalabad to share war stories, smoke cigars, and even presented us with a gift.[2]

Yet when one enemy bullet found its mark and a fellow soldier lay dead or mortally wounded, the adrenaline-fueled euphoria quickly transformed into gut-wrenching pain. Silence and disbelief overwhelmed the cockpit. For me it was a cold burning high in my chest—a pain which only time could heal. *No. Please, God, no!* You wanted to do something, somehow bring him back, but the only alternative was reluctant acceptance.

I internalize the pain. I think of how it might feel if the dead soldier were my son, my brother, my father—someone very close to me. And while that only makes the pain worse, makes that burning in my chest almost unbearable, it somehow seems to me . . . appropriate. It's supposed to hurt. Some child lost a parent. A spouse is at home going about her life with no idea that it is about to be ripped apart. A parent who raised a child from birth, who nurtured him, who loved him, should not have to lose him. But war has taken him.

Our task force tactical operations officer, Chief Warrant Officer 4 Gary Parsons, described the pain he felt this way:

> As a battle winds down, my emotions shift back to that sinking feeling; I almost want to puke. It's the aftermath of it all, whether it's our loss or even theirs [enemy], someone is not going home the way they left that morning. I have arrived on the scene only five minutes after an IED went off and I have seen the blood wash down the street from a triple amputee during a rainstorm. I felt sick and helpless, because I knew I would never find the enemy that placed the bomb, but I tried to provide comfort and security to the survivors. It makes me realize how precious life is and how much the infantry expose their lives daily.[3]

In 2008, I assumed command of an aviation task force in the famed 101st Airborne Division (Air Assault). It was my fifth year serving in the division. I had deployed twice to Iraq as a cavalry squadron operations officer and later as the secretary of the general staff. The year 2009 was to be my first deployment to Afghanistan, and my first combat tour as a commander.

The 101st Airborne Division took great pride in its air assault capability, which traced its lineage back to the gliders used in the D-Day assault and, later, to the use of helicopters in Vietnam. I loved serving in the division, and for the first time in our army career my wife and I had found a place we proudly called home.

My wife, Lisa, and I met at North Georgia College in Dahlonega, Georgia. I had grown up only a few miles from Dahlonega in Ranger, Georgia. I was raised the son of a mill village family—a story I told in a book I called *Southern Roots*. The army took me away from my humble Southern roots and sent me into a diverse world that I'd only previously read about in books and magazines. Lisa had moved around most of her childhood before finally settling in Georgia. Moving with the pace of the army was quite natural for her, but Fort Campbell changed all of that. We bought a house in Clarksville, Tennessee, in 2003. She gave birth to our fourth child, Logan, in 2004, and Clarksville became our home. Our lives revolved around the community and our beloved 101st Airborne Division. We were incredibly humbled when I was selected to command the 7th Squadron, 17th Cavalry Regiment.

In Task Force Pale Horse, we forged a committed team—a team anchored in trust; a team that understood the fine line between flying recklessly and assuming necessary yet calculated risk in order to support the soldier on the ground. We created a team with a cavalry state of mind, as we called it. Everything we did was focused on the infantryman—the guy on the ground. We constantly reevaluated how we did business to ensure that we remained as effective as humanly possible for the infantryman. Army aviation exists for the sole purpose of supporting the soldier on the ground. That's why we were there and we were determined to do our very best to sustain and secure him—to ensure his success and earn his trust.

In the pages ahead you will find our story. We didn't always get it right. We certainly made mistakes but did our best to learn from them and to remain focused on our significant role.

The backdrop for my story is the battles we fought in Afghanistan. The story is told from an army aviator's perspective. Very little has been written about America's most recent war from an air perspective. My intent is to present the army helicopter pilot's side of the war in Afghanistan. Every heroic feat or sacrifice in the air was directly or indirectly performed in support of a soldier on the ground.

Most important, I want the reader, the average American, to close the cover of this book with a better understanding of the soldiers that constitute their army. Ernest Hemingway wrote, "Wars are fought by the finest people that there are, or just say people, although, the closer you are to where they are fighting the finer people you meet."[4]

This book is intended to draw the reader closer to those soldiers, to introduce you to young men and women who had the courage to voluntarily raise their hand to the square and swear an oath to serve their country, knowing full well that they would go to war. They were average young men and women who grew up on the farm or in the house next door.

I was surrounded by an amazing team of extremely talented officers, noncommissioned officers, warrant officers, and soldiers. My operations officer, Jack Murphy, proved to be the glue that held every mission in our area of operations together. He was tireless, and his lovable personality made everyone seek him out for support and advice. Jack was unflappable under immense pressure, pressure that would make lesser men crumble. He is and always will be a dear friend.

My intelligence officer, Jillian Wisniewski, is one of the brightest, if not *the* most intellectually gifted, officers with whom I have ever served. I could provide her a vision, a mere idea, and she would turn it into a masterpiece. Her intelligence assessments never grew stale. She breathed life into them, and they grew, transformed with the operational environment, always providing a current and accurate estimate of the enemy situation. She and Jack were gifted critical thinkers who solved some of the most complex problems we could imagine. Every day I was humbled to serve with them.

I wish I could write about all of my soldiers, but time and space will not allow. We could not have flown, fought, supported, or survived without the tireless efforts of our aviation crew chiefs. They turned wrenches day and night to keep our aircraft flying. Often their innovative fixes got us out of some very tight spots.

I will never forget the day a rocket-propelled grenade (RPG) ripped a hole—over a foot in length—through the rotor blade of a big twin-rotor Chinook helicopter, as it sat in a landing zone near the Spin Ghar mountains in southern Nangarhar Province. We had delivered Special Operations forces to an enemy compound. As our Afghan commando partners were exiting the helicopter an RPG tore through the rotor blade. We frantically sought a repair to get the aircraft off the ground before the enemy had a chance to organize for a follow-on attack. We sent our most experienced Chinook maintenance soldier, Sergeant First Class Sean Claussen, forward to assess the situation. He radioed back to me that he could wrap the blade in duct tape, and it would fly. It was an interesting moment for me. Initially, I wasn't sure if he was joking, so I repeated what he had said back into the radio.

"Duct tape? Are you serious?" I asked.

"Sir, trust me," he replied confidently.

I did trust him. As with all other experts in our task force, we had to rely on the judgment of our technicians. We flew the aircraft safely back to Jalalabad Airfield with a severe vibration but no further damage. It was men like that who kept us in the fight. The troopers who pumped fuel and loaded ammunition onto helicopters in the dead of night when it was twenty degrees outside and drizzling rain, who stamped their feet and blew into their hands to try and stave off the cold yet never complained. It was our signal soldiers, radio telephone operators, electricians, sheet metal repairmen, and communications specialists who made everything we accomplished possible. It was selfless staff officers like Nate Longworth, Tim Speace, and Steve Souza, men who slept very little, drank gallons of coffee, and dipped truckloads of snuff to keep planning and coordinating night after night, only to watch others fly away to execute the mission they had planned. Those soldiers and many others made our contribution to the fight possible. These men and women's contributions will never be adequately quantified. For them I am eternally grateful.

In writing this book I have gone to great lengths to tell our story as accurately as possible; however, I have inevitably erred to some degree. For that I am sorry. I am indebted to a multitude of fellow soldiers who were willing to recollect their view of the events that transpired in 2009. Some of those memories brought smiles and laughter; others brought tears and sadness. One of my soldiers told me, "I've spent five years trying to forget some of the things you're asking me to remember." It is important to note that while we each experienced these events together, as previously mentioned, our perspectives were different. Each of us carries our own unique view of what transpired over thousands of flights and fights in a land far away. And even though we may try to forget, the sacrifice others made is worthy of remembering.

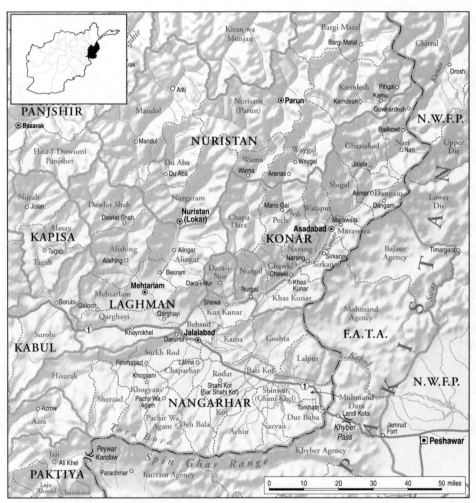

COURTESY OF THE INSTITUTE FOR THE STUDY OF WAR.

Helgal Valley

OP Bari Ali

Darin

Kunar River

MSR California

Nishagam District Center

PHOTO BY THE AUTHOR.

The history we shall make, the record of high achievement we hope to write in the annals of the American Army and the American people, depends wholly and completely on the men of this division. Each individual, each officer and each enlisted man, must therefore regard himself as a necessary part of a complex and powerful instrument for the overcoming of the enemies of the nation. Each, in his own job, must realize that he is not only a means, but an indispensable means for obtaining the goal of victory. It is, therefore, not too much to say that the future itself, in whose molding we expect to have our share, is in the hands of the soldiers of the 101st Airborne Division.[1]

—MAJOR GENERAL WILLIAM C. LEE

SURROUNDED BY TALENT

SEPTEMBER 8, 2009

"Sir, Adam and Patrick just got shot," the battle captain said in a calm but alarmed voice, his eyes glued to the digital map in front of him. Silence fell over the tactical operations center (TOC) and every eye was on me. How would I, their commander, respond? I felt like I'd been stabbed in the chest with an ice pick, like someone was slowly driving it through my sternum.

"Did they crash?" I calmly asked.

"No, sir," he said. "Patrick is still flying it, but it sounds like both of them are shot up pretty bad. They're going to land at Able Main and the medevac helicopter is following them in."

Able Main was a small combat outpost (COP) in northeastern Afghanistan, at the mouth of the valley where Adam Stead and Patrick Benson had just been shot. The digital map enabled us to watch their helicopter, a tiny icon, move in real time across the terrain, from the Shuryak Valley to COP Able Main. Everyone watched and prayed that the icon would not disappear, that it would continue to move until it reached the COP and then stop moving.

The operation was called Lethal Storm—named for Task Force Lethal, Lieutenant Colonel Brian Pearl's unit, which was conducting the operation. We had flown over one hundred of Brian's soldiers, four Chinooks full of them, into landing zones deep in the Shuryak Valley, to landing zones over seven thousand feet above sea level. A low-set western moon cast the valley in the long shadow of Sawtalo Sar, a massive ridge that separated the Shuryak from the infamous Korengal Valley. The insertion went in at 2:00 A.M., and almost immediately our Apache pilots observed Taliban fighters fleeing small villages that clung like beehives to the nearly vertical slopes overlooking the valley. No doubt alerted by the sound of the helicopters, the fighters fled up into the forested mountains to retrieve weapons.

By 6:00 A.M. our Apaches had killed at least ten enemy fighters, maybe more, as Task Force Lethal soldiers had carefully moved to the villages in search of a Taliban commander named Abdul Aziz and his fighters. Despite our best efforts to find and kill them, numerous enemy fighters crept into the forest undetected, where they retrieved hidden weapons and prepared to attack us.

We were operating in the Pech District of Kunar Province—the heart of Al Qaeda and Taliban territory. More specifically, our operation was conducted in the valleys where the attacks of September 11, 2001, had been planned and rehearsed. The terrain had historical significance for both us and the enemy. We did not know it at the time, but we were about to etch an even more indelible memory into our minds, with the blood of our own men.

Task Force Lethal soldiers clumsily struggled to keep their footing on the steep, loose, rocky terrain as they moved to their objectives. It took agility to remain afoot. The ground kept shifting, giving way. It wasn't long until one of the soldiers rolled his ankle, and soon another one became severely dehydrated. Both were unable to continue the mission, leaving us only one option: They would have to be hoisted out of the valley by a cable from our medevac helicopter.

It was a risky mission. The medevac pilots would be forced to hover the aircraft completely still above the trees in broad daylight, with enemy fighters scattered throughout the valley, seeking an opportunity to shoot them down. We were certain that the aircraft would quickly become the primary target within the valley, the focal point of enemy fires, so we had to get in and out of the valley as quickly as possible to minimize exposure time.

Chief Warrant Officer 4 Gary Heine piloted the medevac bird. As he steadied the Black Hawk helicopter at a high hover, flight medic Sergeant Nate Whorton descended seventy feet down into the trees—on a tiny cable the size of his finger. He quickly attached the injured soldiers to the jungle penetrator at the end of the cable, and the crew chief began retracting them up through the trees to the helicopter using a hoist. They swung and swayed like a piñata beneath the Black Hawk as they ascended, but the crew chief eventually pulled them safely inside. Now the cable had to be lowered back down so that Sergeant Whorton could be extracted.

One of Brian Pearl's men transmitted over the radio, "You've got to hurry! The enemy is coming for you. They've told all of their fighters to converge on the helicopter and shoot it down!" and with that the radios came alive with nervous chatter.

Brian's men had been listening in on the enemy's push-to-talk walkie-talkie radios. The message was clear: *They are coming—we have to hurry.* Meanwhile, enemy fighters, like bighorn sheep, ran effortlessly through the rocky terrain trying to reach the helicopter before it departed the valley. We were in their backyard, their childhood playground. Where we struggled to keep our footing, they moved with ease. Several enemy fighters made it into position underneath the helicopter before Whorton could be extracted.

"What was that?" the crew chief asked, clearly concerned. He hoped it wasn't a bullet, but he was sure that it was.

"I felt it in my feet. We just got shot," Gary Heine said. The enemy had made it to their location. They opened fire on the vulnerable Black Hawk with all they had. Bullets hit the nose of the helicopter, yet Heine held his position rock steady.

"He's on the cable!" the crew chief told Gary, letting him know that Whorton was on his way up.

"Tell me when he's clear of the trees," Gary said.

Adam Stead and Patrick Benson flew lead in a team of two OH-58D Kiowa Warrior helicopters charged with protecting the medevac during the hoist recovery operation. When the enemy opened fire, Adam dove his Kiowa without hesitation between the enemy fighters and the medevac. He wanted to draw their fire away from the vulnerable medevac, but more important, he wanted to find and kill the enemy.

As he flew around Gary Heine, the enemy shifted their fire from the medevac to the Kiowa. Both pilots were instantly hit, Patrick through the leg and Adam in the head.

With Adam now unconscious, the nose of the aircraft pitched up and then began to roll right and fall. Patrick, whose leg had literally exploded in the cockpit, quickly took the controls and struggled to keep them from crashing.

"We've been hit. I've been hit. Oh God . . . Adam is dead!" Patrick radioed.

Meanwhile, across the Kunar River Valley, less than twelve miles away, a battle that had raged all morning in Ganjgal village was finally calming down.

"What's happening at Ganjgal now?" I asked the battle captain.

"Sir, Ryan Neal just called us with an update. He's still talking to Highlander Five, Captain Will Swenson, on the ground. It sounds like they are heading back to FOB Joyce now."

The secure phone rang in the TOC. "Sir, it's Colonel Lewis," the battle captain said as he handed me the phone.

"Sir, it's Jimmy. Can I call you back from my office?" I asked, not wanting to disrupt the operations in the TOC.

"Roger, Jimmy. That's fine. Give me an update when you can," he said and hung up. Colonel Ron Lewis was my brigade commander, stationed at Bagram Airbase.

"Sir, Patrick and Adam have landed at COP Able Main. The medevac is on the ground with them," the battle captain told me.

"Roger, thanks."

I turned to my operations officer, Major Jack Murphy. "I need to go update Colonel Lewis. Adam and Patrick are in good hands now. The medevac will take them to FOB Wright. Start working on a plan to get a recovery team up there for their Kiowa. I'll be right back," I said, leaving him in charge.

I walked next door to my office and called Colonel Lewis. "Sir, it's Jimmy."

"Hey, Jimmy. Do you have time to give me a quick update?" he asked. "What's going on in Ganjgal?"

"Sir, it was supposed to be a key leader engagement [KLE]. They planned to go yesterday, but the mission got delayed until today because the Afghan border police couldn't make it. We didn't have enough aircraft to cover it, execute the air assault in the Shuryak, cover our operations up north in Barg-e Matal, and maintain a quick reaction force. It was just too much. These guys were invited to Ganjgal by the village elders, which usually means they don't get attacked. The marine Embedded Training Team [ETT] and the Afghan soldiers went in just before daylight. They were ambushed in the wadi right in front of the village. We launched a team of Kiowas that have been fighting all day. It seems to be over now. They are in their trucks and headed back to FOB Joyce," I said.

"How many casualties?"

"I'm not entirely sure. I know three marines and a navy corpsman led the patrol into the village. Our Kiowas found them about an hour ago. They were killed just outside the village. Ryan Neal is the air mission commander for the Kiowas. He said there were Afghan soldiers lying all up and down that wadi, dead or wounded. We've been flying units of blood from FOB Fenty up to FOB Wright and transferring patients all over the place. They ran out of beds at FOB Wright, so we transferred several patients to the forward surgical team here at FOB Fenty. They were low on blood so soldiers at Fenty have been giving blood throughout the day. It's been a rough morning."

"Okay, you've got a lot on your plate right now. What do you need from here? How can we help?" he asked. It had occurred to me already that if we ended up fighting into the night I would run out of crews to fly the missions. 7th Battalion, the general support aviation battalion, was located at Bagram. They had a large mission load of their own, but they were sometimes used to reinforce our task force when needed.

"Our night Apache teams flew the air assault insertion last night. The day teams are covering our mission at Barg-e Matal. I've got Kiowas fighting in the Shuryak Valley and Ganjgal village now. We'll want to go back in and kill any enemy forces left at Ganjgal tonight, so we will most likely air-assault the Special Forces and Afghan commandos in to clear Ganjgal village after dark. I may need more Apaches for tonight, and I'll need help with Apaches tomorrow for sure. I need to take a closer look at our combat power before I say for certain, but I think I'll need a team of Apaches and another Chinook tonight," I told him.

"Okay, take a look at it and let me know what you need. We'll find a way to help get you what you need," he said.

"Roger, sir," I said, paused for a second, then spoke again. "Sir, Patrick Benson and Adam Stead just got shot."

"What? How bad?" he asked in a clearly concerned tone. "Are they down?" he asked before I could respond, wanting to know if they had crashed.

"No, sir. It just happened. Patrick was able to fly them out of the valley. He landed at COP Able Main. I need to get back to the TOC to see how things are going," I said.

"Okay, I'll leave you alone and let you handle the fight, but call me back when you get a chance and let me know," he said.

"Yes, sir."

I hung up the phone and sat for just a moment, staring at the ply-wood wall in front of me, and for a minute I refused to believe what the outcome of that day might be. I always knew casualties could happen. We had come so close to death all year, yet somehow, by the grace of God, we'd escaped with mere flesh wounds. Our sheet metal repairers were better trained than the fender and bumper boys at Bum-pus Body Shop back in Clarksville. Helicopter after helicopter had returned to the airfield shot up like Swiss cheese. Always, the pilots stepped out of their helicopters wild-eyed and drunk on adrenaline, but alive, perhaps more alive than they had ever been. The mechanics swarmed the helicopters, assessed the damage, and began repairing them.

Adam and Patrick both shot, I thought to myself. How can this turn out well?

I felt a sudden surge of stress and anxiety. For just a second I had a strange urge to explode and let it all out, but I feared where that might take me. Something inside said, "Let go. It will feel good to get it out," but I couldn't. That was a place I'd never gone before and I was terrified of what might be there. So I tucked those emotions neatly away, bowed my head, and prayed for Adam, Patrick, and the boys in Ganjgal.

I prayed for Carrie Stead, Adam's wife, who was back at home carrying out her day with no idea that her husband had just been shot and was reported dead. It hurt to think about it. We had been push-ing hard for eight long months in combat, fighting almost every day. As I thought back over the previous eight months it was hard to put it all into perspective. What we had experienced was like something

I'd seen in a movie as a kid, read in a book, but this had been real—
surreal at times—but real. I was humbled to be able to lead such a
talented group of men and women, men and women who were willing to sacrifice so much. I was amazed at how far we had come since
first visiting Afghanistan on a Pre-deployment Site Survey (PDSS) the
previous year. That was where the story truly began, on that first visit
in the summer of 2008.

PRE-DEPLOYMENT SITE SURVEY

I assumed command of the 7th Squadron, 17th Cavalry Regiment (Task Force Pale Horse) on a cool, rainy Fort Campbell, Kentucky, morning in May 2008. But the ride truly began when I traveled with First Lieutenant Jillian Wisniewski and Chief Warrant Officer 4 Mike Woodhouse to the sweltering July heat of Afghanistan for a reconnaissance of sorts, to prepare for our deployment the following winter.

A quirky, witty former navy corpsman who absolutely abhorred running but loved *Star Wars,* British humor, and restoring old cars, Mike Woodhouse brought color to an otherwise olive-drab world. Mike was rarely if ever in a foul mood and could always be counted on for a laugh. Despite trying to cover it up with a heavy dose of sarcasm, he was a sensitive guy who genuinely loved people, and that appealed to me. Mike and I had known each other and served together for thirteen years. Like me, he flew the Kiowa Warrior helicopter and served as our standardization instructor pilot, the senior instructor in the task force. We expect warrant officers to be masters of their craft—technical and tactical experts in their field. Mike certainly met those criteria, but what set him apart was how passionately he cared. Mike cared about the reputation of our unit as much as any soldier in it. He wanted us to contribute to the war in ways in which an aviation unit never had before—to make a quantifiable difference.

Jillian Wisniewski was a petite, blond-haired, blue-eyed intelligence officer from West Virginia who had graduated from West Point in 2006. Smart and athletic, yet quiet and unassuming, she had a degree in operations research and a natural affinity for data analysis, systems efficiency, and pattern development. Innately inquisitive, Jillian was a natural problem solver—ideal qualities for the challenges we would face in 2009. Academically she thrived in the hard sciences, yet she wrote poetry, ran cross-country, played volleyball, Ping-Pong, Scrabble, and Cornhole, and was a self-proclaimed connoisseur of hot tea, designer coffee, and food. She made daily trips to FOB Fenty's Green Bean Coffee stand, where she would order a hot cappuccino, light on the milk and robust with espresso, no sugar, and then, after a few hot sips, she'd proclaim it "delectable!" She was the perfect lead for our intelligence team, upon which we would lean heavily in the following year.

After a painfully long flight around the globe, which seemed to grow exponentially more difficult for me with each passing year of my life, we finally landed at Bagram Airbase. The first few days in Afghanistan were spent with the 101st Combat Aviation Brigade (CAB). I made my way around Bagram to visit all of the senior leadership in CJTF-101 before moving on to Jalalabad Airfield to spend time with our sister unit, 2nd Squadron, 17th Cavalry Regiment (Task Force Out Front).

Our division headquarters, the 101st Airborne Division, was already in Afghanistan serving as the Regional Command East (RC-East) Headquarters, also known as Combined Joint Task Force 101—CJTF-101. The 101st CAB, the other aviation brigade in our division, was deployed as well, providing aviation support for all of the ground forces in Afghanistan. Both the CJTF-101 headquarters and the 101st CAB headquarters were located at Bagram Airbase. The 101st CAB's subordinate aviation battalion task forces were strewn across Afghanistan, supporting infantry brigade combat teams in various provinces of the country. Task Force Out Front, which we would be replacing, was stationed at Jalalabad Airfield in Nangarhar Province. Due to the challenging terrain, weather, and vast distances that prevented the battalions from mutually supporting one another, each aviation task force had a complement of Kiowa, Apache, Chinook, Black Hawk, and medevac helicopters.

The site survey was our opportunity to gain firsthand insights into how TF Out Front was conducting operations within Nangarhar, Nuristan, Laghman, and Kunar (N2KL) provinces as we prepared to take over the mission from them in January 2009.

TF Out Front was responsible for rotary-wing aviation support to 3rd Brigade, 1st Infantry Division—TF Duke, the brigade responsible for stability and security in N2KL. TF Duke was arrayed across N2KL with a battalion roughly responsible for each of the four provinces. Their brigade headquarters resided at FOB Fenty, at Jalalabad Airfield, where Task Force Out Front was also located.

As I had previously served as the unit's operations officer in Iraq, and later as the squadron executive officer, 2nd Squadron, 17th Cavalry held a special place in my heart. I had many wonderful memories from my time in the unit. In fact, most of my insights for air cavalry capabilities in the counterinsurgency environment were shaped during my time with 2-17 while serving in Iraq. Many of the soldiers, noncommissioned officers, and warrant officers with whom I had previously served were still in the unit, so I looked forward to seeing a lot of familiar faces in Jalalabad.

Mike, Jillian, and I put our rucksacks on our backs and headed out to the flight line. Lieutenant Colonel John Lynch, the commander of Task Force Out Front, sent a Black Hawk to pick us up.

"What do you think?" I asked Mike, as we stood at the passenger terminal, looking out across the airfield.

"I think that's a big friggin' mountain is what I think," he said.

Mike was referring to the massive mountains to our immediate north that peaked at fifteen thousand feet. It was July. Sweat ran down my nose and dripped onto the scorching tarmac, yet the gray massif towering over us was still covered in snow. Bagram sits in a huge bowl surrounded by the Hindu Kush mountains.

"Here they come," Jillian said, nodding to the Black Hawks that were now ground-taxiing toward us.

The crew chief saluted as I approached the bird. I shook his hand, and he helped us get our gear settled in the helicopter. We were given headsets so we could speak with the crew.

"Welcome to Afghanistan," a voice said over the headset. It was the senior pilot.

"Thanks. It's good to finally be here," I said, genuinely happy to be visiting.

"Sir, we'll be flying you to JAF. We'll leave the doors open so you'll have a good view. It's a pretty amazing flight," he said.

"Roger that."

Prior to our trip I had read countless books and articles in which authors attempted to describe the terrain of eastern Afghanistan. I had also spoken with other soldiers who had served there. From their descriptions I tried to picture the terrain. They really hyped it, saying, "You just have to see it to believe it." Seeing it firsthand in the summer of 2008, I realized that they were absolutely right: It was simply impossible to articulate adequately the feeling of standing in the midst of the Hindu Kush mountains. The peaks were majestic from a purely observational perspective, yet it was humbling to consider a seasoned, indigenous enemy force that intimately knew how to use the terrain to their advantage in battle. This was the historic arena for numerous epic battles and home of America's longest war. It was beautiful yet deadly.

At the time of our site survey nine Medals of Honor, our nation's highest award in combat, had been earned since the global war on terrorism began in 2001. Four of those medals were earned in battles fought in N2KL; four more would be awarded for battles fought during our deployment to that area. Eight of the thirteen—over half—would be earned in Kunar and Nuristan provinces alone.

"Look at that lake," Jillian said.

She pointed out the door at Sarobi Lake. The water was a beautiful emerald green. The earth rose quickly from the lake, forming mountainsides, until the brown dirt transformed into sheer gray rock. The terrain in N2KL climbs and plummets across 15,600 square miles of eastern Afghanistan. At its eastern extreme lies a roughly three-hundred-mile border—a porous, ill-defined, and largely ignored boundary between Afghanistan and Pakistan. Visualized on a map of the United States, the Afghanistan–Pakistan border, within our area of operations, would stretch from Washington, DC, to Raleigh, NC. The problem with the border was that it sliced through Pashtun tribal areas, thus separating them from one another by a Western-imposed international boundary. Very few roads crossed the border, but a web of trail systems crisscrossed back and forth across the boundary, making control of cross-border foot traffic nearly impossible—a reality exploited by enemy fighters.

In contrast to the lush mountains of northern Georgia, where I grew up, a place where massive oak trees sink their roots deep into the ground to secure the rich, fertile soil to the earth, everything in Afghanistan is hard as steel. From the granular moving sands of the desert region that blot out the sun in a storm to the sheer gray rock walls that disappear into the clouds, everything is hard, including the people who live there—life is hard in Afghanistan. The Hindu Kush mountains rose like the earth's spine in the center of our area of operations, climbing higher and higher until peaking in Chitral, Pakistan, at 25,230 feet, and eventually anchoring itself on the Himalayas. Foreign soldiers had occupied the Hindu Kush since the time of Darius the Great. These rugged, rocky mountains had tasted the blood of countless soldiers from myriad ethnicities over the centuries. Persians, Greeks, Macedonians, Mongols, Brits, Russians, and then Americans, French, Poles, Germans, Australians, and many others had fought, bled, and died there.

The Spin Ghar mountains stood like a giant partition between Nangarhar Province and the Kurram and Khyber agencies of Pakistan, marking the southern boundary of our area of operations. Tora Bora, the mountains that caught America's attention in 2001, anchored our southwestern boundary, while the historic Khyber Pass cut through the Spin Ghar mountains in the southeastern corner of Nangarhar Province. The Khyber Pass has always been an important trade route, linking southern and central Asia via the Silk Road. The pass is legendary as the route through which Alexander the Great and Genghis Khan marched their forces, bound for India. It was simply the most challenging and humbling terrain I'd ever seen, at once beautiful and ominous.

We followed the Kabul River to Jalalabad. As we flew into the Nangarhar bowl I saw Jalalabad sprawling to the south. "Sir, if you look to our ten o'clock you'll see the mouth of the Kunar Valley. That's where the real trouble lies," the pilot said.

After we landed at Jalalabad Airfield, John Lynch met us with a smile and a firm handshake. "Welcome to Jalalabad," he said.

"Thanks, John."

"How was the trip?"

"Good. It actually went very smooth. I'm just all jacked up from the time zone changes."

"Yep. I'm sure you are. We'll get you settled and then we'll eat some lunch. You hungry?"

"Starved."

"Good. Let's go," and he showed us to our rooms.

Mike, Jillian, and I spent our first day with 2-17 Cavalry receiving briefings, and having passed through ten time zones, it was a challenge to remain awake—I stood through most of the meetings. By the third day it was time to get out and see the country firsthand. Our first flight was in a Black Hawk. The crew met us at the TOC,[1] where we received a mission briefing from the battle captain and various other staff officers and noncommissioned officers. They discussed our flight route, told us what U.S. ground patrols would be out on the roads, told us where fighting had already occurred that day, and provided the status of all artillery and mortars in the area of operations. It was a thorough briefing intended to arm us with the most accurate picture of the battlefield before we left the base.

After the mission briefing we moved to the helicopter for a crew briefing delivered by those who would fly us on our battlefield tour. I noticed that the pilots walked with a certain swagger. You could sense both pride and confidence in their body language. It wasn't a distasteful, cocky pride but rather a visible confidence earned through hardship and experience. They reminded me of cowboys I'd been around in the past. They were in their element and we were visitors on their ranch—the new guys. They had the advantage in every way. They knew where we were going. We didn't. They knew where danger lurked, when and where to be concerned. We sensed danger everywhere. I wondered how long it would take our crews to gain their level of confidence. In many ways it's good to remain cautious for as long as possible. Those who grow too comfortable too quickly assume too much risk too early.

Following the crew briefing, we departed Jalalabad Airfield and flew northeast, almost directly over the location of the first successful Stinger missile engagements of the Soviet–Afghan War.

"Right over there is where the first Stinger missiles were used in combat," I told Mike and Jillian.

"On the Russians?" Mike asked.

"Yeah, on September twenty-fifth, 1986. Eight Soviet Hind helicopters were flying to Jalalabad Airfield when they were shot down."

The contrast of the whole situation was fascinating to me. On that day several heavily bearded men who most likely could not read or write, men who lived in rock houses glued together by mud, pulled the trigger on the most sophisticated heat-seeking surface-to-air weapon on the planet and turned the tide of a war. Five missiles were fired that afternoon; three of them brought down helicopters, each in a ball of flame.

"I'm not too worried about Stinger missiles today," Mike said. "I don't think we've given any more out since then."

"Me neither," I said. "Thank goodness."

While we were not concerned with Stinger missiles that day it was still unsettling to know that we could be engaged by an ever-present enemy at any moment. A very real, living, breathing enemy was trying to kill us every day in Afghanistan.

We flew northwest up the fertile green Kabul River Valley to Laghman Province, flew over the capital city of Mehtar Lam and then north, through the Alishang and Alingar valleys. The Alingar drew very narrow at the northern end. A strip of blue water and a dirt road all but disappeared into the wall of mountains that led into Nuristan.

"Sir, we don't go any further north in the Alingar. That's where Commando Wrath took place," the pilot said as he pointed into the valley.

Commando Wrath was a Special Forces operation to kill or capture Hezb-e Islami Gulbuddin (HIG) leader Haji Ghafour in his Shok Valley lair. The operation had taken place in April and was still fresh in everyone's mind for several reasons. The Shok Valley was essentially a giant slot canyon. Haji Ghafour's compound was perched on the high ground overlooking the deep narrow valley below. TF Out Front was forced to insert two Special Forces detachments, along with their Afghan Commando partners, into the bottom of the valley because it was the only place to land.

The mission went wrong from the start. Bad weather had forced them to delay the operation a week, but even a week later the weather was far from ideal. The landing zones were expected to be in a dry wadi, but when they got there the "dry wadi" was a raging river. The helicopters could not even land, so the men had to jump off the ramp of the Chinooks while the pilots held steady at a hover. Ghafour's fighters were hidden in cracks and crags of the rocky cliffs above, already in place when they arrived.

As the Green Berets attempted to climb the near-vertical switchback trails, Ghafour's men ambushed them. They battled for six and a half hours before TF Out Front could get out of the valley. Every member of the team was injured to some degree, but the story they all so vividly remembered, and frequently recounted, was that of Sergeant John Wayne Walding. Who would expect anything less than gallantry in battle from a native Texan, born on the Fourth of July, named John Wayne? Near the top of a mountain, Sergeant Walding was shot in the knee, his leg all but severed. He self-injected morphine, folded the lower portion of his leg up, and tied his foot off to his thigh with his boot string. He then fought his way back down the mountain while scooting on his bottom.

Ten Green Berets were later awarded the Silver Star for their actions in the Shok Valley. John Lynch and one of his medics were awarded the Bronze Star for Valor for running throughout the valley, helping load and evacuate the wounded. Operation Commando Wrath further proved a lesson learned centuries prior and relearned countless times through the ages—in Afghanistan terrain means everything.

I stared out of the door like a kid on a school bus, taking in all the sights as we flew from Laghman to Kunar Province. The Kunar River winds and twists its way south from glaciers in Pakistan, warming itself with every mile it flows until finally it empties into the Kabul River just outside the gates of FOB Fenty. The Hindu Kush mountains rise abruptly on the northwest side of the valley. The Pakistan border sits atop the ridgeline only a few kilometers east of the river. As we traveled northeast up the Kunar, the valley grew considerably narrower and the river's current significantly increased.

Our helicopter began to slow and descend as we prepared to land at the forward arming and refueling point (FARP) on FOB Wright, which sat just south of Asadabad—the Kunar Provincial capital. The FARP was manned with soldiers equipped to pump fuel and load ammunition on all types of helicopters operating in Afghanistan. A FARP is an aviation unit's gas station on steroids, designed to execute its mission like a NASCAR pit crew. As the FARP personnel heard the distinct *whap whap whap* of rotors, they donned helmets and gloves and ran out to their assigned pads. The FARP provided fuel, bullets, water, and also a field-expedient latrine.

"Look, piss tubes," Mike said, surprised that they still existed.

When the global war on terrorism first began we had no other alternative than to relieve ourselves wherever we could: behind a tree, a rock, or beside our own vehicles. Women held up ponchos for each other to provide a little privacy, guys just turned their backs. Once we settled into fixed bases in 2003, we built our own outhouses, which provided privacy and a place to sit—a hole in a piece of plywood over a fifty-five-gallon drum cut in half and filled with diesel fuel. We took shifts burning it every evening—a delightful duty. It wasn't until the fall of 2003 that we celebrated the arrival of the Porta-Potty, or "blue canoe," as we called them, but even then we held on to our piss tubes. Piss tubes were waist-high PVC pipes sunk several feet into the ground. In 2009, there were three tubes still in use at FOB Wright. Some things just seem to have sentimental value and ease of use.

We got off the Black Hawk and waited in a holding area as the helicopter was being fueled. The perimeter wall that surrounded FOB Wright was less than twenty yards from the fueling points. To the west the terrain climbed straight up, almost vertically. I watched heavily bearded men with turbans on their heads herding goats along switchback trails just outside the FOB. The men walked slowly with their hands clasped behind their backs. One old man squatted on a large rock. He stroked his long whiskers as he stared down at us. Another ancient-looking man with a long gray beard, who reminded me of Gandalf, sat on his haunches and thumbed through a string of prayer beads. I wondered what they thought about all of this, of our being there.

Afghanistan is a place where the people dream of a better life, but it's just been so long since they've seen peace that they've forgotten what it looks like. They know what fear is. They have felt that. They know what death is. They've seen it, and they intimately understand war. Perhaps a better life would simply be the absence of the things they know so well, the things they've learned to live with, to endure.

Suddenly, soldiers scrambled out of a small block building, donning helmets as they ran toward two 155-mm howitzers, large artillery pieces that sat about fifty meters from the fueling pads. The guns were oriented northwest, over our aircraft. I figured out rather quickly that they were about to shoot, so I plugged my ears and braced myself as the massive barrels recoiled and a shock wave, visible in the dust, pulsed across the FOB.

Mike Woodhouse laughed out loud. "I love it!" he said, catching a glimpse of what we'd trained for, for so many years.

The crew chief signaled for us to get back into the aircraft so we strapped in and prepared for takeoff. With a roar the helicopter lifted off, and again I heard the loud concussion of the big guns. It was the first time I had flown underneath a gun target line—it would not be the last. We were finally about to enter the area we had heard and read so much about.

We flew to the north over Asadabad, where the Pech River empties into the Kunar. Then we turned west and followed the Pech River into the valley, at which time our flight profile noticeably changed. There were many places in Afghanistan where we did not fly without an armed escort. Two Apaches flanked our Black Hawk on either side. As we entered the Pech the Apaches began varying their airspeed and altitude. They were above us then below us, on the right and then the left, flying lazy S-turns. The Black Hawk pilots increased the speed of our helicopter as well. I looked over at Mike Woodhouse, who had his arms folded across his body armor and his feet kicked out on the seat in front of him. He looked back at me, gave me a thumbs-up and smiled, then said, "Here we go."

Below us the Pech River flowed fast and strong. The Pech Valley ran from its mouth, where it joined the Kunar Valley, west into the heart of the Hindu Kush mountains. As the valley snaked its way into the Hindu Kush, other, smaller valleys branched off to the north and south, each presenting a uniquely different yet often linked enemy problem for coalition forces. Each valley displayed differences in terrain and enemy activity, and villages of varying personalities with diverse tribal and cultural customs.

Some valleys were more accessible by ground and air than others. Some had sheer rock walls that could not easily be traversed, even on foot. Others were laden with gentle wooded ridges and a web of trail systems, making it easy for the enemy to slip in and out of the valleys undetected. Some valleys were home to large populations that were willing to cooperate with coalition forces; others detested the U.S. presence and would fight to remove it. Some resisted extremist groups for various reasons; others were more than willing to accommodate them.

As we continued into the Pech, I saw a string of simple villages whose residents farmed the lush river valley. They lived in humble structures and carried out a straightforward existence, yet the complexity of the situation revolving around their villages could not be overstated. While many of the inhabitants lived in the valley with access to the river and the road, others lived in clusters of homes on the steep slopes of the mountains, clearly constructed with security in mind. Very few trails led to their mountain houses, which were built out of logs, rock, and mud. The roofs were flat, with the roof of one home often serving as a walkway or an open patio for the family living on the next layer of structures. In some cases trees growing out of the rocky slope served as ladders, enabling the villagers to climb from one level to the next.

It was baffling to look down on the area and realize that the attacks of September 11, 2001, were conceived in that environment. Somehow this extraordinarily primitive area had gained the attention of the world due to global attacks that had emanated from here. It was an extremely difficult concept to wrap my mind around.

Flying into the Korengal Valley for the first time, I was nervous yet curious, like I feel when I wade out into the ocean. Being in the water certainly appeals to me, but once I am waist deep I feel like I've entered the food chain. It didn't help that the pilot climbed higher in the air and sped up, partly because the terrain had begun to rise, but more so due to the danger inherent to the valley. I had read a lot about the deadliest piece of terrain in Afghanistan since 9/11. The Korengal was hell with the lid off, but as scary as the place was, I figured that experiencing hell on earth would make me appreciate the good life in America a little bit more.

As we flew into the valley, Sawtalo Sar, the large ridge that separated the Korengal and Shuryak valleys, was out my door. It was where Navy SEAL Marcus Luttrell's reconnaissance team was compromised and subsequently ambushed, leaving him the lone survivor, during Operation Redwing in June 2005. It was where the 160th Special Operations Aviation Regiment's (SOAR) Chinook was shot down trying to rescue Luttrell's team, killing all nineteen servicemen on board. Just over the ridge, near the Chowkay Valley, was where Lieutenant

Colonel Joe Fenty and nine others were killed in a Chinook crash as they attempted to depart the area after Operation Mountain Lion in May 2006. From the air, the place seemed benign, but in the coming months I would learn that seemingly benign places in Afghanistan could open a trapdoor to hell in seconds.

As we flew over the Korengal outpost, I saw the men of Viper Company, 1-26 Infantry. Several men manned machine guns on the perimeter, anticipating enemy contact—a daily occurrence. I wanted to get a good feel for the layout of the terrain and our U.S. outposts within the valley, so I asked the pilots to circle one more time so I could take a closer look at the KOP, OP Restrepo, OP Dallas, and Firebase Vegas. "Sir, we don't spend too much time hanging out in the Korengal," the pilot said, indicating his desire to depart the valley.

"Roger, just one more pass and I'll be good."

I knew why he said it. If we went down in that valley, help would never get to us in time, not before the enemy did. The lucky ones would die in the crash.

It wasn't always like that. There was a time when the people of those mountains met strangers with smiles, extended hospitality, and shared what little food they had with Western travelers. In 1960 three diplomats, an American, a Brit, and a German, traveled up the Pech to Nangalam. They parked their vehicles and spent ten days walking through Chapa Dara, up the Wama Valley, across the ridge to Waygal, and back down to Nangalam. The setting of Kipling's *The Man Who Would Be King* was just up the valley in Nuristan, but war changes people. I suspect that many if not most of the people living in those isolated villages desperately miss the days when it was safe to welcome strangers into their villages. They didn't change on their own. They had been acted upon by extremism. War and hatred found its way up the secluded valleys and left a stain. It altered people.

From the Korengal we flew to FOB Blessing to meet with Lieutenant Colonel Brett Jenkinson, who commanded all the soldiers in the Pech and Korengal valleys. We landed at the FARP, which sat about two hundred vertical feet below his headquarters. His executive officer met us with an outstretched hand and a smile. "Hey, sir! Welcome to Blessing."

"It's good to be here. Thanks for giving us a few minutes of your time. I know you're busy," I said.

"No problem, sir."

I was amazed at how close they lived to the locals. I'm not sure why, since I had been in outposts in Iraq that were built in the center of cities like Mosul and Tikrit, but it seemed uncomfortably close here in the heart of bad-guy country. Afghan men with weathered, expressionless faces sat on walls outside the wire, staring at us as we climbed the hill to the command post. I noticed that a few of the men sported flaming red beards that had been dyed with henna—a tradition from the time of the prophet Mohammad. I even saw a red-haired goat with ruby eyes, bangs, and a bell around its neck. A lone donkey stood in the corner eating grass along the perimeter wall.

The TF Out Front executive officer accompanied us on the trip. He pointed to the donkey. "See that donkey, sir?"

"Yeah."

"It used to be a marijuana-eating donkey," he said.

"What?"

"They had a big patch of marijuana growing in the corner of the FOB and the donkey used to graze on it. It was the mellowest donkey in Afghanistan, but a sergeant major made them cut the marijuana down and burn it, so now the donkey is perpetually pissed off," he said with a smile.

I laughed and shook my head.

I had been a long-distance runner my entire life. In fact, I had once run a marathon in two hours and thirty-three minutes, yet I was absolutely winded when I reached the top of the hill. Climbing the mountain at just under four thousand feet above sea level with full combat equipment was like trying to run uphill with a gas mask on, but I had no mask on at all. There simply wasn't enough oxygen to breathe, even in the shadow of the valley. I could only imagine how tough it would be to fight in the mountains that towered over us.

Brett Jenkinson met me at the door.

"Brett Jenkinson," he said with a smile, reaching to shake my hand.

"Jimmy Blackmon. Thanks for seeing us, Brett."

"I'm glad you could stop by. Come on in," he said as he turned and walked toward his conference room. Pointing at a cooler: "Can I get you something to drink? Soda, coffee, water?"

"No thanks, I'm good."

Brett was a tall, lean, and lanky infantryman with a tightly cropped, high and tight haircut. He was full of energy and purpose. He and his operations officer, Major Tito Villanueva, briefed us on their area of operations with an enthusiasm we had not yet experienced on our visit. Having only recently arrived in theater, Brett's unit had taken responsibility for the bloodiest piece of terrain in which our army was then engaged. It was not only an extremely complex area, but also home to a well-financed, disciplined, and determined enemy.

The depth of knowledge that Brett's team demonstrated was impressive. He contended that "we can't kill our way to victory in this war." There were obviously areas in which he felt we could and would make progress, yet he made it abundantly clear that the blood feud with the Korengalis was irreconcilable.

"We're fighting every day in the Korengal. We've talked to them. We've tried to repair the road going into the valley, tried to convince them that it's for their benefit, but they don't care. They attack the road crews. We're never going to get anywhere in that valley."

His demeanor visibly changed as we spoke about the Korengal. "We need to get the hell out of there now. I'd like to build a wall between them and the Pech," he said.

His men were taking fire multiple times each day and he was acutely aware of how much blood had already been spilled in that valley. He did not want to shed another drop of American blood in the Korengal. He wanted out of the valley as soon as possible.

"We can't sit in these outposts and just take their attacks. We've got to get out and patrol—kill these guys. We've got to pick up the pace offensively," he said.

I just listened and wholeheartedly agreed. If you sit in a FOB or COP and wait, they will attack on their terms, but if you get out and disrupt the enemy, kill their leadership, keep them looking over their shoulder, then you create space to maneuver.

After the briefing, Brett walked me back down the hill to the helicopter. We had to meet the birds as they landed and depart the FOB immediately or the enemy would begin shooting mortars and rockets at us.

"Thanks again for taking the time to show us what's going on in your AO," I said.

"No problem."

"I guess we'll see you in about four months," I said.

"We'll be here." Brett smiled warmly and shook my hand. He looked me in the eye and said, "So long."

I left FOB Blessing with one certainty in my mind: We would be fighting alongside Brett Jenkinson and his men a lot in the coming months. It was clear to me that Brett wanted to increase the operational tempo as soon as possible—to take the fight to the enemy. Brett had no intention of letting his men sit in their outposts, wringing their hands, waiting for the next attack to occur. He wanted to put pressure on the enemy, and he wanted our support doing it. I planned right then and there to see that he got it.

We departed FOB Blessing and flew east. I looked out my door and saw the Waygal Valley running north. At that time some of the only remaining 173rd Airborne Brigade soldiers, having not yet been relieved by the unit replacing them, were beginning work on an outpost just up the valley near Wanat village. Soon they too would be heading home. As we continued down the Pech toward the Kunar, Mike Woodhouse keyed the mike on the internal communication system (ICS) and, referring to Brett, said, "He likes to fight."

I looked over at Mike and smiled. "Yep. I've got a feeling we are going to be fighting a lot in this valley," I said, and looked back out the door.

We exited the Pech River Valley and flew back out into the Kunar, then turned left and proceeded north. We followed the valley to FOB Bostic, near the city of Nari, where we landed to refuel and receive a briefing from Lieutenant Colonel Jim Markert, commander of 6th Squadron, 4th Cavalry (Task Force Raider). As I exited the helicopter I noticed that Bostic sat in a bowl. I felt vulnerable staring up at towering mountains on every side, but I had no idea how that would compare to what I would see in a few short hours.

One of Jim's officers met us at the landing zone. After brief introductions he led us through a maze of plywood buildings to their command post. We met Jim, his executive officer, command sergeants major, and his operations officer, who presented their briefing on northern Kunar and Nuristan. Again, we witnessed an incredible depth of knowledge acquired in a very short period of time. Jillian was a bit overwhelmed at how well versed everyone was with regard to their operational environment. It seemed as if they could have spoken for days about the terrain and the enemy. Listening to their briefing put the weight of preparation into perspective—a common experience when you deploy into a combat theater of operations and meet the team already in place. They named every ridge, hilltop, valley, road, insurgent leader, financial backer, and bag boy in their area of responsibility. I too felt an overwhelming need to study, but I also had the benefit of having done this before. Being "in the fight" has a way of making you very smart, very fast. I knew that after about a month of being in the lead we would be just as well versed.

Jim Markert's depiction of his area was much more somber than Brett Jenkinson's. As Brett had described his area, he'd used a healthy portion of sarcasm, cracked a joke or two, and then got deathly serious. Brett's briefing was a roller coaster ride with peaks and valleys, smiles and frowns. Jim Markert, on the other hand, presented the challenges he faced matter-of-factly. He genuinely looked forward to working with us and appreciated our visit so we'd better understand his team's challenges. He knew that his men would depend on our ability to fight our way into his outposts and resupply his men. He knew our Apaches and Kiowas would respond when his men were in a fight and that our medevac helicopters would risk everything to save his wounded troopers. Jim had inherited the most challenging terrain in Afghanistan, with the highest elevations and most restrictive, canalized, isolated valleys in the country. His outposts sat primarily in these deep, narrow valleys, dominated by enormous mountain ridges, with only one way in and out.

The remote and challenging terrain made Jim's area a natural haven for the enemy. They could move freely through the mountain trails and hide out in isolated villages. The terrain also isolated Jim's forces. Five of his outposts were not accessible by ground vehicles, requiring our helicopters to resupply them. No one had driven a vehicle through the Kamdesh Valley since early 2008. The road simply couldn't hold up under our heavy combat vehicles, and the mountains were crawling with enemy forces with itchy trigger fingers. Helicopters were essential to sustain Jim Market's soldiers, and so anything that prevented their routine resupply meant they assumed much more risk to the force.

From FOB Bostic we flew north, up the Kunar River and into Nuristan. We passed over the village of Bati Kowt. Just past Bati Kowt the valley forked. The Kunar River itself angled to the northeast and crossed the border into Pakistan toward Drosh. We passed over the Gowerdesh Bridge and flew the crevasse that turned west—the Kamdesh Valley, along the Landay Sin River.

Again, the pilot accelerated, showing clear concern that we could be shot at any moment. He flew about one hundred feet above the river, which in retrospect probably wasn't the safest choice. As I sat in the back of the Black Hawk, watching the rock walls speed by, it seemed that our rotors were less than a foot from the mountain at times. I was reminded of a story someone had once told me about the Russian experience in this area. Russian helicopters were allegedly taken down by fighters throwing rocks through the rotor blades from above. I don't know if that story is true. I had never found any evidence to support it, but flying through the narrow valley made me realize that it was a real possibility.

Initially, the Russians had embraced the nap-of-the-earth (NOE) method of flying while they were in Afghanistan—flying low to the ground and conforming to the contours of the earth, thus minimizing exposure. They believed that flying low and fast gave them the advantage of surprise.[2] While this is true, there is always a compromise associated with NOE flight. First, flying NOE puts the aircraft within the range of enemy machine guns. Until the mujahideen received American-made, heat-seeking Stinger missiles, the only significant threats to their helicopters were machine guns, RPGs, the terrain, and weather. Had they flown at higher altitudes they could have mitigated the risk of being shot down, but they would have lost the advantage of surprise. Once Stinger missiles were introduced into the war, limited exposure became the key to their survival, so NOE would have indeed been the best option. The Russian pilots had a choice—fly low and risk being shot with machine guns and RPGs, or fly high and risk being shot with a Stinger missile. Ultimately, most Russian pilots chose to fly high and trust their aircraft survivability equipment (flares) to defeat the heat-seeking missiles. "No longer did helicopters come cruising in on a straight, gradually descending flight path, but rather in a tight, twisting spiral from a great height and firing flares every few seconds."[3] The flares were designed to burn hotter than the helicopter engines, thus attracting the heat-seeking missiles.

Another key change following the Soviet war in Afghanistan was the proliferation of cell phones and handheld push-to-talk radios. By

2009, enemy fighters and their supporters carried a means to communicate easily with one another. Using cell phones and radios, the enemy reported our movements from the time we departed our FOBs until we disappeared from their sight. The only way to achieve surprise in 2009 was to fly on dark nights and to use deception as part of the mission plan. On that July day we flew NOE in the middle of the day down a very narrow and deep valley.

We passed over COP Lowell first, named for Private First Class Jacob Lowell, a soldier in 1-91 Cavalry who was killed only a couple of days after his unit assumed responsibility for the area in 2007. Formerly known as COP Kamu, COP Lowell was adjacent to the small mountain village of Kamu. The COP appeared to be extremely vulnerable, sitting in the bottom of the deep, narrow Kamdesh Valley, but nothing compared with COP Keating, which we saw next. I didn't even notice it on the first pass because it was very small and I couldn't believe it would be located in such a vulnerable place. The pilot brought us back around and pointed it out once again. It was hard to believe soldiers had survived so long in an outpost so clearly exposed, but when these outposts were built the threat was much different than in 2008. The leaders who chose to build them built them for a reason, and based their decision upon the threat assessment at that given time. In 2008, the environment had changed significantly, and it would be our responsibility to adjust accordingly.

Named for First Lieutenant Benjamin Keating, who was killed on November 26, 2006, when his military vehicle plummeted from the narrow rocky road into the river a short distance from the outpost, COP Keating was nothing more than a postage stamp in the bottom of a deep, narrow gorge adjacent to a tiny, isolated village. The road, which followed the river through the valley, seemed to disappear into the outpost then reemerge on the other side. In fact, the road squeezed between the outpost and the river on the north side. At that location sparse green trees somewhat hid the road from view from the air.

Outside the outpost, on what appeared to be a sandbar by the river, sat the landing zone and a small footbridge that crossed the river. Typically, a landing zone is built inside the COP, but there simply wasn't room inside Keating. The south side of the outpost was pressed up against a mountain that climbed vertically for several thousand feet to a ridgeline above. A switchback trail zigzagged like a snake from the outpost up to the top of the ridge.

We climbed out of the valley from Keating to OP Fritsche, which sat atop the southern ridge, and it was like going from Dante's Inferno to Paradise in a matter of seconds and a few thousand feet. We had been flying through a jagged slot in the earth. Suddenly, as we exited and looked out across the valley, into Nuristan, Himalayan images from the pages of *National Geographic* flashed into my mind. From the top of the ridge it looked and felt like we were in British Columbia. Huge timber-lined and snowcapped mountains surrounded us. A frigid wind filled the cockpit as we flew past small popcorn clouds that floated like cotton balls suspended in air. Jagged, snowy peaks pointed heavenward against a bright blue sky as far as the eye could see. Postcard perfect. From this perspective it was easy to imagine Afghanistan's potential. With security and investment Afghanistan could be an outdoor paradise. I could easily envision whitewater rafting, snow skiing, mountain biking, adventure racing, hiking, fishing, and rock climbing as a booming industry. We slowly circled back to the south, where white slowly turned to green and then brown again.

As we flew back down the Kunar Valley no one spoke. I thought about Brett Jenkinson and Jim Markert. I wondered what the future held in store for us. In hindsight it seems surreal that on that day we had no knowledge of the events that would unfold in the coming months.

WANAT

Back at FOB Fenty, Mike, Jillian, and I met for dinner to compare notes and unwind a bit. I had still not adjusted to the time zone changes, so by early evening I was falling asleep while eating, yet I knew I'd be wide awake at 3:00 A.M. Lieutenant Colonel John Lynch and his senior staff officers lived in a bee hut together—a bee hut is nothing more than a wooden box built to house eight soldiers stuffed in like sardines—and they kept a few open bunks for visitors, so that's where Mike and I slept.

John's flight surgeon also lived in his bee hut. He was on medevac call 24/7. When a medevac request came in, the battle captain would call over a handheld radio for the crews to report. Doc would listen to the nature of the call and determine if he wanted to go along on the mission or only send a flight medic. He almost always went when there was a U.S. casualty, and particularly if there were gunshot wounds or potential amputations. He carried a Motorola radio with him everywhere he went, and at night he sat it beside his bed. It chattered throughout the night, making sleep nearly impossible. My only hope for some rest was Ambien, but I planned to fly the following day, so that night I didn't take one—thank goodness.

Early in the morning of July 13, I heard Doc's radio crackle to life. It was a medevac request for the Waygal Valley. Doc, who slept in his uniform, exploded out of his bed and ran out the door. Before the door slammed behind him, I thought I heard the words "mass casualty," so I pulled on my shorts and a T-shirt, wiped the sleep from my eyes, and hurried to the TOC.

Major Bernard "Bernie" Harrington, the task force operations officer, sat beside the battle captain. Having just been awakened, he too was in shorts and a T-shirt. Bernie was an Apache pilot and one of the most competent field-grade aviators I knew. Another officer with a love for long-distance running, he calmly gave guidance and direction as the medevac and Apaches were launched. He asked the battle captain if a full-motion video feed from an unmanned aerial vehicle (UAV) was available to view, but there wasn't one in position yet. They were told that a Predator UAV was on the way.

Second Platoon, Chosen Company, of the 2nd Battalion, 503rd Infantry Regiment had begun establishing COP Kahler in the Waygal Valley near Wanat village. They named the outpost after Sergeant First Class Matthew Ryan Kahler, who had been killed on January 26 of that same year, several miles farther north in the valley at COP Bella.[1] Due in large part to the significant threat, TF Out Front, using their Chinooks, had moved the platoon from COP Bella to the new location on July 9. Their mission was to secure the site while a local national contractor built the outpost itself. The men of second platoon spent every hour possible digging to exhaustion in the rocky terrain. They had not been shot at once since arriving at Wanat, but the anticipation of an attack fueled their desire to dig, to fortify.

Specialist Christopher McKaig served as an assistant gunner on a machine gun team in second platoon's weapons squad. Though he was born in New Jersey, McKaig's family had moved to Oregon during his junior year of high school. A city boy who had been baptized in the great outdoors, Chris McKaig was born again, and the lush green forests of Oregon were his paradise. Rather quickly he'd fallen in love with hunting and fishing. His father bought him a bow and a dozen arrows. He practiced every day improving his accuracy with the bow until his father finally agreed to let him hunt whitetail deer.

Hunting became an obsession. He spent every available hour in the woods with his bow. He also wrestled and played football and hockey. He liked the contact sports and despite being of average stature, he always felt a sense of pride when he stood up for the underdog. Chris would later tell me, "I believe God put a warrior's spirit in me."[2] On July 13, 2008, his warrior spirit would be tested like he could never have imagined.

Despite experiencing daily contact with the enemy for fifteen long months, "every one of us was scared—really scared," he told me.

"We knew there was gonna be a fight," he added. "It was just a question of when."

They established an observation post farther up the mountain where Specialist McKaig and eight other paratroopers were located. They called it "Topside," from a parachute mission that their unit had conducted on the island of Corregidor, during World War II. It was painfully hot to dig under the searing July sun. McKaig squinted through dark sunglasses and wiped sweat from his face as he dug and sipped water throughout the day.

As all good combat soldiers do, the paratroopers executed "stand-to" at 3:00 A.M. Soldiers have been taught for centuries that the enemy prefers to attack just before dawn, so they increase their security and prepare themselves for an attack well before dawn. All of the men of 2nd Platoon were alert, lying down in their fighting positions and scanning for the enemy in every direction. They looked through night-vision goggles for movement or anything out of place, anything that didn't seem right. To McKaig it was a lot like deer hunting. He examined the ridges closely, looking to catch even the slightest hint of movement.

At 4:30 A.M. there was enough ambient light to see with the naked eye. The men decided to remove their night-vision goggles. Just as they were taking them off, anticipating another scorching day spent scratching in the dirt under an unbearably hot Afghan sun, the valley exploded with gunfire and RPGs. They took fire from every direction at once, including from the village.

Though somewhat confused at how the enemy had surrounded them without being seen, the paratroopers instantly responded in kind, shooting back in every direction. Specialist McKaig fought alongside his buddy Specialist Ayers, who manned the M240 machine gun. It was terrifying. "The enemy fire was so intense I couldn't stop shaking. I got tunnel vision," said McKaig. It was like he was looking through a straw with no peripheral vision. Sometimes everything seemed to slow down, like the fight was in slow motion. "I actually saw a bullet exit one of my friends and hit a sandbag behind me—or so I thought," he recalled. "Then the fight would speed back up and it was chaos again, with enemy in every direction trying to kill us all."

An RPG impacted just below McKaig, and then another one exploded just above him; the concussion lifted him off the ground. He went through magazine after magazine of ammunition, fighting back—killing. His elbow burned. His assault pack was on fire. On some subconscious level, he understood that he had been wounded. The rational man would have stopped fighting for a second, checked his wounds, at least screamed for a medic, but he didn't react as he would have otherwise—he was swimming in a pool of adrenaline. *I wasn't trained for this,* he thought to himself, *not this.*

Simple, routine tasks such as changing a magazine in his rifle suddenly became difficult for McKaig. He kept thinking, I have to focus or I am going to die. Perhaps that was the training kicking in. For the first time in his life he encountered fear in a commanding way, fear that would shrivel the guts of the strongest men. The overwhelming urge to curl up in a ball and await his fate was almost impossible to resist. He desperately wanted to hide, somehow disappear, but in his heart he knew that succumbing to such weakness would bring certain death. He had to focus and fight.

The battle came in flashes of images that he could focus on only for a split second. He was bleeding and needed to bandage his wounds, but he realized that it didn't really matter that he was wounded because nothing could be done about it, considering the situation they were in. It was probably better that he didn't know if he was critically wounded or not. He was jolted back into the fight by the deafening sound of machine gun fire and RPGs. Chips of rocks, dust, and debris flew through the air. His body ached from the blasts all around him, and his ears rang with the deafening sound of war. He was being pummeled inside and out. Focus, Chris. Focus or you are going to die, he told himself. What a shitty place to die.

He dug deep within and focused harder.

"We've got to work together," McKaig told Ayers. They were hunkering down behind a small bit of cover provided by rocks. "Let's divide up our sector. I'll take three o'clock to nine o'clock," he said, pointing, "and you take ten to two."

"Okay," Ayers said. "Sounds good."

Face-to-face, the two men stared at each other, almost touching noses. The nervous anticipation of exposing themselves was painful to bear. McKaig counted: "One, two"—their hearts raced—"three," and both men rose up, identified enemy fighters, and began shooting.

They each fired eight to ten rounds at the enemy, who were quickly closing in on their position. After shooting they ducked back down, wild-eyed, panting, and scared out of their wits. They had exposed themselves for a few seconds and cheated death. Now they must do it again.

"You ready?" McKaig asked Ayers.

"Yeah."

"Okay, let's go. One, two, three," and both men rose again, firing at the approaching enemy, then recoiling back down behind the rocks.

"Again. One, two, three," McKaig counted, and up they rose.

This time when they ducked back down, Ayers looked different. He had a scared expression on his face; something was wrong. He coughed and "what seemed like a cup of blood came up." The bullet had hit him just above his body armor, beneath his collarbone. He was dead in less than twenty seconds.

Suddenly, something changed inside Chris McKaig. He seemed to focus harder, more clearly. He screamed at the top of his lungs, "Ayers is dead!" but the noise of battle was so loud he could not hear his own scream. Then, with an absolute clarity of purpose, perhaps given only to soldiers in close combat, he heard the enemy. They were close enough that he could hear the ominous sound of their bodies crawling through the rocks and the timbre and the emotion of their shouts. He peeked above the rocks, exposing only the top of his head and his eyes, and he saw an enemy fighter tangled up in the barbwire about one meter from McKaig's Claymore anti-personnel mine. He grabbed the firing device and prepared to squeeze it, but for some morbid reason that he didn't fully understand, he wanted to watch as he blew the Claymore on the man.

It was risky. He was terrified to raise his head above the rocks. Every time he rose up to shoot he assumed he'd be shot in the head, but he was terrified and wanted to know that the man had died when he blew the Claymore—that he was no longer a threat. McKaig was willing to risk another peek just to make sure.

From behind the rocks he squeezed the firing device and watched the explosion. Sparks flew and he saw the man receive the full force of the blast, saw shoes fly from the dead man's feet. Like an injection of morphine, he felt cool relief for a split second. Then, just as quickly, terror returned—an emotion he could not have previously conceived, that no man should have to experience.

Bullets began to rain down around Ayers's body so McKaig pulled him closer to him. Every few minutes he reached down and checked Ayers's pulse, just to be sure. He didn't want to believe that his buddy had been killed.

He could hear the enemy talking again. He threw two grenades at them, but then realized that they were so close that they had time to dive for cover before the grenades actually exploded. He pulled the pin on another grenade and let it "cook off" for a couple of seconds, then threw it up high into the air so the shrapnel would explode in every direction. It worked, and again he felt momentary relief.

Suddenly, Specialist McKaig saw several objects arc through the air and land all around him. "Grenade!" he yelled, but quickly realized that they were rocks. They had thrown rocks at him! Then it clicked: They had thrown the rocks in hopes that he'd think it was a grenade. They wanted McKaig to expose himself by leaping out from behind cover and running.

Everyone at OP Topside was either killed or wounded within the first twenty minutes of fighting. "Where are the birds?" several of the men screamed in anger. Helicopters and artillery were game changers in Afghanistan. The men needed them badly, and they needed them now. What they didn't know was that TF Out Front was in the middle of a shift-change briefing when the medevac request came into the command post. The night crews were ending their duty period and the day crews were just coming on shift. They were in the process of reporting to the command post to receive a briefing, which officially began their day, when they were notified of the attack. It was terrible timing, but they were racing to respond.

The day crews immediately ran to their Apaches. Chief Warrant Officer 3 Brian Townsend and Chief Warrant Officer 2 Theiman Watkins were crewed together. Chief Warrant Officer 3 Johnny Gaveraeu was in the other Apache. His fellow pilot had some difficulty with his flight gear, so Chief Warrant Officer 3 Jimmy Morrow, who had been on shift all night, jumped in the front seat of Gaveraeu's helicopter so they could respond faster. The Apaches were in the air within minutes, but it was a thirty-minute flight to the valley. The pilots flew the birds as fast as they would go, but it still seemed to take too long to get there. It seemed like an eternity to the men fighting for their lives and praying for help in the Waygal Valley.

At OP Topside, Specialist McKaig and his buddies fought on. Six or seven muzzle flashes could be seen sparking like cigarette lighters in a window of a mud hut only seventy meters away. McKaig picked up a light anti-tank weapon (LAW) and fired it into the window—direct hit. The enemy stopped shooting for a few seconds. It was like the power blinked off and all was quiet for just a split second, and then suddenly an RPG exploded right beside McKaig and his crew, killing Specialist Phillips.

Someone yelled, "They've got Zwilling!" Specialist 'Gunnar Zwilling was a twenty-year-old black-headed paratrooper from Florissant, Missouri, who had been with the unit for two years. The one thing soldiers fear more than death itself is being captured—a prisoner of war.

McKaig realized that he was at a decision point. He had two magazines of ammunition left. He could risk death by running to COP Kahler to get more ammunition, or he could hunker down and await certain death. As hard as that decision was, he knew what must be done. He looked across the rocky ground at Sergeant Gobble and yelled, "Do you want us to all fall back, or do you want us to go get more ammo?" Sergeant Gobble wanted them to get more ammo and bring it back to Topside, but no one appeared to be overly excited to run the gauntlet down the hill with McKaig, and it was a two-man job to get more ammo. The speedball resupplies were kept in large MK-19 ammunition cans, too heavy and bulky for one man to carry.

McKaig heard his platoon leader, Lieutenant Jonathan Brostrom, and Specialist Jason Hovater yelling. Fully recognizing that they might die trying, Brostrom and Hovater had run up the hill under intense enemy fire to save their buddies, for a very simple reason—that's what soldiers do for each other in a crisis. It was a heroic move.

Tragically, neither Lieutenant Brostrom nor Specialist Hovater would come back down the mountain under his own power. They would be carried down the mountain by the men they sacrificed their lives to save. Brostrom, Hovater, and McKaig's team leader, Corporal Pruitt Rainey, were all killed trying to save their fellow soldiers at OP Topside.

McKaig told himself three times to go before his body actually followed the command. He ran, zigzagging down the mountain as fast as he could go. The bullets, each carrying death with it, whizzed by him as he ran. He could hear them missing him by mere inches. His body ached yet he felt as if he were flying. He saw the concertina wire that surrounded the perimeter ahead. He would have to jump it and thought it just might be possible at a full sprint. Like a long jumper he planted his left foot in the rocky soil and lifted his right knee high into the air. His body departed the earth and took flight, then quickly dropped to the ground, like a sandbag thrown out of a second-story window. He landed in the middle of the wire and panicked.

He was stuck and the more he fought to try to free himself, the more entangled he became. He was a sitting duck, certain to be shot. Like someone drowning, he frantically fought to free himself, but the longer he fought, the stronger he felt the searing pain of fear in his chest—the fear of dying.

An enemy fighter in the second-story window of a building in Wanat village took aim. McKaig knew he was about to be shot through the back. He was certain the enemy had seen him run down the hill, tried to shoot him as he ran, then watched as he had become entangled. He imagined the enemy fighter smiling and thinking to himself, I've got you now.

McKaig fought hard to free himself, but it was impossible. Over the roar of the battle he heard the shot that was meant to kill him. He felt the bullet pass through his trousers at his calf. He felt the stinging in his calf, but amazingly the bullet had only brushed his skin as it passed his leg. *He missed me,* McKaig thought to himself.

The enemy fighter hastily popped off several more errant shots that hit noisily but harmlessly in the dirt next to McKaig.

Suddenly, a hand took hold of him and snatched him out of the wire. It was Specialist Hamby, and to McKaig he was heaven-sent. Hamby had sprinted down the hill with McKaig, only a few meters away the entire time, but McKaig hadn't seen him. He had not seen anything or anyone as he ran. He just ran.

Once he had safely arrived behind the sparse protection of the sandbags, McKaig was surprised to see Sergeants Gobble and Stafford there as well. They had been at Topside when he'd left. He hadn't seen them run with him either, yet they were already there. What he hadn't realized was that both of them had been right on his heels all the way down the hill, until he'd become entangled in the wire, that is. They'd managed to get over the wire and make it to the patrol base ahead of him.

The enemy fighter in the second-story window continued to shoot into their fighting position. Despite the fact that the shooter appeared to be a bad shot, McKaig knew that it was only a matter of time until he got lucky and hit one of them. McKaig told the M-203 gunner to put a round in the second-story window. The gunner had only two rounds remaining—a flare and a high-explosive round. He loaded the flare first and put it right in the window—a perfect shot. Smoke billowed noiselessly out of the window, and for a moment, all was uncomfortably silent. McKaig looked through his sights, waiting for the enemy soldier to come out, to give him a shot, but he never emerged.

"Shoot the HE round," McKaig said, still looking down his sights as sweat steadily dripped from his nose to the stock of the rifle. The gunner then shot the high-explosive round. It was another perfect shot and this time, the building went silent for good.

With the shooter silenced, McKaig had work to do. He ran to a vehicle to get more ammunition. He found a speedball can filled with grenades and machine gun ammo, specifically prepared for emergency situations such as this one. He gathered all he could carry, stuffed his pockets full, and then began mentally preparing himself for what he feared but knew must be done—the trek back up the hill to Topside. He was about to begin up the hill when suddenly he saw something he couldn't believe. It was too good to be true, but it was. First Platoon, Chosen Company, pulled up to the outpost in four vehicles. He felt something strange stir within him, a feeling almost foreign that he realized he had not felt to that point in the battle—hope. For the first time since stand-to, he actually thought he might live.

The machine guns on the vehicles began to lay down a heavy base of fire. Then he noticed something else for the first time: the blissful sound of an Apache's 30-mm cannon. The cavalry had arrived and the tide of the battle was slowly beginning to turn. That knowledge alone gave him strength. He had allowed himself to venture dangerously close to despair. At times he had almost crumbled under the stress of battle, but mentally he had fought hopelessness, and now he realized it was all worth it. He suddenly moved with renewed speed and purpose.

The Apaches quickly went to work engaging enemy forces on the ridges. It was easy to find enemy fighters to shoot at, but the shots made the pilots nervous because they were so close to the perimeter, where the men of Second Platoon were located. The pilots feared that they would hit the paratroopers. Someone transmitted over the radio to the Apaches, telling them to "shoot the building. It's full of enemy."

Jimmy Morrow confirmed the request, observed effective enemy fire emanating from the building, and engaged, killing everyone inside.

"Artillery! Lay down flat on the ground," someone yelled. McKaig suddenly feared that he might die from friendly fire. The Apaches were shooting enemy fighters right outside the wire, and now artillery, shot from FOB Blessing, was about to rain down almost on top of him. Trying to protect himself, McKaig frantically began trying to dig into the ground with his hands, tried to scratch out a place to hide, but it was no use. Suddenly he realized that he was meant to live or die in this valley, and all he could do was wait and see. The thought was somehow liberating. In some strange way it eased the burden of survival. All he could do was fight the enemy, kill as many as possible. If he was meant to die at Wanat, then he would most certainly die at Wanat. If not, then he would see this morning of hell to its conclusion, and he would leave the valley alive.

His body suddenly lifted from the ground; he seemed to hover for a split second, then he slammed back down into the rocky earth as artillery exploded with a deafening crash. His ears rang and his body ached from the concussion and hours of fighting, but he was still alive and able to fight back.

The men wanted the Apaches to know exactly where they were, so they threw an orange VS-17 panel made out of nylon into a small tree to mark their position—a bright orange piece of nylon that screamed out for attention against the gray rocks and wiry green scrub in the Waygal.

The pilots received a "danger close" request at Topside, which meant that the soldiers on the ground wanted the Apaches to shoot so close to their position that they too would be in danger of being hit by the rounds. Enemy fighters were that close to them. A fighter with an automatic machine gun and a two-man RPG team slithered through the rocks, closing in on the OP.

"We are beside the VS-17 panel. I'm going to throw a smoke grenade towards the enemy. Shoot fifty meters east of the smoke," one of the men told the pilots. The Apache pilots saw the smoke and immediately shot a burst of 30-mm cannon. The men on the ground were terrified of the Apaches. Several of them screamed out "Lie flat!" as the Apaches flew straight at them, cannon thumping away. The rounds impacted the rocks and exploded like grenades, sending shrapnel and debris through the air with enough force to take a man's arm or leg off. It was a devastating weapon.

Despite the battle that continued to rage, the men of Second Platoon knew they had to get the medevac helicopter in soon or the wounded would die of their injuries. The Apaches suppressed the enemy, trying to force their heads down, as the medevac made its approach to a landing zone between Topside and COP Kahler. One of the heroes of the day was a flight medic in TF Out Front, Staff Sergeant Matthew Kinney. Staff Sergeant Kinney would later receive the Silver Star and Air Medal for Valor for hoist extractions in the Korengal Valley.

I had known Matt Kinney since he was a private first class in Germany. We had served together in 4th Brigade, 1st Armored Division in the 1990s. We had both been competitive runners and lived near one another, so we ran countless miles across the German countryside together. We had no idea that a decade and thousands of miles later we would be reunited.

As they flew into the Waygal Valley they radioed the men on the ground. "Hearing them ask for a medevac, knowing they needed us but hearing all the machine guns in the background, sends a chill through your body. It's a scary thing. You know you have to go, but you also know you may die. Once you're on the ground you just go. It's the anticipation that's the worst," Kinney said.

The medevac pilot flared the bird at the bottom of the approach and sat it down right outside the wire. Kinney exploded out of the helicopter, jumped the concertina wire, and ran through a storm of bullets to carry wounded soldiers back to the bird. Time and time again he sprinted around the perimeter, asking soldiers where the wounded were located. Several times the soldiers pointed to a row of bodies. "I can't help them," Kinney shouted above the noise of machine guns and helicopter rotors. "I need your wounded! We'll come back for them."

Kinney loaded the aircraft with injured men and then quickly departed. Along the perimeter Sergeant Hissong told the men to get back up the hill to OP Topside to recover their fallen. McKaig now had eight grenades and two cans of ammunition for his machine gun. Two other soldiers, Tinnin and Green, said they'd go with him. Hissong then looked McKaig in the eye and said, "They're all dead, McKaig. Don't look at them when you get up there."

"Yes, sergeant," McKaig answered in disbelief.

"You and Sergeants Gobble and Stafford would be dead too if you didn't get down here when you did," he added.

They ran as fast as they could up the steep hill, carrying a heavy ammunition can in each hand. McKaig suddenly realized that he didn't even have a weapon with him. In an adrenaline-raged state he had run up the hill to help recover his buddies, leaving his weapon behind. Green and Tinnin protected him as he lumbered forward. As he approached he could see that the OP was completely destroyed, and then he saw his fellow soldiers. Just as Sergeant Hissong had said, they were all dead.

They found Zwilling's body near a bush several meters away. While they were relieved that he had not been captured, the pain of his loss cut them to the core.

Staff Sergeant Phillips and a marine had made it up the hill ahead of McKaig and fought from what cover they could find. Phillips, McKaig, Green, Tinnin, and the marine fought on for a while before returning to Kahler. Staff Sergeant Kinney made trip after trip into the valley, retrieving wounded soldiers, flying them to the forward surgical unit at FOB Wright, then returning. Slowly, enemy gunfire began to dissipate. McKaig heard the medevac pilot over the radio: "Are there any more wounded?" he asked. "There are," Sergeant Hissong answered, "there's one more."

Staff Sergeant Phillips helped McKaig to the helicopter. He had sustained his energy to fight through adrenaline and sheer will, but he was slowly beginning to wither both physically and emotionally. The pilot pulled in power, and the medevac bird began to climb out of the valley. Stafford lay wounded on the floor of the helicopter, and McKaig sat beside him. The crew chief handed McKaig a bottle of water, but he couldn't stand the thought of drinking in front of his wounded friend. He looked down at Stafford, whose lips were cracked and bleeding, his face smeared black with blood and dirt. McKaig opened the bottle and poured the tiny cap full, a mere thimble of water, and poured it over Stafford's lips. They both wept.

Sitting in the command post at FOB Fenty, I felt overwhelmed with emotion. I had served two tours in Iraq, but I had never experienced anything like that. I felt fear for the men in the valley, yet I felt completely helpless to do anything for them. I was crawling out of my skin, anxious, overpowered with tension. Throughout the battle I was praying that it would end, that the tide would somehow turn, that something, anything, would happen to stop it, but it went on and on. It had a profound impact on me. I hoped I would never experience that feeling again.

In the hours that followed, casualty notification teams visited nine families. They knocked at doors bearing news that all families dreaded receiving. *If they call you on the phone, your soldier is okay*, families would tell each other. *If they knock at the door in dress uniform, it's the worst.* It was a tragic day for many Americans, particularly those who fought alongside and lost fellow soldiers. "Those images will never leave my mind," McKaig later told me. "They are forever a part of me."

The battle at Wanat was the single deadliest attack since the war in Afghanistan had begun. We lost nine American heroes that hot July morning.

> First Lieutenant Jonathan P. Brostrom, 24, of Hawaii
> Sergeant Israel Garcia, 24, of Long Beach, California
> Corporal Jonathan R. Ayers, 24, of Snellville, Georgia
> Corporal Jason M. Bogar, 25, of Seattle, Washington
> Corporal Jason D. Hovater, 24, of Clinton, Tennessee
> Corporal Matthew B. Phillips, 27, of Jasper, Georgia
> Corporal Pruitt A. Rainey, 22, of Haw River, North
>   Carolina
> Corporal Gunnar W. Zwilling, 20, of Florissant, Missouri
> Specialist Sergio S. Abad, 21, of Morganfield, Kentucky

Everyone in Task Force Out Front's command post was devastated; however, having listened to the battle unfold and watched the gun tape videos, it was clear to me that every American soldier in that valley fought heroically. I listened intently as multiple levels of close air support (CAS), unmanned aerial vehicles, and Apaches were coordinated for and sequenced into the fight. I saw the work in the command post, felt their emotion, as they coordinated and synchronized assets. I now clearly understood the complexity of fighting a determined and disciplined enemy in incredibly challenging terrain. I departed with a revised and sober perspective of the importance of preparation in the months to come.

Later that evening Mike, Jillian, and I went to dinner together. Mike didn't crack his usual jokes, and I had nothing optimistic to offer. We ate in silence, Jillian poring over the enemy in her mind, Mike and I silently asking the same question: Is our team ready for a fight like this?

Two days later, on July 15, Mike Woodhouse and I joined Chief Warrant Officer 4 Anne Wiley and Chief Warrant Officer 4 Mike Slebodnik to fly an orientation flight around Nangarhar and Kunar provinces in Kiowa helicopters. The cavalry community is rather small and the 101st Airborne Division Kiowa community is even smaller, so Mike Woodhouse and I knew Anne and Mike very well. We'd all served together in the past.

Mike Woodhouse and Anne decided to fly lead while Slebodnik and I took trail. It was great to get out and fly with pilots we knew and to get their firsthand personal perspective of the fight. Slebodnik and I laughed and reminisced about past deployments to Iraq and field training exercises at Fort Campbell. Both Mike Slebodnik and Anne had taken the opportunity, as many soldiers do, to focus on fitness during their deployment. Obviously, fitness is an important part of a soldier's life; however, "fitness" is a relative term. Both Mike and Anne had significantly raised the bar in that regard.

We met them in the team room where the pilots kept their flight gear. Slebodnik had put his tight-fitting army combat shirt on.

"Dude! Look at you. You are *fit*," I said, and poked his chest.

A huge smile emerged on Mike's face. "I've been working at it," he said, proud yet almost embarrassed that I was making such a big deal of it.

I pulled my camera out of my pocket. "Let me get a picture," I said.

We sat down at their planning table and they methodically walked us through the planning and briefing process they used to prepare for each flight.

"Which seat do you want to fly in, sir?" Mike Slebodnik asked.

"Are you kidding?" I said. "You're not really asking that, are you?" In a Kiowa the pilot in the right seat does most of the flying and is the only one of the two pilots who can shoot the weapon systems. The left-seat pilot is primarily responsible for navigation, tuning radios, running the sight, and backing up the right-seat pilot.

"That's what I figured you'd say," he said, laughing. Then he leaned in and said, "If you think Anne is going to let Woodhouse fly right seat, you are crazy."

Mike and Anne took us up the Kunar River Valley to see all of the FOBs and COPs. We flew up the Pech River Valley again, filled up with gas at FOB Wright, and then headed back down to Nangarhar Province. We flew to the Torkham Gate so we could view the Khyber Pass from the Afghan side. It was a great flight, providing us with a much better understanding of the environment in which we would soon be operating. I gained clarity as to the tactics the 2-17 CAV pilots were using by flying with Mike. The flight also helped us shake the funk we'd been in after Wanat.

AIR CAVALRY RECONNAISSANCE, SURVEILLANCE, AND TARGET ACQUISITION

The following day Mike, Jillian, and I met in the dining facility and ate breakfast together. We discussed what we had seen so far, and of course spoke at length about Wanat, this time trying to capture the lessons we had learned. Later that morning we sat in on the TF Out Front targeting meeting. The targeting meeting was an important synchronization effort that enabled the team to focus their reconnaissance assets in order to better understand the enemy and answer the commander's information requirements. I was very interested in their process because I felt that it was one of the most important meetings held in a cavalry unit. It determined their focus and resource allocation in order to obtain information about the enemy. The results of the targeting meeting became the reconnaissance priorities.

Helicopter crews were assigned specific tasks based on the meeting's outcome. Without this meeting, well-intentioned aircraft were merely sent out on the battlefield to troll for the enemy. If the targeting meeting was conducted properly, then the crew would review the results of their reconnaissance efforts since the last meeting. They would determine if they had answered the questions posed previously about the enemy. It might be that they were trying to determine the routes that the enemy used to travel from one area to another—where they crossed the Kunar River, for example. At the conclusion of the meeting they would decide if they needed to continue collecting data in order to answer those questions or if they needed to shift their collection efforts to another location. It was refreshing to see the progress of an intelligence-collection process that I'd helped to create in 2-17 Cavalry years before.

I served as the operations officer of 2-17 Cavalry from 2003 to 2004, while deployed to Iraq. I had joined the squadron at Qayyarah Airfield West, south of Mosul, in June 2003. While the 101st encountered significant fighting at each major city as they pushed north through Iraq, the initial push went surprisingly smoothly. Once they captured Mosul, the fighting subsided somewhat. But after a relatively calm summer, enemy activity abruptly increased.

Once the division was established in northern Iraq, 2-17 Cavalry was tasked to work directly for 2nd Brigade Combat Team (Strike). That fall Strike began encountering IEDs, ambushes, and mortar and rocket attacks, all on a more frequent basis. We kept our Kiowas in the air around the clock. We covered ground patrols when they went out, we provided aerial security for meetings, and we conducted reconnaissance around our FOBs, but we rarely caught anyone in the act of emplacing IEDs or rockets. We seemed to show up always right after an attack had occurred. Faced with the dilemma of how to "get left of the boom," as we called the process of trying to determine what the enemy would do before he did it, the intelligence officer Captain Candy Smith and I began trying to find patterns in enemy activity.

At that time we had no tools to help us with trend or pattern analysis other than an army field manual. We were certain that the enemy was no different than every other living thing on the planet: they were creatures of habit, they set patterns, and it was our job to find those patterns and exploit them. Certainly, enemy actions could be more accurately anticipated if we could determine a precedent in time, location, or routes.

As we brainstormed the problem, Captain Smith's assistant said she thought she could write a program or build a database that would allow us to record all of the attacks and overlay them onto a map. We would then be able to plot attacks by type, time, size, etc., and color-code them. Once we began compiling the data, we began to notice clear and distinct patterns in locations and times—where and when the enemy preferred to attack us.

Armed with this information, we were then able to task Kiowas with specific reconnaissance objectives. We didn't immediately begin killing the enemy as they prepared for attacks, but what we quickly experienced was a reduction in attacks due to our presence in the right place at the right time. We forced the enemy to operate where they preferred not to operate. We interdicted their timelines, and clearly, our actions began to deter their attacks. That alone saved lives. We had found a way to become more effective for the soldier on the ground.

Our actions were not novel by any stretch of the imagination. We implemented simple pattern analysis that already existed in army doctrine at the time. What made it unique was that we made it work, albeit at the elementary level, despite lacking the technological tools to exploit our ideas fully.

In 2003, we had limited technological systems in our command posts. Few units even had Internet access—only those supported by large signal corps assets, and that wasn't many. Intelligence collection was done at the unit level, and there were few databases below the division that held a repository of intelligence data collected. We used the manual approach. Each day we contacted the infantry battalions and asked for a roll-up of all enemy activity in their area for that day. We copied down the location of attacks, number of fighters, weapons used, and time of the attacks. Our soldiers then manually input the raw data into our database. We were trying to transform that data into actionable intelligence—to make sense of it all.

What we did in 2-17 Cavalry turned the light on for me personally. It helped me realize that our potential was far greater than we had previously realized. With the right tools we could exploit the raw data even further to answer much more complex questions about the enemy. I did not have all the answers, but I had many questions and ideas, which I took with me to 7-17 Cavalry.

By my second tour in Iraq, under the direction of General Stanley McChrystal, joint fusion cells were established in Iraq and Afghanistan, which brought all collection, not only army but also joint and other governmental agencies (OGAs), together. Bringing all the various sources of intelligence together, "fusing them," made joint fusion cells a game changer. A fusion cell had been established at FOB Fenty and I looked forward to exploiting its resources to make us a much more effective cavalry task force and valuable asset to the forces we supported.

Moreover, our command posts, at the battalion task force level, had become much more capable since the war began. The technology resident in a battalion in 2008 rivaled, if not exceeded, that found in a

division in 2003. Our senior leaders saw the power of pushing access
to systems down to the lowest possible level, thus enhancing understanding and enabling targets to be prosecuted in a much timelier
manner.

As Jillian, Mike, and I sat in on 2-17 Cavalry's targeting meeting, it
was exciting to see how far they had advanced our original systems.
Aviation units do not "target" per se, but TF Out Front used the
targeting process to focus their reconnaissance and surveillance assets. Jillian's goal, and mine, was to gain as comprehensive an understanding of their process as possible in one targeting cycle (seven
days of input/analysis/output). We would then take that process back
to Fort Campbell and begin trying to take it to the next level.

Jillian's experience thus far had been academic and in the garrison
environment. PDSS was her first trip to a combat zone. She saw the
environment through the lens of potential. Her mind was filled with
ideas, but she was somewhat concerned that her being only a lieutenant in an aviation unit would somehow hinder her ability to do
all the things she wanted to do. Jillian didn't like parochialisms. She
liked transparent, straight-shooting, honest feedback, and she welcomed it from all players regardless of rank and position. She hoped
to play a key role in the process, despite preexisting notions about
inexperienced lieutenants.

During my first few weeks of command she had clearly demonstrated what kind of officer she was. She had sent a document to my
office for review. It was a good product, but I had numerous questions, which I wrote in red in the margins of the paper. When I finished making notes and asking questions, I had filled the margins with
red ink. My adjutant returned it to Jillian later that afternoon. She
walked straight to my door and knocked.

"Yes, Jillian," I said.

"I just wanted to thank you," she said with genuine sincerity.

"For what?"

"For this," she said and held the paper up. "This is the first feedback I've received on my products since I've been in the army. I can
work with this." She smiled and walked out. I knew she would thrive
as our intelligence officer.

Because I didn't have the answers, I knew it was critical that I ask
the right questions. I felt that if I could adequately articulate the

vision I had for what we could do, and get the intelligence team to fearlessly attack the problem before us, we would make huge strides and contribute immensely to the fight in eastern Afghanistan. I didn't want them to fear failing, nor did I want them to hold back in exploring their ideas. Immediately following TF Out Front's targeting meeting I pulled Jillian aside.

"Jillian, there is a wealth of raw data in the fusion cell that we can use."

"Sir, are they even going to let me in those meetings?" she asked, half joking but with obvious reservations. When she attended the fusion cell meeting with 2-17 Cavalry's intelligence officer, she said that most folks wrote off the aviation intelligence section, except to ask for operational-type input. The fusion cell focuses primarily on targeting high-value individuals, and aviation intelligence focuses more on the big picture of enemy trends. She had come back from the meeting with the realization that she needed to listen intently to the input from each unit and use that to piece together an understanding of the enemy holistically.

"I think we can exploit the intelligence they offer to create a macro-perspective of enemy activity in our area and not just focus on high-value targets," she said, "but it isn't going to be easy. My shop is small."

"Well, what if I found you more people?" I offered, knowing she wanted and needed a larger team. The more we brainstormed about what was possible, the more work it created, and we were authorized only Jillian, her assistant, one sergeant, and two analysts. We needed more analysts.

She thought about it then looked directly at me and said, "If you give me more people, I will definitely put them to work." She discussed her vision for how her shop would work through the tasks of deliberate operation planning, intelligence collection, database management, and current operations and intelligence tracking. She was already noting how each person's tasks would fuse with the others' to eliminate redundancies and run efficiently. I listened, content with her plans, while thinking about the enemy we would face.

"You know," I interrupted, "the question isn't *where*—we can easily see where the enemy is attacking us in the Kunar and Pech river valleys. What we need to know is *how* they are sustaining the fight.

Are they using the timber-smuggling money to finance it? If so, how does it work? What routes are they using to smuggle to and from Pakistan?"

She nodded, excited to discuss the threat, and added, "I agree that those are questions we can help answer as the aviation task force. We can *see* some of those indicators—how are they bringing weapons and materiel into the Pech from the Federally Administered Tribal Areas (FATA)?"

"They are exposed the most at the river crossings," I added. Since flying over and observing our area of operations for the first time, my focus had immediately gone to the river. Why focus on the porous, "official" border when we could focus our resources on the natural obstacle—the river—and narrow the enemy's options down?

She nodded and added, "I think we can figure this thing out, but it's going to require a focused methodology to help confirm what we see through visual indicators using the other collection means, like human and signals intelligence, and of course all of the ground units."

The questions we discussed that day would form the basis of my intelligence priorities later on—what I as the commander wanted to know about the enemy. We had to understand the enemy's modus operandi, understand what they knew about us, and then interdict them both physically and psychologically. I knew that it would not be easy and that many people might think that an aviation unit could not possibly do this, but I believed we could. We would determine the enemy's pattern of life, interdict their communications and logistics, surprise them, then keep them off balance, thus forcing them to act counter to their desires.

I could see that Jillian was initially a bit unsure as to how we would answer all these questions, but her whole demeanor had changed as we spoke. This was right up her alley. She loved the complexity of the problem, and I knew her team would thrive solving such intricate problems.

There were a lot of collection assets within our area of operations. We had to maximize the use of those assets and form quality relationships with everyone else in our area, others who were studying the same tactical problem. I wanted to create an environment where she and her team were not afraid to explore their ideas. I wanted them to start solving the puzzle a piece at a time. We would be flying all over the N2KL daily. Every crew would be a sensor and would be looking for something based on where they were going to fly and the time that they would be there. It would be up to Jillian's team to put them in the right place at the right time with the right focus.

At the end of July, our site survey was complete. It was time to return to Fort Campbell and make our final preparations for deployment. John Lynch's guys flew us back to Bagram Airfield to catch an air force jet to Manas, Kyrgyzstan. When we arrived at Bagram we entered the air force system of personnel movement. I had used the system many times before, traveling in and out of Iraq, where in 2004 my Gerber multitool was confiscated because the security folks apparently feared that I might use it to hijack the very plane that was taking me home after a yearlong deployment in Iraq. I realized everyone had to do their job and follow the rules, but I'll admit that I had a bit of a sour taste in my mouth.

The airforce passenger terminal folks took us to a fenced-in compound where a young airman told us, "This is the holding yard. Wait in here until you are called forward to manifest. Do not leave the area."

We filed into the small holding area feeling like caged dogs, and what I saw made me sick to my stomach. The waiting area was nothing more than a large cement pad inside a fenced area. There were a couple of metal benches under a small shed, but most of the pad remained outside, under the pitch-black Afghan night. There, laid out on the cement or propped against rucksacks, was a large group of clearly weathered soldiers. A few of them stared off into the night, detached. I perceived that their thoughts were far from where we sat. But most of the men were in a deep sleep. One soldier, on the cement slab, sat flat on his butt, his legs stretched straight out in front of him and his feet crossed. He leaned back into his rucksack. His arms were folded across his chest, and his patrol cap was pulled down over his eyes. At least fifty of us dragged our bags in and tried to find a place to relax. He didn't move. He appeared to be in a coma, oblivious to everything around him.

The men's uniforms were salt encrusted, their hair matted and greasy. They looked as if they had walked there from whatever outpost they had occupied for the past year. They had basically done just that.

These men wore the patch of the 173rd Airborne. A helicopter had picked them up at FOB Blessing. They'd flown to Jalalabad, where they'd caught another flight to Bagram. Now, these American heroes, who had spent fifteen months in a remote outpost fighting for their lives on a daily basis, were lying on a cement pad and getting barked at by a cleanly washed air force sergeant who worked a shift. I was sickened.

I approached the sergeant. "Don't you realize that these guys just rolled in from being in an outpost for over a year? Do you not have a classroom or someplace with chairs where they can wait?" I asked.

"No, sir. This is how the system works," he said.

I shook my head and walked away. I sat down, leaned back against my rucksack, turned on my headlamp, and began trying to capture more notes from our visit. After several hours of waiting, we were told to line up for manifest. They began moving us forward into a large processing center. Quietly, the men got up and began forming a line. No one had complained about having to wait on concrete. In fact, they had not spoken much at all, not even to one another. These men were going home. They were used to such a sparse existence that this seemed somewhat normal, if not better than what "normal" had become. I then saw a few men go back to the fence and move nine wooden crosses forward. They were ceremonial stands used to hold the Kevlar, dog tags, and weapons at memorials for fallen heroes. And then it struck me: These men were not just any soldiers, in from some remote location. They were the men who had lost nine of their brothers in the Waygal Valley just a few days prior. These were Specialist McKaig's platoon mates. They were headed home and taking the memorial stands with them. As we moved forward in the line, several soldiers silently continued to move the wooden stands along with them.

It was a stark reminder of the tragic realities of war. The scene clearly demonstrated the contrast between those who fight from remote locations in the heart of enemy territory and those who don't. Nonetheless, I fully understood and respected the fact that everyone had a role to play in the war. The soldiers and airmen who worked in offices on Bagram were no less important. Their work contributed to the overall success of the war. Those who ensured that we got mail to the front lines affected morale perhaps more than they could imagine. Nevertheless, frontline soldiers dating back to Vietnam have looked down on those who did not leave the big bases, those who are not directly involved in fighting.

We boarded an air force C-17 and flew in silence to Manas, Kyrgyzstan, lulled to sleep by the roar of jet engines. In Manas, while we waited for a flight back to the States, we played cards, and Mike and I reminisced about our days together in the 1st Squadron, 1st U.S. Cavalry. I also had time to look carefully over my notes and assess where I thought we were in terms of preparation, and what needed a bit more attention prior to our deployment. I had gained a much greater appreciation for the complexity of the fight we'd face in Afghanistan. Words can't truly describe the breathtaking, beautiful, yet treacherous terrain in eastern Afghanistan, nor can one fully understand the difficulty of fighting a largely indigenous, disciplined enemy that is battle-hardened and knows how to use the terrain to his advantage. I already had great confidence in our crews. I felt that we had prepared ourselves thoroughly for the deployment; however, I left Afghanistan knowing that we must ensure that our air mission commanders, those pilots in charge of teams who make critical, tactical decisions with potentially strategic implications, understood the importance of their decisions on the battlefield.

Our pre-deployment site survey was complete. In my mind it was a huge success and an eye-opening experience for me personally. I was excited to return to Fort Campbell and put the final touches on our training.

A CAVALRY STATE OF MIND

Cavalry units conjure up images of the Old West, where leaders like Phil Sheridan, Jeb Stuart, and Nathan Bedford Forrest led elite forces deep into enemy territory to terrorize supply trains, attack the flanks, and report on their enemy's whereabouts and disposition. They were known for their red and white guidons,[1] cavalry hats, sabers, and spurs. These men and their units serve as an inspiration for the modern-day cavalryman. But the cavalry panache can be taken to an extreme. Sure, it's exciting to live the flamboyant lifestyle of a cavalryman. Riding into battle behind the red and white guidon, wearing a big Stetson hat with crossed sabers on the front and golden spurs strapped to cavalry boots, jingling as you charge into battle on a trusty steed can be intoxicating, but that is not what makes cavalry special.

It's true that cavalrymen passionately cling to the traditions of their forebearers. The Stetson hat and spurs are coveted accoutrements proudly worn by contemporary cavalrymen, but I have become somewhat well known for repeatedly reminding my cavalry troopers that, "cavalry is not about horse shit and gun powder. It's about standards." What sets quality cavalry units apart is that they establish high standards, and demand that all of their troopers must consistently meet those standards.

Task Force Pale Horse was an air cavalry squadron. Our crews knew how to conduct their primary missions of reconnaissance and security. I was confident in their technical abilities, but in my mind the tactical tasks of reconnaissance and security were only half of the equation. There is something called the "cavalry mentality," and this term cannot be downplayed or understated. Historically, a cavalry unit is the eyes and ears of the commander. In a reconnaissance role they are sent ahead of the main force to scout out terrain, determine route suitability, bridge serviceability, and, most important, find the enemy. The cavalry scout is trained to see things others might miss, notice what is out of place, analyze a situation, and report his observations. In a security role, the cavalry protects the main force by finding or interdicting an approaching enemy force. In Afghanistan we protected convoys by looking for ambushes and IEDs.

While cavalry scouts operate independently, they are not to become decisively engaged with the enemy unless absolutely necessary or required by the mission. Tasked with a specific purpose, yet entrusted with the ability to adjust their mission as necessary to achieve the commander's broader intent, a cavalryman is afforded tremendous trust and latitude, something he takes very seriously and must never violate.

Our steeds have changed over the years. Today the air cavalry's primary helicopter is the OH-58D Kiowa Warrior. Due to the vast distances and mountains in Afghanistan we "task organized" our units. Back at Fort Campbell our battalions were structured around one aircraft type, except for 7-101, the general support aviation battalion. 7-17 cavalry had thirty Kiowas, 3-101 had twenty-four Apaches, 4-101 had thirty Black Hawks, and 7-101 had a company of Chinooks, a company of Black Hawks, an air traffic control company, and a medevac company. In Afghanistan we gave ten Kiowas to 3-101 and ten to 7-101. In return they gave us Apaches, Black Hawks, and Chinooks. Task organization meant that we reorganized ourselves to best meet the specific requirements of the ground force brigade commander.

A task-organized unit is called a task force. Task Force Pale Horse was comprised of AH-64D Apaches, OH-58D Kiowas, CH-47F Chinooks, UH-60M Black Hawks, UH-60L Medevac, and Hunter unmanned aerial vehicles (UAV). While each aircraft was designed for a specific role, I required all of the aircrews to think and act like cavalrymen. It wasn't the type of helicopter that made us cavalrymen but rather our attitude, our mentality.

The Black Hawk is an assault helicopter, designed to move an infantry squad around the battlefield. I wanted the pilots to do more than just move soldiers and supplies on the battlefield. I wanted them to scout as they flew from one place to another. I wanted them to notice patterns of life in the various villages and the Afghan country-side. I wanted them to observe activity along their route of flight: how the locals responded when they flew over, what appeared to be lashed to donkeys on the mountain trails, and people who looked out of place. Most important, after each mission, I wanted them to report what they saw in great detail. Their observations were invaluable.

My assault company commander bought into my idea wholeheartedly, often transmitting over the radio, "You Kiowas guys go do your thing, and we Black Hawk pilots will come in and clean up the mess behind you." He was fond of saying he thought like a gun pilot but flew a Black Hawk.

The Apache helicopter is unquestionably the most lethal killer on the modern battlefield, but it is also very good at reconnaissance. In fact some units use Apaches as their cavalry platform. Sensors enable the pilot to slew the 30-mm cannon to their helmet, thus the gun points where the pilot looks. This technology allows the pilot to quickly en-gage enemy forces. Once an Apache pilot locks onto an enemy fighter it is almost impossible for him to get away. The faster they run, the hotter they glow in the thermal system. But the Apache cockpit is a tandem two-pilot cockpit—one pilot sits in front of the other. The cockpit design prevents the pilots from easily observing things outside of the helicopter with the naked eye.

OH-58D Kiowa Warriors are equipped with a 50-caliber machine gun. The gun is fixed forward, meaning it points forward and can't be moved in flight; therefore, the pilot must maneuver the aircraft to adjust the impact point of bullets when engaging targets. This makes it less accurate than the Apache, but the highly maneuverable and agile Kiowa is a fantastic scouting helicopter. Kiowa pilots have tre-mendous visibility from the cockpit, particularly since they remove the doors when flying missions. Kiowa pilots are trained to be in-quisitive.

Afghanistan's heavy lifter is the Chinook. Without her the mission in Afghanistan would be nearly impossible. Only the Chinook can carry heavy loads of personnel and equipment into the high moun-tainous terrain. While the Chinook's primary role is lift, the pilots can also pay attention to what they see and report their observations back to the intel team. The Chinook has a crew of five—potentially a lot of eyes observing the battlefield. I did not want Chinooks and Black

Hawks assigned specific reconnaissance missions; I wanted Jillian to develop a collection plan that required the Chinook and Black Hawk crews to pay particular attention to certain locations based on the time they were flying. They would then be required to report what they had seen in their debriefing following the mission. If we were to maximize our capability it would mean that every pilot was a scout to some degree—a battlefield sensor. For us, cavalry was not a helicopter. Cavalry was a state of mind.

There were certainly challenges that I knew we would have to overcome. I was keenly aware that our pilots were products of their previous experiences, which would make some of them resistant to change. The majority of our pilots had one or more combat tours in Iraq, but we had very few pilots with Afghanistan experience. Aviation operations in Afghanistan, particularly Regional Command (RC) East, differed vastly from those in Iraq. Fighting in Iraq had taken place primarily in an urban environment. In RC-East the majority of our fights would occur in the mountains and valleys outside of villages.

Kiowa teams in Iraq commonly departed their FOBs with a specific mission but almost always deviated when a "troops in contact" (TIC) was declared, and ground forces were engaged with the enemy. Due to the distances, complex terrain, and limited rotary-wing assets available in RC-East, prioritization of assets was essential. I knew that crews would naturally want to "run to the sound of the guns." While this was a common practice in Iraq it was not always what ground force commanders wanted in RC-East. TICs occurred in many locations multiple times daily. The use of artillery and mortars normally silenced the enemy in a matter of minutes. If our Kiowas deviated from an assigned mission to help troops in contact at a COP or FOB, while seemingly logical to the pilot, it could potentially detract from the brigade's larger mission and priorities. We would have to educate battle captains and aviators that deviating from assigned missions required brigade authorization unless lives were at risk on the ground. Clearly subjective, that would not be an easy call for our teams to make.

In a counterinsurgency fight, every soldier on the battlefield is a sensor. Perhaps the most underutilized collection assets were the rotary-wing aviation aircrews. Helicopters traverse and observe more of a brigade's battle space daily than any other sensor on the battlefield. It is essential to integrate them into the collection plan, give them specific reconnaissance objectives, and thoroughly debrief them after each flight. In 2009, we were determined to prove just how valuable an aviation task force could be, not only for air assaults, convoy and patrol security, and hasty attacks, but also as a collection asset. In order to achieve success we had to get genuine buy-in from our crew members. They had to commit to the cavalry mentality.

I would soon see our crews embrace the cavalry way of thinking quite well, as evidenced in this journal entry from First Lieutenant Aaron Nichols, a Black Hawk platoon leader in our task force.

14 Feb 2009

SPC A.J. Mick pointed out a HUGE train of donkeys headed into Pakistan. Each donkey (est. 150–200 donkeys) was packed with large yellow bundles of stuff . . . not sure exactly what the "stuff" was. Mike Downing and I whipped the aircraft around and got some pretty good pictures for the S2. We'd already done quite a few recons with Special Operations Forces guys before, but this was the first time where we found some possibly shady activity. Our crew felt pretty good about the whole venture, and felt even better when the S2 drummed up a pretty in-depth story-board for BDE about what we found.

—Aaron Nichols

A HATEFUL DAY

On September 11, 2008, I crawled out of bed at 5:00 A.M. and went for a run on a Tennessee back road. The deployment was on my mind. Over the years I have found that I do my best thinking during a run. That particular morning, I recall going over our training program in my mind. Had we done everything we could to prepare our men and women for the terrain and the complexity of the fight we would face? We had a phenomenal team, and I had great confidence in them. It was as if the universe had tilted and brought us all together at one place and time. I was incredibly proud to serve in their ranks, but I always asked myself that question—had we done enough?

Later, as I drove to work, I reflected on the fact that we'd been at war for seven long years. I'd been working in Alexandria, Virginia, when it all began. Driving to work on I-495, I listened as Jack Diamond announced over the radio that a plane had struck the World Trade Center. I clearly remember smirking as I pictured in my mind the tail of a Cessna airplane sticking out of a window a hundred stories up. I assumed that some knucklehead had gotten the bright idea to fly downtown and crashed his plane into the building. I imagined the pilot's face would be all over the news by the time I got to my office.

After parking and walking across two acres of asphalt to the Hoffman Building, I rode an elevator to the fifth floor just as a plane impacted the second tower. Not long after, as I stood in front of the television in disbelief, I felt the explosion and looked out the window to see thick black smoke billowing into the skies over our nation's capital.

Impossible, I thought. This cannot be real. At that time I could not comprehend how my life had changed in an instant. Nor was it possible to comprehend how many American servicemen and -women would die and suffer life-altering wounds in the coming years.

As I drove to work seven years later, I tried to imagine how different my life would have been had 9/11 not occurred. Like so many other service members, 9/11 was not simply a tragic historical event for me. Rather, it was the day that my life took a significantly different path. I went to war, which meant my life would forever be affected by what I experienced. Now, seven years later, I had two memorials to attend. I would first go to the annual 9/11 memorial service at the 101st Airborne Division headquarters, then attend the 4-101 memorial in remembrance of three of our own soldiers that had been killed exactly one year prior. I wanted to pay my respects, knew that I must attend, but admittedly did not look forward to that ceremony. The memory of their deaths was still fresh in my mind. It would be an emotional day.

Some say that the crash on September 11, 2007, was just coincidence. Others said it was ill fated. Regardless, all agreed that it was a tragedy. The soldiers were in C Company, 4th Battalion, 101st Aviation Regiment, and had departed Fort Campbell as a flight of three Black Hawks on what was supposed to be a simple cross-country training mission to Chattanooga. However, somewhere south of Nashville they encountered bad weather that got progressively worse the farther south they flew. They tried to avoid it, but conditions worsened to the point that two of the three Black Hawks committed to instrument flight. They punched into the clouds, transitioned to their instruments, and called air traffic services for vectors to an airfield. Those two aircraft were able to land safely at the nearest airfield, but the third helicopter crashed in rural north Alabama, killing the entire crew.

Captain Scott Shimp, the company commander, was one of the pilots. Scott was an all-American kid who grew up in Bayard, Nebraska, graduated high school in 1998, and left Nebraska for West Point that summer. Shimp was a good-looking, fit young man who was the salutatorian of his high school class. He played football, wrestled, sang in the choir, was an Eagle Scout and a member of the National Honor Society. Shimp was a natural athlete with an intellect to match.

A 2002 graduate of the United States Military Academy, Shimp was a member of West Point's bicentennial class. Just above the Hudson River, where countless historic American leaders had preceded him, President George W. Bush presented Shimp with his diploma. Armed with a degree in electrical engineering and a commission in the United States Army, Shimp embarked upon an army career. Passionate about everything outdoors, he liked to snowboard, Jet Ski, ride motorcycles, camp, and hike. Scott was a man's man and a natural-born leader. His men responded to his leadership. They wanted to perform for him. Flying with Scott, and serving as the pilot in command of the Black Hawk, was Chief Warrant Officer 2 David Stanley. Dave was a native of Niceville, Florida, where he was known for his skills on the baseball diamond. He'd already proved himself as a superb combat pilot during two tours in Iraq. He played an important role in preparing his fellow pilots for the upcoming deployment to Afghanistan. Dave was thirty-three years old and married with two children—a husband, father, and a damn good soldier.

The crew chief on board, Sergeant Jeffrey Scott Angel II, was a baldheaded sergeant from Gauley Bridge, West Virginia. Sergeant Angel graduated from Valley High School, where he was the quarterback of the football team and captain of the baseball team. When he wasn't playing sports, Jeffrey could be found chasing whitetail deer through the mountains of West Virginia or pulling fish out of a lake near Gauley Bridge. It was impossible to dislike Sergeant Angel, who always wore a disarming smile on his face. He was twenty-four when he died, and left behind a wife and a young daughter.

The deaths of Scott Shimp, Dave Stanley, and Jeff Angel devastated C Company. In the year since their crash the emotional wounds had not fully healed, so I knew the memorial would be a very tough ceremony for everyone involved. Those thoughts filled my mind as I stopped to show my identification card at the Fort Campbell gate. Just as I passed through the gate my BlackBerry rang. It was my brigade commander, Colonel Ron Lewis.

"Hey, Jimmy, can you swing by the office? There has been an incident in Afghanistan. I'll tell you more about it when you get here," he said.

Colonel Lewis is one of the most talented officers I know. He is intellectually gifted and possesses a work ethic with which few officers can compete. A Chicago-born African American, Ron's parents taught him from childhood that there are no ceilings in life. He is a 1986 graduate of West Point. Of average height and possessing no excess flesh, he is lean and fit—a natural athlete who can play any sport from Ping-Pong to football equally well. I had served as his deputy prior to taking squadron command and had a great relationship with him. We generally saw things the same way, which made commanding under him very comfortable.

As I made my way to Colonel Lewis, Major Jack Murphy, my task force operations officer, stood in a silent command post thousands of miles away, with Bernie Harrington, Task Force Out Front operations officer, and his team. Jack had been unable to accompany me on my PDSS so he went later, on a separate trip. He was in Jalalabad with TF Out Front. I was safe on U.S. soil, unaware that the command post had just received a text—"Mike Slebodnik has been shot in the leg." Harrington later told me that upon receiving the text he thought, Mike is probably really pissed off and trying to find the guy that shot him in the leg. His injury couldn't be serious. Everyone in the command post waited with nervous anticipation for the next report, but all felt certain that it was a flesh wound. Mike would be all right.

Soon the 2-17 Cavalry Australian exchange officer who was flying as Mike's lead called Bernie and told him that Mike did not look good, that it was a serious wound. Still Bernie didn't think the injury could be life-threatening, or perhaps he just didn't want to believe it could be. The aviation brigade launched a medevac from Bagram. It would fly to COP Nagil, where Mike was being treated, and move him to the Bagram hospital. The chaplain entered the command post and Bernie, along with five or six others, stepped aside, closed their eyes, and bowed their heads. The chaplain led them in prayer, while others silently pleaded with God for Mike to survive.

After the prayer, Bernie remained in the command post, seated beside the battle captain, until they received the text stating that the medevac had landed safely at Bagram. He then went to his desk, which sat right outside the command post entrance, and began sorting through the other missions for the remainder of the day. He kept thinking, There's a combat support hospital there. They have everything needed to save lives. Mike is in good hands now.

Then, in a low voice the battle captain announced, "Attention in the TOC," and mumbled something. It always irritated Bernie when someone mumbled. He liked soldiers to sound off with "ATTENTION IN THE TOC!" to get everyone's attention. The TOC is a busy, often noisy place, with soldiers coordinating, radios squawking, and multiple phone conversations taking place simultaneously. We use the command "Attention in the TOC" to silence everyone when something important has happened and everyone needs to hear it. Bernie was soft-spoken himself. I'd never heard him raise his voice, but if you needed the attention of everyone in the command post then you had to sound off and be heard. He yelled into the TOC from his desk, "Sound off so everyone can hear!"

"ATTENTION IN THE TOC!" the battle captain repeated, much louder this time. "Mr. Slebodnik has died of his wounds." Silence fell like a blanket over the TOC.

Back at Fort Campbell I walked into Colonel Lewis's office. He shook my hand and pointed to the couch. "Have a seat. Out Front just lost a Kiowa pilot and we need you to select a chief warrant officer 4 from your unit to serve as the casualty assistance officer."

"Mike," I whispered, while staring at the wall. "Mike Slebodnik," I repeated, louder, and turned my eyes to him.

"They are saying he was shot through the femoral artery. Did you know him well?" he asked.

"Yes, sir. A very close friend. I flew with him while I was on PDSS."

I don't know how I knew it was Slebodnik, but his face flashed into my mind. I could suddenly see his smile. Smiling came easy to Mike. Images of time spent together, events we shared, raced through my mind like an old carousel slide show. I saw him in his Stetson hat, head cocked to the side and a toothy grin on his face. I saw the picture I had taken in the gear room at Jalalabad. He was in his tight-fitting army combat shirt, and as I was picking on him about looking so fit I had snapped a picture—a huge grin on his face. I felt almost numb, detached, as those images ran through my mind, and then I imagined him trying to put a tourniquet on his leg, knowing that if he didn't hurry he might bleed to death. I could see him struggling, his movements frantic as he tried to stop the flow of blood. I saw fear in his eyes, a stark contrast to his warm smile. The images were so real in my mind, perhaps because of the pain I felt as they flashed in and out. A softball-size lump ached in my throat. The pain inside needed to get out. I felt like I wanted to explode, but I held it inside, fought the emotion until it eased.

Mike had been flying a routine reconnaissance mission in Laghman Province, which was a relatively calm area northwest of the city of Mehtar Lam. As he flew down the road he had seen a man who seemed to be harmlessly walking south. Just as Mike passed overhead, he watched the man raise an AK-47 machine gun and shoot at the aircraft. A single bullet hit the helicopter. It passed between the armor side panel and the seat, striking Mike's leg. The round passed through his leg and severed his femoral artery. As the copilot raced for the closest outpost, Mike attempted to put a tourniquet on himself, but there was too much blood and too little time. We lost an American hero, a father, a husband, and an incredible friend that day. Sadly, he wouldn't be the last.

I sat through the 4-101 memorial in dismay, numb to almost everything around me. Reflecting on the loss of those three young men, of wives without husbands and fatherless children, combined with this most recent loss of my close friend, gave September 11 an even more repulsive taste for me. I had lost one more friend and fellow cavalryman. I kept seeing Mike's face and it made my chest burn. I wanted to throw up.

I had assigned Chief Warrant Officer 4 Ed Walker to be the casualty assistance officer. I knew that Ed would take care of Mike's family and ensure that they received all of their benefits and entitlements. When a soldier deploys, he wants to be sure his family is taken care of, and that loved ones back home understand what to do if something bad happens to him; however, few actually sit down with their families and explain all of the entitlements.

That evening as I drove home on I-24, I knew that there was a very real likelihood I would endure this experience again. I hated the thought of losing another soldier, but I knew that it could happen. As I turned my car toward home, the question from earlier that morning remained: Had we done everything we could to prepare our soldiers?

I knew the answer. We *had* done everything we could to prepare our soldiers for war. I believed that we were better trained than any unit with which I'd deployed, but that did not mean that the enemy would not have some victories and inflict casualties. At the end of the day, the enemy gets a vote. We can train as hard as we want to, but sometimes training isn't enough. The reality was that we were deploying to the most violent place in the world, to fight an incredibly hardened, battle-tested enemy. We would fight every day. We would do well, but the likelihood of losing soldiers was and is very real.

LEAVING

By November our training was complete. We were as ready as we would ever be, and it was a good thing because flights were departing every day.

Leaving is never easy. It was my fifth deployment; I'd made two trips to the Balkans, spent two years in Iraq, and now Afghanistan. Over the years, the way in which we separate families from their soldiers has evolved. In the early years of the war it was not uncommon to see wailing wives and children clinging to a chain-link fence as soldiers walked across the flight line to board a jet. It was a pitiful sight that always made me cringe. The army decided that there had to be a better way to facilitate a more graceful, less tearful separation. Nowadays, families are invited to a hangar on the airfield. Soldiers report to their unit areas for accountability, drop off their bags, and draw their weapons from the arms rooms. They are then transported to the hangar, where they can visit with their families for a short while before being called to formation. Once in formation a designated senior commander bids the soldiers farewell, reminds them of the importance of the mission they are going to do, and thanks them for their willingness to serve. This is done in the presence of family. Then soldiers file onto buses, which move them to a passenger terminal where they will wait for their flight. When they board the buses for the terminal it's the last time they see their families before returning for midtour leave—two weeks of leave during the yearlong deployment.

My wife, Lisa, and I have found that it's easiest for us to say goodbye at home the night before and for me to get up early and leave before the kids wake up. Some families like to hang on for as long as they can.

Whether it's a soldier's first or fifth deployment, leaving is always difficult and separation's iron weight presses down most heavily upon the wives and children.

One bitter-cold November night I addressed a formation of my soldiers and their families as they prepared to say their final goodbyes. It was late at night, as it seems is the case with all deployment flights. As I spoke, I noted that many young wives held tissues in their hands and stared at their soldiers as they secretly longed for me to hurry up and finish. A few children ran around in the hanger, oblivious to the fact that Dad or Mom was about to leave for a year and go off to war. Most of the soldiers seemed to listen to what I had to say, which of course made me feel good, but there was another group that thoroughly sized me up. Fathers and grandfathers were intent on hearing what I had to say. When I concluded my remarks I gave the command for the chalk leader to take charge of the formation.

As the soldiers filed out of the hangar, family members sobbed and whispered, "I love you," through quivering lips. As they did so, a man approached me with his hands in his pockets. He was a small, lean man with a beard and mustache. He wore jeans and a black jacket that was buttoned at the bottom and flared open, with his hands in his jeans pockets. He seemed nervous as he approached me, shaken. He extended his coarse, trembling hand and took my hand in his and then held on to it. With tears trickling down his cheeks he looked at me through small blue eyes and said, "You take care of my son. You bring him back to me." He had no pride, no shame—only a boy, whom he had raised from birth. This father was counting on me, a total stranger, to take care of that which was most precious to him.

I will never forget that moment as long as I live.

At that moment I felt the weight and responsibility of command like I had never experienced before. When I faced difficult decisions in Afghanistan, I would see that father's face every time. He had gone on to tell me that he was a Vietnam veteran. He wanted me to know that he understood the nature of war. We were both fully aware of the inherent danger his son would be in, but I also knew that he was counting on me to make sound decisions with regard to his and everyone else's sons and daughters. After that night in the hangar, I never saw the man again. To this day, I do not know his name, but

I am grateful for the impact that he had on me, in that moment and for the rest of my career.

Like most families in our task force, we had Christmas a couple of weeks early in 2008. Military families have grown accustomed to celebrating birthdays, anniversaries, even Christmas on alternate dates. From 9/11 to 2008 I had missed three Christmases, two anniversaries, and seven birthdays. Soldiers adapt; so do soldiers' families. It was time to go to war.

My old college buddy Colonel Bill Gayler spoke to our task force just before we boarded the plane. Bill was then serving as the deputy chief of staff of the 101st Airborne Division. I had known him for over twenty years, since our days in the corps of cadets at North Georgia College, and we were close friends. Bill was the corps commander at North Georgia my freshman year. I'd looked to him as a guy I wanted to emulate. He was an Apache instructor pilot, which was not all that common for a commissioned officer. He was smart, charismatic, and articulate, but what appealed most to me was his authenticity. Bill Gayler loved soldiers. It showed in the way he treated them and how they responded.

After he spoke to our unit, he and I stepped aside and he told me that I was doing a great job in command. "Just take care of your soldiers and be yourself, Jimmy. You guys will do great over there."

Figure 1: The author and SSG Christopher McKaig in Afghanistan 2014. Photo by Ronald Dvorsky.

Figure 2: The Intelligence team (Left to right: Capt. Jillian Wisniewski, Staff Sgt. Jay Karvaski, Spc. Jacob Andrews, 1st Lt. Andrew Campbell) Photo by the author.

Figure 3: Barg-e Matal in January 2009. Photo by the author.

Figure 4: The Nuristan Mountains in January 2009. Photo by the author.

Figure 5: Maj. Jack Murphy and Capt. Jillian Wisniewski. The last day at Jalalabad. Photo by the author.

Figure 6: OH-58D Kiowa Warrior in the Kunar Valley. Photo by the author.

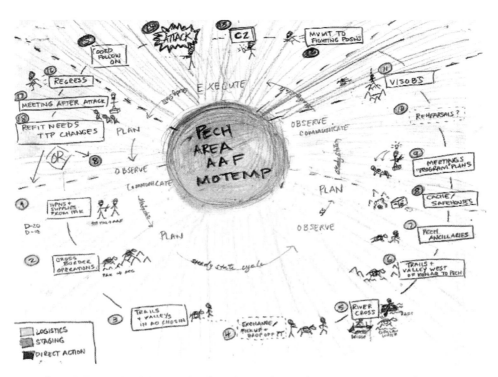

Figure 7: The result of the Intel Shop's brainstorming session. The Modus Operandi Template for the Central Kunar Valley. Photo by Jillian Wisniewski

Figure 8: Sarobi Lake. Photo by the author.

Figure 9: Staff Sgt. Azad "Oz" Ebrahimzadeh during the Helgal Valley air assault. Photo by Russell Klika.

Figure 10: Apache helicopter in the Hindu Kush Mountains. Photo by Russell Klika.

Figure 11: A Chinook conducts a resupply to Special Forces soldiers in the Helgal Valley. Photo by Russell Klika.

Figure 12: Blowing up a weapon cache in the Helgal Valley. Photo by Russell Klika.

Figure 13: The lady of the Helgal. Photo by Russell Klika.

Figure 14: Afghan soldiers exit a Chinook during the Helgal Valley air assault. Photo by Russell Klika.

Figure 15: Air Assault in the Helgal Valley. Photo by Russell Klika.

IT ALL BEGINS

The flight to Afghanistan is a two-day haul. We flew to Germany on a Boeing 747. After six hours there we swapped crews and flew to Incirlik, Turkey, then to Manas, Kyrgyzstan. Forty-eight hours after leaving U.S. soil, we landed at Bagram Airbase, Afghanistan.

Our helicopters moved by sea to Rota, Spain. From there, air force cargo jets fly transports to Bagram. The bulk of our personal gear was containerized at Fort Campbell, moved by trucks to the port at Jacksonville, Florida, and loaded onto ships. Less than a month later personal items arrived at Karachi, Pakistan, where it was transferred to trucks and driven through the Khyber Pass to Jalalabad. By mid-December helicopters, crews, and equipment were assembled at FOB Fenty, where we began the process of taking the reins from Task Force Out Front.

John Lynch sent a Black Hawk to Bagram to fly me to FOB Fenty. My operations officer, Jack Murphy, met me at the helicopter.

"Hey, sir," he said with a warm smile. "Welcome to Jalalabad." In the summer of 2008, I had been looking for an operations officer, whom we called an S3 in the army. I had scoured the list of candidates attending the staff college, but I only knew two of the officers on the list, and both of them were committed to the 160th Special Operations Aviation Regiment. I called an old friend, Lieutenant Colonel Frank Muth, whom I had previously served with in the 3d ACR. Frank was serving as the aviation branch chief at Human Resources Command at the time. "Yes! The guy you want is in Rhode Island. He's attending the Naval Post Graduate School. His name is Jack

Murphy. He has his mind set on going back to the 82nd Airborne Division, but if you call him I bet he'll change his mind."

Frank gave me Murphy's number. I called him immediately.

After identifying myself I said, "Frank Muth told me to give you a call. He said you had worked for him before, and that I should recruit you to be my S3."

"That's kind of him, sir, but I'm sure he exaggerated," Murphy said and chuckled.

There are officers in the army that seem to try and fulfill a stereotype. They behave the way they think they are supposed to versus just being themselves. I was looking for a guy who was comfortable in his own skin, an authentic leader, someone I could trust to make good decisions in my absence.

After twenty minutes of small talk I put the pressure on. I needed an answer. "Jack, we're deploying in November to eastern Afghanistan. It's going to be a heck of a year, and I need a good field-grade officer, someone I can count on. I was told you want to go back to the 82nd, but what if I told you that if you come to work for me you'll go directly into the job, and we'll deploy to the toughest fight in the world a few months later?" I asked.

In a calm and sincere tone he said, "Who would say no to that, sir? I'm honored that you called."

And just like that, Major Jean-Jacques "Jack" Thai Murphy became my S3. God could not have personally issued me a better one. The son of a Vietnamese librarian and a first-generation Irish-American cartographer, Jack is one of a kind. I saw him as a contradiction of the stereotypical army officer—diametrically opposed to the Hollywood image of a ranting meathead that views everything in life as black and white. Jack was laid-back and easy-going, collegial, and quite liberal for army standards. Yet despite his success and tremendously positive reputation it seemed that while he loved the army, he could take it or leave it. If the army stopped tomorrow, Jack Murphy would shrug his shoulders and go snow skiing or kayaking, while he decided what to do next.

My guess is that on the angriest day of his life, Jack Murphy did not raise his voice. I certainly never saw him do it. Yelling wasn't Jack's style. He took everything in stride. He was the big brother in the Jack and Jill relationship. While it was in Jillian's blood to lash out against the army rules that she considered to be silly and pointless, Jack, who frequently agreed with Jillian's reasoning and logic, chose to follow the rules simply because it wasn't worth the energy to sweat the small stuff. "Is it really that big of a deal?" he'd ask when Jillian became frustrated.

Jillian's typical response was, "It's not that it's a big deal, sir. It's the point: that policy makes no sense." She was born to challenge the status quo and demand "why." Jack was her perfect counterbalance and she, his. I was thrilled with them both.

We had decided it would be better for Jack to travel to Afghanistan ahead of us, to prepare to receive the rest of the unit. As soon as Jack hit the ground he began synchronizing the relief in place, which was a two-week process during which time we conducted a deliberate transfer of responsibility from one unit to the other.

Initially, TF Out Front remained in the lead, calling all the shots on missions as our soldiers shadowed them. They made all the tactical decisions with our soldiers learning their processes. During the second week we assumed the lead role and they sat back, offering advice and counsel. At the end of the two-week process we would conduct a transfer of authority ceremony, which signified the official shift of responsibility from one unit to another. 2nd Squadron, 17th Cavalry Regiment had written another historic page in their unit's history, and 7th Squadron had begun yet another historic journey.

"Come on, I'll take you to your room and you can put your rucks down," Jack told Command Sergeant Major Thom and me at the helicopter.

Eric Thom and I roomed together in a walled-off section of a bee hut, which would be our home for the next year. Eric Thom was a super battle buddy and a senior noncommissioned officer, but an even better friend. I had known him for several years. When I became the brigade operations officer in 2006, he was my operations sergeant major. My wife, Lisa, and I were great friends with Eric and his wife, Samantha.

Eric was lean and fit. He could max the army physical fitness test without breaking a sweat. He had run a sub-three-hour marathon, yet he was built more like a bodybuilder than a long-distance runner. A tight, blond flattop sat atop his fair-skinned, muscular body. Incredibly smart and well rounded, he was finishing the last requirements of his master's degree online when we deployed. Our soldiers were blessed to have such a professional, caring leader as their command sergeant major.

The early morning sun reflected off the snow-covered mountains, lighting up the valley on January 6, 2009—a picture-perfect backdrop for the ceremony. As Command Sergeant Major Eric Thom and I unfurled the 7th Squadron, 17th Cavalry Regimental colors at Jalalabad Airfield, I was reminded that it was the first time the 7th Squadron colors had been flown in combat since they were cased in the spring of 1972, in Vietnam. I thought of Private First Class Garfield Langhorn, who gave his life for his fellow troopers.

On January 15, 1969, almost forty years ago to the day, a C Troop Cobra helicopter flown by First Lieutenant Sterling Cox and Warrant Officer 1 Birch Petteys went down in the heavily forested jungles of Vietnam. A rescue team was quickly deployed. The team made its way to the crash site but found both pilots dead. They prepared the bodies and began moving to the landing zone but came under heavy machine gun fire. In short order, they were surrounded and began taking casualties. As the men fought valiantly to defend themselves against superior numbers, an enemy soldier threw a grenade into their perimeter. It landed near several of the wounded men. Knowing for certain that he would die, yet without hesitation, Garfield Langhorn threw his body on top of the grenade, giving his own life so that his fellow cavalrymen might live. I could see his face in my mind's eye that morning, a twenty-year-old African-American male in 1969. At a time when too many Americans still judged a man by the color of his skin, at a time when there was still too much hate in our society, Garfield Langhorn demonstrated infinite love—a soldier's love. What an incredible legacy to carry forward.

Eric Thom and I slowly unfurled the regimental colors, a flag that represented the history of those who fought before us. It was now our turn to write another remarkable chapter in the history of our great squadron. I knew many of the men who had fought with 7-17 Cavalry in Vietnam, and I knew with certainty, though seven thousand miles away, January 6 was a special day for them as well. I sensed both their pride and their presence.

Task Force Pale Horse consisted of sixteen OH-58D Kiowa Warrior helicopters, six AH-64D Apaches, six UH-60M Black Hawks, four CH-47F Chinooks, three UH-60 medevac helicopters, three Hunter unmanned aerial vehicles, and a pathfinder detachment, which consisted of seventeen highly skilled and specially trained infantrymen. Almost six hundred men and women from all walks of life, unified in purpose. On that sunny bluebird day John Lynch bid farewell to the men and women of Task Force Duke, whom they had supported, and I committed Pale Horse to giving 100 percent in support of TF Duke from that day forward. It was time to go to work.

COUNTERINSURGENCY

Our first large-scale, deliberate operation came just two days after the transfer of authority. It was called Operation Able Reach—an air assault with Brett Jenkinson's Task Force Spader—designed to "disrupt the enemy's pattern of life" in the village of Aybot, on the high eastern ridgeline in the Shuryak Valley, an ancillary valley near the mouth of the Pech River Valley as it winds westward from the Kunar River Valley. Simply conducting an operation in the village would disturb the enemy's normal activities. No roads accessed the village, so the enemy operated freely without fear of being attacked.

We planned to insert Able Company into a landing zone on the ridgeline about eight hundred meters above the village. Brett's men would set up several positions on the high ground so they could cover the main force as they walked down a small, steep trail to the village.

I learned an important lesson about Chinooks and landing zones that day. In Iraq most every landing zone (LZ) was on the flat desert floor, but in Afghanistan it was difficult to find a flat place anywhere to land. Every helicopter has a slope limitation, except the Chinook. A Black Hawk, for example, cannot land on a surface with a slope greater than fifteen degrees. For Operation Able Reach we selected an LZ in the back of the Shuryak based on imagery, but we had not put eyes on the actual LZ. A couple of days prior to the mission I decided to fly over the area to take a look. When I saw the proposed LZ, I did not believe that any helicopter could land there. It was a steep slope covered with scrub bushes. Jay Vollmer, our Chinook instructor pilot, was with me: "No problem, sir. We can get it in there."

At first I thought he was kidding. "Are you being serious?" I asked.

"Sir, you can land a Chinook almost anywhere."

"Yes, but I'm going to be on this Chinook with you, so I want to know we can land there."

"Trust me, sir," he said and smiled.

Landing zones aside, it was a pretty straightforward mission—a daytime operation—and we did not expect to meet significant enemy resistance. It was the perfect mission for us to cut our teeth on—a gentle start to what would become a very challenging year.

Able Reach allowed us to plan, brief, rehearse, and execute our first large-scale combat operation in tough conditions. It enabled us finally to execute the tactics, techniques, and procedures we had spent so much time training for back at Fort Campbell.

As a part of our preparation for Afghanistan we had reflected on eight years of combat experience gained in both Iraq and Afghanistan to determine what we felt would be the optimal way to operate in such challenging terrain. The mechanics of an air assault were relatively straightforward; nothing really changed in that regard. What was more difficult—a topic we spent a great deal of time discussing— was the effects of aviation on the Afghan population.

I felt that it was critical that our crews fully understood that their actions would have a profound impact on the local populace we sought to support. As we discussed the effects of aviation operations back at Fort Campbell, prior to deploying, Colonel Lewis had coined the phrase "COIN at altitude," which was a way of noting that aviation units played a significant role in the counterinsurgency fight. COIN at altitude ultimately made its way into both Colonel Lewis's and my commander's intent for our enduring operational plan in Afghanistan. Too many times in both Iraq and Afghanistan our aviators' actions, often in ignorance, infuriated the local populace, thus damaging the objectives of our counterinsurgency strategy. While not commonly discussed within aviation units at that time, our objective was to ensure that our pilots knew that their actions in the air had a direct impact on the ground. A pilot who scattered a shepherd's sheep by flying right over the top of them made enemies, not friends. Blowing over clotheslines or scaring farm animals with our helicopters was obviously rude and did not advance the ground commander's counterinsurgency objectives. Civilian casualties and inconsiderate flying would not help our cause in any way.

The Afghans who had lived through the Soviet occupation vividly remembered the destruction Soviet gunships left in their wake. Their humble homes were destroyed, and countless women and children were killed in their attacks. We did not want to repeat the mistakes of the Soviets. To that end, the commander of the International Security Assistance Force (ISAF) published a tactical directive. The tactical directive was a document that provided guidance and intent for the employment of force. While not inhibiting a soldier's right to self-defense, it provided guidance for shooting artillery and air-to-ground munitions from helicopters and jets. It addressed proportionality and consideration of collateral damage. It drove the methodology for our direct fire engagements, but in no way did the tactical directive avert inconsiderate flying in the midst of people who were previously terrorized by Russian helicopters. That would require education and understanding on our part.

We made it clear to our crews that it was better to let one bad guy get away rather than shoot a missile into a building, killing the enemy, but also wounding a dozen women and children in the process. We had to know when to shoot and when to break contact with the enemy. All of these things—considerate flying, proportionality, and noise abatement—contributed positively or negatively to the counterinsurgency fight writ large.

It was a fact that our actions would have an impact on the local populace. What we had to do was to make choices that would minimize the negative impacts. It was critical that all of our crews had a firm understanding of the overall counterinsurgency strategy, and that we operated within the intent of that strategy. Being careless in the air could destroy any progress made on the ground in a matter of seconds. We felt that our pilots would make better decisions if they at least had a base understanding of the culture and tribes in Afghanistan.

There were numerous tribes throughout Afghanistan, including: Pashtun, Tajik, Hazara, Uzbek, Aimaq, Turkmen, Baloch, and Nuristani, to name only the largest tribes. The majority of the people in our area of operations were the Nuristanis and the Pashtuns. Pashtunwali would play a large role in how the Pashtun tribes in our area would react to our operations. Pashtunwali is an "alternative form of social organization,"[1] that is to say, the "keystone of the Pashtuns' identity and social structure, and it shapes all forms of behavior from the cradle to the grave."[2] It is a very powerful, self-enforcing code that is so religiously adhered to that, once truly understood by our soldiers, it enabled us to be predictive in our operations.

For example, when the local leaders invited us into their village or agreed to a meeting, we could rest assured that our forces would not be attacked while in the village. Hospitality, even to the enemy, was a social requirement. That did not mean that enemy forces, including men from the very village we were visiting, would not position themselves to ambush our soldiers as they departed the village. In fact that was normally the case, but they would not attack us *in* the village—a custom that had not changed since at least the 1830s. In his account of *Sale's Brigade in Afghanistan*, Chaplain G. R. Gleig noted, "If you throw yourself upon them in their own homes, you may almost always assure yourself of protection; but it does not by any means follow that, having escorted you to the extreme limits of their territory, and seen you fairly across the line, they shall not fall upon you in the next minute and plunder you of every article of value that you possess."[3]

Or in our case ambush or blow us up.

This knowledge enabled us to focus our attack helicopters on the areas where our forces would most likely be attacked as they departed the villages. As ground force commanders met with locals inside the village, our helicopters paid close attention to signal intercepts and searched for potential enemy activity in the terrain that the enemy would most likely use to try and attack our soldiers as they departed. It also enabled us to conduct refuel operations and team sequencing, which ensured that our air assets were at the right place with a full load of ammunition and fuel when enemy contact was most likely to occur.

Another important element of the Pashtun code is vengeance. Revenge for the killing of an Afghan is essential. Even Afghan mothers will insist that their children avenge their fathers if they are murdered. "Hence revenge becomes, among the Afghans, a point of honour which no man may waive except with disgrace."[4] Failure to avenge a family member can result in being cast out from the village—a shameful penalty. To lose one's honor is a disgrace. A family without honor is "unable to compete for advantageous marriages or economic opportunities, and is shunned by the other families as a disgrace to the clan."[5] This knowledge helped us educate our crews about the significance of collateral damage. We could not afford to inflict civilian casualties on the battlefield, even if it meant letting an enemy fighter escape into a village.

The greater question was how we could apply the counterinsurgency tenets of clear-hold-build in Afghanistan. The terrain made engaging the local populace painfully difficult. First, there were no roads to the remote mountain villages, only trails. Access to the villages would, in the remote mountains and valleys, require either an air assault to access them, which we could not feasibly accomplish on a daily basis, or dismounting our vehicles and walking in. The latter forced our ground forces to assume unreasonable risk since most foot marches took all day and the enemy would certainly attack our forces from the dominant high ground as they moved back to their vehicles.

Second, the population in N2KL, outside of the major river valleys such as the Kunar, was dispersed across a very large area. Villages literally dotted every remote ridge, mountain, and valley in our area of operations. It was nearly impossible for us to interact with them on a regular basis, much less live among them as we had in Iraq. As we would later see, it was all too easy for the local insurgent leaders to order their fighters to observe our movements into local villages and then attack us all the way back to our bases. Furthermore, the enemy could move through the villages and influence the Afghans without us being able to interdict their actions.

Finally, we did not have the troop strength or an adequate number of helicopters to live among the populace. Unlike Iraq, where established road systems gave access to large population bases, Afghanistan was difficult to navigate. If effective counterinsurgency meant routine contact with the local populace and earning their trust, I did not see how we could do it outside of the major cities—not with the troop strength we had. I certainly didn't have the answers, but I knew that it was critical that we, as an aviation force, avoid negatively affecting the hard-earned progress made by our brothers and sisters on the ground. We had to enhance their operations on the ground and protect them from the enemy when necessary, and it would require discipline in our cockpits.

We made several decisions with regard to tactics before deploying to Afghanistan. We decided to fly transient flights at altitude (1,500 to 2,000 feet above ground level) in order to mitigate the effectiveness of small-arms and RPG attacks on our aircraft. We flew low to the ground only when landing, or when our Kiowas and Apaches were conducting reconnaissance operations.

Since we were task organized with both Apaches and Kiowas in Pale Horse, we trained to conduct team "pure" missions (two Kiowas or two Apaches) and mixed teaming (one Kiowa and one Apache), which we called "Pink Teams." This was a throwback to the days of Kiowas and AH-1 Cobras. The scout (Kiowa) would conduct reconnaissance and the gun (Cobra) would do the shooting. It was a very effective way to operate; however, I found that using a "high team" of two Apaches and a "low team" of two Kiowas together worked best for us in N2KL. Our Apaches were equipped with the newly fielded Modernized Target Acquisition Designation Sight (M-TADS). The resolution of the new sight gave the pilots incredible visual fidelity. In order to maximize the sight during deliberate air assault missions, we generally put the Apaches at a higher altitude and tasked them to maintain contact with any suspected enemy fleeing the objective. We also tasked them to isolate the target areas, thus ensuring that no enemy reinforcements showed up unexpectedly. Due to the high elevation of the terrain in RC-East this often put the Apaches at ten thousand feet or higher.

We used the Kiowa team in close, over the objective. They flew directly over the ground forces as they performed their mission. A Pink Team concept would have forced the Apache to cover his wingman (the Kiowa over the objective), thus preventing the Apache from being able to utilize his sight to its full potential. Having a team of Kiowas gave the ground forces a sense of security in a close fight and early warning from the Apaches, which closely observed all of the terrain surrounding the objective. It was the best of both worlds. If the Kiowas made contact they could engage with their own weapon systems or, preferably, conduct a target handover with the Apache team.

One of the things we didn't rehearse prior to arriving in RC-East was how to operate with an extremely dispersed ground force. Back at Fort Campbell we were able to pick the entire ground force up at a single pickup zone and then fly to the objective. But due to the ground force's geographically dispersed basing in Afghanistan, they could not assemble at one location, nor could all the forces come from a single outpost. Many combat outposts housed a large platoon or small company (eighty personnel). They had to maintain a minimum force at the outpost in order to protect themselves, should they be attacked while a large portion of their men were executing operations away from the base. Also, because they conducted daily patrols in the countryside, it was common for the staff or select individuals to plan an entire operation for their company. They would brief the leaders on the plan and we would fly to their location for a rehearsal. Again, due to dispersion, we often picked up numerous elements from several outposts before finally flying to the objective to conduct a mission.

Initially, the aforementioned process seemed cumbersome, with the planning and rehearsing being less than ideal; but after a few iterations we established a comfortable routine. The key to success was that we reached out with our planners and did as much of the work as possible for our ground brethren. We had the luxury of living on an airfield with a large force of soldiers securing us. We had time and manpower to plan. We also had helicopters, which made mobility easy. We commonly flew one of our planners out to COPs to plan with the infantry. The relationships we built with our brothers on the ground were absolutely critical to our success on the battlefield.

The one thing I knew for certain was that I didn't have all the answers to the tactical problems we would face in Afghanistan. I desperately desired to create a climate where everyone felt free to think creatively. For the team to be successful we needed problem solvers, soldiers who were constantly coming up with new and innovative ways of doing things better, smarter. They had to feel free to live in a world with fewer fences, run free like a horse in the open prairie, in a time before barbwire. When they encountered the occasional fence I wanted them to press against it. I was ever-mindful that it was my responsibility to serve as the governor of the engine I was creating, but I was careful not to let them feel the bits in their mouths unless the reins were in my hands.

I was reminded of my first National Training Center rotation as a second lieutenant and how that experience shaped my approach to creative problem-solving for years to come. I had been sent to a cavalry troop just weeks prior to our rotation. I was excited to get to play war against a living, breathing opposing enemy force—the Crasnovians, as we called them, an army built around the Soviet doctrine.

I had not yet taken over as the scout platoon leader, so I served as the troop executive officer for that particular rotation. I was amazed that we applied our army doctrine, and the Crasnovians applied Soviet doctrine, yet they kicked the living crap out of us every day. The Crasnovians were just another army unit that used Soviet weaponry and played the role of trainer for our units, but they were excellent at what they did.

Each day they would punch a hole in our lines, then race to our command posts and logistics support bases. By noon the Crasnovians were driving victory laps around our tactical operations centers, and helicopters littered the battlefield—victims of their surface-to-air weapon systems.

To make matters worse, the Crasnovians were horrible sports. Back then we set up tactical assembly areas. Our perimeter was about a half a mile across. The troops formed a circle, and the squadron headquarters was set up in the command post in the center. To communicate with the command post we used TA-312 radios. The squadron ran a switchboard. The troops had to run wire from their troop command post to the squadron command post in order to connect to the switch.

When you wanted to talk you cranked the dial sending electricity through the wire to the switchboard. The electricity lit up a light and buzzed the switchboard operator. He'd pick up and ask who you wanted to talk to. Then he'd connect you, physically, by wire.

Laying wire was laborious, and we only had a limited supply. When the Crasnovians penetrated our perimeter their favorite little trick was to drive their tracked vehicles in a circle around our command post, cutting all of our wire, a subtle way of shooting us the bird. Yet the next day we would valiantly repeat the same thing all over again. I recall thinking, isn't this Einstein's definition of insanity? We do the same thing over and over, yet expect a different result.

After we returned home from that humbling experience I spoke to my troop commander, a larger-than-life Texan named Karl Kearney, who was an incredible leader and athlete. Karl was well known throughout the 3rd Armored Cavalry Regiment as a charismatic team builder who was once the quarterback at Oklahoma Panhandle State University. Possessing a cannon for an arm, he was the natural choice as the quarterback and captain of our officer football team for the annual Regimental Turkey Bowl.

Karl Kearney was a winner. It didn't matter what the challenge was, he was as serious as a heart attack on Sunday morning about winning. I told him that in order to figure out how to win next fall at the National Training Center we had to be creative, find a way to gain an advantage. Each month a new unit arrived in town to play on the Crasnovians' home turf, and every month the visitor received a thorough butt kicking. The Crasnovians knew every goat trail, hiding place, and secret path on the battlefield. We had to find a way to level the playing field. Karl and I brainstormed for weeks, and one day one of us, I do not recall which, came up with an idea.

We decided to buy forty power telescopes. We could land our helicopters on the mountaintops, where ground forces could not get to us and they could not shoot us down. The scopes would allow us to spot the enemy and call for artillery on them.

We flew with enlisted aerial observers back then. I was flying with Staff Sergeant Henson. As soon as the observer controllers said we could begin movement Staff Sergeant Henson and I flew forward, under the cover of darkness, and landed just on the back side of a mountain peak overlooking the enormous valley known as the central corridor. Staff Sergeant Henson and I shut the helicopter down, set up our FM radio, and called our squadron headquarters to tell them we were in position. I couldn't wait for the enemy to arrive.

As the sun rose we had a perfect view of the entire central corridor. We would be able to see the Crasnovian tanks and armored personnel carriers as soon as they began to move into the valley, and that's exactly what happened. Just after daylight we began to see them line up to move forward. Staff Sergeant Henson and I reported everything we saw. Our ground forces knew exactly where the enemy was and how many vehicles were coming. From our vantage point we could literally read the bumper numbers on the vehicles.

There was a narrow gap, a pass, which the enemy would have to travel through. We knew that if we destroyed their vehicles at that location it would take them a while to figure out a way to get through the pass. While they were trying to figure it out, we would rain steel down on them from above.

We called for artillery and began to pound them. We called artillery on every formation that tried to move forward that morning and reported their every move to our squadron headquarters. We had perfect situational awareness. Sergeant Henson and I were as giddy as schoolkids.

I had not flown more than fifteen minutes in my helicopter that morning, but I had found a way to win, and that is exactly what I wanted in Pale Horse.

KORENGAL—LEARNING THE HARD WAY

When we took over the mission from the 101st Combat Aviation Brigade they were conducting resupply operations during daylight hours only. Flying in the Hindu Kush mountains on dark nights was like flying into a black hole, or as our pilots said, "It was like flying in a paper bag." The 101st CAB had built a system of low-illumination routes, which they flew on dark nights. The routes were set up so that pilots could display them in the cockpit. A line on their moving maps depicted the route they were to fly. All they had to do was fly the line at the assigned altitude and they were guaranteed obstacle avoidance. This procedure effectively mitigated the danger of darkness. The routes were established in the most commonly flown valleys, which allowed pilots to essentially transition from forward operating base to forward operating base. Due to the risk, deviating from the routes was rare, but that was about to change.

Many of the FOBs in Regional Command East were air-centric. In order for the soldiers to survive they required routine aerial resupply. There were very few roads in Afghanistan and those that did exist followed the valley floors. FOBs built in the valleys, where roads could support them, were vulnerable to enemy attacks from high ground. Outposts built high in the mountains had the inherent tactical advantage of being on higher terrain but required helicopters to resupply them regularly, which resulted in risk to the aircraft. The enemy could pattern our resupply efforts very easily and plan aerial ambushes.

The General Support Aviation Battalion (GSAB), based out of Bagram Airbase, was tasked with the mission to resupply units in the Korengal Valley, despite it being in Pale Horse's area of operations.

The Pale Horse Chinooks were needed to resupply the even more remote outposts in the Kamdesh and Gowerdesh valleys, which lay far to the north in Nuristan Province. These missions were aptly named the Korengal resupply and the KamGow resupply respectively. The valleys in which these outposts resided were extremely narrow and long.

The 101st CAB's Chinooks were CH-47D models. We deployed to Afghanistan as the first unit equipped with the new CH-47F model, which gave us the advantage of glass cockpits—digital instrumentation and multifunction displays. The instrumentation and multifunction displays in the CH-47F made it much safer to operate at night. Initially, we didn't realize that the enhanced capability of the CH-47F enabled us to change the ways in which we executed missions. Sometimes it takes a significant event to spark change.

In the wintertime, snow, fog, and low-lying clouds made it difficult, if not impossible, to fly from Bagram to Jalalabad. In late January 2009, the men living in outposts in the Korengal Valley were in desperate need of resupply, and as fate would have it, weather was less than favorable for flying that day. It looked as though we would have to conduct the Korengal resupply ourselves. Depending on how many sling loads were needed, the Korengal resupply could take four to six hours to complete. Supplies—ammunition, water, mail, and food—would be transported to FOB Blessing by truck and prepared for sling loading. We would then use our Chinooks to deliver the sling loads to Firebase Vegas, OP Restrepo, OP Vimoto, OP Dallas, and the Korengal Outpost (KOP.) The Korengal Valley is not overly large, so we usually conducted the mission with two Chinooks. One Chinook delivered supplies in the valley while the other Chinook picked up its load at FOB Blessing. We also used the resupply flights to move soldiers into the various outposts and transport those who needed to depart the valley.

The Korengal resupply was set for January 17, 2009. The morning revealed low-lying clouds and haze. Gray skies produced an off-and-on drizzle throughout the day. We assumed Task Force Eagle Lift would not be able to get through the passes from Bagram to conduct the mission, so we called our crews to the TOC to prepare them to conduct the mission. TF Blue Spaders needed five turns into the Korengal Valley and two to other COPs outside the valley. We decided to conduct the mission with one Chinook, protected by a team of Apaches. Chief Warrant Officer 2 Joe Mosher, a quiet, prior-enlisted noncommissioned officer, was the pilot in command of the Chinook, crewed with Chief Warrant Officer 2 John Taylor. In the back of the aircraft were Sergeant Jonathan McLawhorn, the flight engineer, Specialist Kenneth Mason, the crew chief, and the door gunner, Specialist Leandro Garcia.

After the mission briefing, the crews conducted a team briefing so that every crew member, Chinook and Apache alike, fully understood how they would go about accomplishing every aspect of the mission. Takeoff time was set for 8:30 A.M. The crews gathered their gear and headed to their aircraft around 7:45 A.M., but when they contacted the TOC for radio checks they were told to stand down.

"The guys at Eagle Lift are saying they will make it. They want to do the mission so just hang tight for a while," the battle captain said to Joe Mosher.

Joe Mosher rolled his eyes and let out a sigh. "They're not going to be able to make it. If we're going to do this I want to go now. I don't want to wait until every enemy fighter up there is up and looking to shoot at us," he said to Taylor. "We're going to end up doing this. We all know it, so why don't we just go do it now?"

Mosher didn't like the idea of spending time in the Korengal Valley during the middle of the day. Two hours passed and it became clear that Eagle Lift, as Mosher predicted, would not make it. "Flex 6-4," the battle captain called over the radio, "Eagle Lift isn't going to make it. Go ahead and execute the mission." Each aircraft in Afghanistan was assigned a call sign. Mosher and crew were flying Flex 6-4 that morning.

"I told you they weren't coming at eight thirty this morning," Mosher mumbled.

Mosher didn't like it. He felt relatively comfortable going into the Korengal early in the morning, but not in the middle of the day. Still, he knew the resupply was desperately needed, so he pressed on. His crew departed FOB Fenty three hours after the originally planned takeoff time.

After a quick stop at FOB Joyce in the central Kunar to drop off some supplies, they crossed the river and entered the Pech River Valley. "When we get to the Korengal let's take a quick look into the valley. I want to make sure we've got the ceilings to get in there. It looks like there's a pretty low cloud layer," Mosher told the crew.

As they passed the entrance to the Korengal they diverted to take a quick look into the valley. A low, scattered layer of clouds hung in the valley, but it didn't look like the weather would interfere with the mission. As they approached FOB Blessing they could see the hookup team prepared to attach the loads to the cargo hook under the belly of the aircraft. Sergeant McLawhorn made his way to the center of the aircraft and laid down with his head over the "hellhole," which is a square hole in the floor of the helicopter through which the crew chief looks to see under the aircraft in order to give directions to the pilot.

Mosher slowed the big Chinook down and came to a hover over the load.

"Come left two," McLawhorn said over the Chinook's intercom system, indicating that he wanted Mosher to move the helicopter two feet to the left.

"Back three," he then directed.

"Hold, that's good. Slings on," said McLawhorn, indicating that the soldier underneath the aircraft had hooked the sling legs onto the cargo hook.

"Up ten for slings tight. Eight, seven, six, five, four, three, two, one. Slings tight," McLawhorn said. The slings were connected to the cargo hook and the slack was out of the sling legs. Joe Mosher then pulled in power to climb. The load teams shielded their faces with their arms to protect themselves from the dust and sand blown up by the Chinook's massive rotor blades.

"Here we go," Taylor said, as they departed Blessing for the Korengal.

They flew back east to the entrance of the valley. The first set of three slings was to be dropped at the Korengal Outpost. The first turn went off without a hitch, smooth as glass. It was a good start.

"Flex 6-4, the guys on the ground are picking up some chatter. Nothing too serious right now, but sounds like the enemy is talking about us. We'll escort you to the mouth of the valley, and while you pick up the next load we'll stay here and look for the enemy," Chief Warrant Officer 2 Kevin Clark told Joe Mosher. Kevin was the air mission commander of the Apache team.

"Sounds good. These next loads are going into Restrepo, so watch that area close," Mosher said.

"Roger. We've got it."

Flex 6-4 returned to FOB Blessing, but this time they landed and picked up two soldiers before attaching the sling loads. One of the soldiers needed a ride to Firebase Vegas, and the other needed to get back to FOB Fenty in order to depart theater for a midtour leave. With the two passengers on board, they picked up three more sling loads and departed for a second turn into the valley. As they departed it Joe called Kevin Clark on the radio.

"You guys seen anything?" Mosher asked.

"Negative. They obviously see us and they are talking, but they haven't said anything too alarming," Clark said.

"Okay. We'll fly past Restrepo and circle back to the north to drop the slings," Mosher said.

"Roger, we will pick up your twelve and six inbound," said Clark, indicating that one Apache would lead them in and one would cover their trail as they made the approach. OP Restrepo was a tiny out-post. To drop the sling loads precisely where the men on the OP could get to them would require a slow and deliberate approach. The valley was dark. It began to drizzle and gloomy clouds loomed overhead.

As they entered the valley, John Taylor noticed a white truck parked on the side of the road with its hood up. While it didn't alarm him, it stuck out in his mind because during their mission brief Jillian's intel folks had mentioned that the enemy often used this tactic as a way to cover their true intent of observing coalition forces, or worse, to wait for an opportunity to shoot at them. Jillian's team was beginning to understand the enemy and how they operated; more important, they were providing meaningful briefings to the pilots who were actively looking for the indicators.

Taylor kept his eye on the truck but didn't observe anything overly concerning. Mosher made the final turn and saw where he needed to drop the slings. He proceeded inbound with caution, and the entire crew was calm and deliberate in their actions. About four hundred meters prior to the touchdown point the crew suddenly saw a bright flash, heard a loud explosion, and felt the aircraft jolt. For Joe Mosher, time instantly slowed down. We didn't just get hit, did we? he thought.

The aircraft was still flying fine and for a moment Joe thought, We can still drop these slings and depart the area. What Mosher did not realize was that an RPG had hit the aircraft and blown a large hole through the fuel cell. Flames blew out of the bottom of the aircraft like a torch as fuel spilled from the tank and ignited.

John Taylor snapped his head to Mosher and said, "Cut the load!"

"No," Mosher said, "hold the load," which Sergeant McLawhorn reluctantly did.

Suddenly, another RPG passed just under the front of the aircraft and exploded in the hill adjacent to them. Taylor pointed at the RPG impact. "There goes another one!" he shouted.

"Cut the load!" Mosher ordered.

Sergeant McLawhorn immediately jettisoned the sling loads free from the aircraft and they plummeted into the valley below. Specialist Mason, manning the right-side machine gun, began shooting into the valley.

"Do you see them?" Taylor asked Mason, meaning the enemy.

"No," he replied, "but I'm pretty sure I know where they shot from."

Joe Mosher broke right and quickly decided where he was going to attempt to put the helicopter down. He later recalled thinking that the Korengal Outpost was the largest landing area available, but if the aircraft blew up they might burn the whole outpost down. His instincts told him to land immediately. Every fiber of his body wanted out of the burning aircraft. As long as they were in the air, a crash was still a possibility, and burning was about the last way he wanted to go out. He knew that if he landed in the valley no one would get out alive. The enemy would swarm them before help could arrive. He had to get as close as possible to friendly forces. Firebase Vegas was their best bet so he quickly decided to head in that direction.

Mosher accelerated to get out of the engagement area. He got the Chinook up to one hundred knots airspeed. Flames were shooting out of the belly of the aircraft as fuel continued to pour from the tank, and enemy forces continued to engage them with large- and small-caliber machine guns and RPGs. Suddenly the left engine, fuel starved, shut down. The helicopter instantly dropped about thirty feet, but nonetheless it remained in the air. Joe knew the aircraft could hover on the power of a single engine.

"We've got to land!" Taylor yelled to Mosher.

"We need to get to Vegas," Mosher replied as he pulled up on the collective control lever to get more power and pushed forward on the cyclic to gain airspeed. Airspeed would get them out of the area faster, but if the only remaining engine quit, Joe would have to slow the aircraft down quickly before hitting the ground.

Smoke began to fill the cockpit as the fire continued to burn in the back of the helicopter. Sergeant McLawhorn disconnected his safety strap and retrieved an extinguisher. He fought the fire as they flew on toward Vegas.

"Open your window so we can clear this smoke," Taylor told Mosher, but that would have required Mosher to let go of the cyclic and he was scared to take his hands off the controls. Taylor then jettisoned his door, which drew the smoke out, helping to clear the cockpit enough for Joe to fly and for them to breathe.

"We've got to get this thing on the ground. My neck is burning," Taylor said, fearing more for the men in the back of the aircraft than for himself.

Just then Mosher saw the landing zone at Vegas. "There! I'm going to put it down right by the wire, on the edge of the perimeter," Mosher said.

He rapidly slowed the aircraft and made a quick ninety-degree, right turn. If the aircraft rolled he wanted his side to be down, so they could exit out of Taylor's now-ejected door. He and Taylor both braced themselves, not knowing if the aircraft would land level or roll over. Mosher got both back wheels down, but the front of the aircraft was sitting on some small scrub and a tree. As he continued down, Taylor released his seatbelt and prepared to shut down the remaining engine. As Mosher reduced the collective control, allowing the aircraft to sit on the ground, the aircraft suddenly rolled right. Taylor managed to shut down the engine before being thrown across the cockpit into the windscreen on Mosher's side. Sergeant McLawhorn, who had been fighting the fire, was thrown out of the back of the aircraft.

With the aircraft on the ground, Taylor scrambled out the door and Mosher followed. Garcia, Mason, and one of the Blue Spader soldiers they had picked up at Blessing followed them out through Taylor's door.

Everyone except McLawhorn met at the front of the aircraft. "Where is McLawhorn and the other passenger?" Mosher asked everyone, then ran to the back of the aircraft to search for them. He saw Mc-Lawhorn lying in the bushes about thirty yards from the aircraft. "I've got McLawhorn!" he yelled. "He's hurt."

Sergeant McLawhorn's back was broken and his teeth were chipped. He couldn't walk, but he was alive. They would need a litter to carry him out. They were still missing Sergeant Dawson, but the aircraft was already a ball of flames. They tried to get close, but it was now impossible.

Sergeant Ezra Dawson was the thirty-one-year-old son of a preacher from Oklahoma. He'd later moved to Las Vegas, where he worked as a waiter and part-time comedian before joining the army. He was a handsome, African-American infantryman with a smile that would light up a room. He was headed home for midtour leave, but he didn't make it out of the Korengal Valley. The crew was devastated. They were certain that Sergeant Dawson was in the helicopter. Soldiers from Firebase Vegas, having watched the entire ordeal in the small valley, rushed down the hill to do what they could to help, but there wasn't much left that they could do.

"Flex 6-4 is down in the Korengal!" the radio telephone operator (RTO) reported in the command post back at FOB Fenty.

"Go get the SCO [squadron commander] and the S3," the battle captain ordered one of the other RTOs, who ran from the TOC to get me.

I ran back to the TOC with him. The battle captain had already briefed the medevac crew. They were preparing to launch as I entered the TOC. We had a team of Kiowas in the FARP at FOB Wright, so I told the battle captain to have them wait and escort the medevac to Firebase Vegas. The soldiers at Vegas reported that they had recovered the crew, but one of the passengers was still missing.

"Get the Pathfinders ready to go. We'll need to send them in and recover what's left," I told the battle captain. Since I had about thirty minutes before the medevac and Pathfinders arrived at the Korengal, I thought through the situation. The crew was secure at Vegas. The Pathfinders were being spun up. The medevac was on the way. It was time to take a breath and slow things down. I went to my office to call Colonel Spiszer, the Task Force Duke commander, and Colonel

Lewis to explain what had happened and what I had already put in motion.

"Colonel Lewis," he answered.

"Sir, I have launched a medevac to go get the crew. We're briefing the Pathfinders on the situation now. I plan to take them in on a Chinook once it's dark so they can go through the wreckage and recover what we can."

"Okay. We'll need to find the black box so we have the recordings of what happened," he said.

"Roger, sir. We are showing the Pathfinders what it looks like now and we are going to take them out to a Chinook to show them where it is located on the aircraft. Once the fire is out and the wreckage has cooled they should be able to recover it."

"What about Sergeant Dawson?" he asked.

"I think the soldiers at Vegas will recover him. We'll bring him out when we put the Pathfinders in."

"Okay. Be careful going in there—in and out quickly. We don't want to give them another target to shoot at."

"Yes, sir."

Colonel Spiszer informed Major General Jeff Schloesser, the commander of CJTF-101. General Schloesser directed him to destroy the aircraft completely, so it could not be used as propaganda against us.

Captain Matt McNeal was the air mission commander of the Kiowa team at FOB Wright. He linked up in flight with the medevac, and they flew to Vegas to recover the crews.[1] As they flew in, smoke billowed from the smoldering Chinook, which was already unrecognizable. The medevac brought the entire crew back to the aid station at FOB Fenty.

That evening I flew in the jump seat on the lead Chinook as we inserted the Pathfinders to recover the downed aircraft. We landed in the LZ at Vegas, and after the Pathfinders exited the helicopter, we respectfully loaded Sergeant Ezra Dawson and flew his body to FOB Fenty.

The following morning the Pathfinders sent back pictures. They had recovered the black box. Only a few scraps and melted sheet metal remained of the helicopter. General Schloesser ordered us to bury what was left.

We learned many lessons from the Flex 6-4 shoot-down, lessons that were not lost on our men. In fact, Flex 6-4 entirely changed how we operated, and forced us to reevaluate how we were conducting all of our missions.

It was clear that, like the Crasnovians at the National Training Center, the enemy were observant; they had noted the pattern of multi-turn, day-only resupply missions into the Korengal Valley for quite some time and had elected to act. They took advantage of the situation. Since arriving in theater, the Blue Spaders had received multiple pieces of intelligence stating that the enemy wanted to shoot an aircraft down in the Korengal.[2] We knew that the enemy were always watching us and reporting our actions to their leadership. It would be tragic ever to think that we had found "the" way to execute a given mission.

In war, what works today is obsolete tomorrow. We learned that we had to develop systems that would force us to challenge our assumptions and tactics systematically and continually.

A couple of weeks after the attack several things were proven true. The enemy had been studying our resupply missions and had used our patterns against us. They had not only achieved a tactical success but also an information-operations success; Al Jazeera aired a video of the Flex 6-4 shoot-down. The event was video-recorded from at least three positions.

General Schloesser was correct in his assessment that they would try to use the wreckage as a propaganda tool. The video showed our soldiers burying what was left of the charred and burned aircraft. It gave us insight as to the complexity of the attack. They had strategically placed shooters on both sides of the approach path to Restrepo to engage the aircraft. In the days that followed, we obtained a copy of a sketch they had drawn as they planned the attack. From that document we clearly saw the in-depth planning, briefing, and rehearsing that the enemy had conducted. It was a sobering discovery. The shoot-down had been planned for quite a while, and the level of planning was possible due to our predictable pattern.

We had assumed responsibility for the Korengal resupply mission and never questioned if we could do it differently than our predecessor. In hindsight it's easy to say that it should have been apparent to us, that we could have executed the mission at night using the increased capability of our newly fielded CH-47F Chinooks. The new aircraft gave us tremendous capability. It had a fully integrated, digital cockpit management system, a common aviation architecture cockpit, and advanced cargo-handling capabilities that complemented the aircraft's advanced mission performance and handling characteristics. It was ideally suited for dark nights with no ambient illumination.

The loss of Flex 6-4 forced us to consider thoroughly every mission enabler on the battlefield, such as close air support and UAVs, and how we could use them to reduce risk and increase capability. From that point forward, UAVs, various intelligence-collection assets, infrared illumination rockets, and fixed-wing aircraft would help us perform what we coined "conditions-based" turns when executing multiturn resupply missions.

We felt relatively certain that we could execute the first turn into a valley such as the Korengal without any issues, but after the first turn the likelihood that the enemy would attack increased. We had to use every tool at our disposal to gain situational understanding, which would enable us to evaluate the risk with each successive turn. The Flex 6-4 shoot-down drove us to operate almost solely at night, and later in the deployment we would use only "red illumination" (new-moon phase, with zero illumination) to execute repetitive-turn resupply missions. Previously, aviation had not flown freely throughout the area of operations with limited illumination, but we trained, utilized the systems in the aircraft, maximized the use of infrared illumination rockets, and began flying on the darkest nights to reduce the enemy's ability to observe and shoot us. The utter darkness of the mountain valleys, which we once feared, became our greatest protection against a determined enemy.

Most important, we adopted an approach that forced the enemy to become reactive in nature. We constantly asked ourselves what we could do differently that would prevent them from discovering patterns they could potentially exploit. "Keep him guessing" became our mantra.

The Flex 6-4 shoot-down also reminded us how easily we could die, how quickly a seemingly routine mission could become a life-and-death situation. In fact, it helped us to better understand that *nothing* was routine in Afghanistan.

COWBOYS AND INDIANS

I've known how to fight all of my life. It's always seemed natural, and pretty darn simple, to me, yet as I participated in mock battles at the army's combat training centers, I noticed something unusual. Many of our soldiers overthought strategy. They made things more complicated than they really were or had to be. After the initial fight at my first National Training Center rotation, in 1993, where the army tested us against an opposing force, it dawned on me that war with real guns was really no different than playing Cowboys and Indians with my cousins in our grandfather's backyard. I had watched it, learned it, from a black-and-white, secondhand Zenith television since I was old enough to remember. Whether it was Hoss Cartwright and his brothers, Tonto and the Lone Ranger, or Marshall Matt Dillon and his sidekick, Festus, the principles of fire and maneuver to gain a position of advantage had not changed much at all over time.

My first battles were fought in the 1970s, on a forty-acre farm in Ranger, Georgia. My team would hunker down behind the woodpile and come up with a plan. "Okay, Jimbo," my oldest cousin—the alpha male—would instruct, "me and Brian are gonna stand up and throw rocks as fast as we can at 'em. That'll get their heads down. When they duck for cover you run to that big pine tree over thar, that'un with all them green pinecones under it. Once you're thar you pile up a bunch of them pinecones and get ready."

He grabbed me by the shoulders and pulled me in uncomfortably close to make sure I understood his instructions. Sweat poured off the end of his nose, which was now a mere two inches from mine. "When I holler you start throwing at 'em. They'll lay down and hide 'cause them ole green pinecones hurt. When they duck fer cover Brian'll run around on the other side of 'em, behind the well house, and we'll have 'em surrounded. You got it?" he said with his brow furrowed.

"Yeah. I got it," I said, knowing I'd better not screw it up. He didn't like being let down.

It was nothing more than a childhood game to us back then, but in truth it was building a foundation of tactics. Once, I even conducted a one-pony cavalry charge. When I was about eight years old my grandfather bought me a Shetland pony. I named him Sugar Babe, and at that time I was convinced that he was the meanest creature God had put on this earth. He would bite me, kick me, slap me with his tail, and when he had had enough for one day he would make a run for home and no amount of pulling or jerking on the reins would deter him.

About that same time I also acquired a new weapon. I don't recall how I came by it, but I became the proud owner of a pistol BB gun. It looked just like a six-shooter that John Wayne carried in the movies. With my Daisy lever-action BB gun, and my pistol hanging at my side, I felt invincible.

Since I was the youngest and smallest combatant, my neighbors and cousins allowed me to fight mounted from time to time. On the day of the infamous charge, my friend Jeff Sanford and I fought against his older brother David. David, whom we called Davy, was holed up in a brush pile, and any time we got close he opened fire on us. I got the bright idea to take my Daisy in one hand and my pistol in the other. I held the reins with my teeth like Rooster Cogburn and put the heels to that little pony. I remember feeling like I was a hero. Being the youngest, I always had to prove myself, show everyone that I was just as tough as the older kids. Davy was the oldest kid around, so I was excited to go head-to-head with him. It was the closest I've ever come to feeling like I was in the movies. I felt like a real live cowboy, nobly charging the bad guys' hideout.

I could not cock the gun while riding. I knew that I had only two shots—one from the pistol and one from the rifle—and I had to make them count. I waited until I could see Davy hiding behind a log in the brush pile, then I brought the six-shooter up and let fly with a BB. Missed.

At that point it dawned on me that I had not practiced mounted marksmanship, a lesson that I put in my kit bag of knowledge. I raised the rifle and shot my one and only BB, which also missed.

Davy, on the other hand, remained behind the cover of the log, waiting until my weapons were empty. Once I was at close range, he calmly rose and took careful aim. I was right on top of him at that point. That was when I felt a cold burning in my chest and a surge of adrenaline.

I pulled hard on the reins, then urged Sugar Babe to turn and run for all he was worth. I tried to make myself as small as possible on that pony's back. It was no use. It was too late. The tactical blunder was already made. Davy shot me in the right thigh from about fifteen feet. The BB sunk deep into my leg. I squealed in pain and rode away, having lost the fight.

I learned many tactical lessons growing up in those Appalachian foothills. Just as in real war, I learned that logistics are important. We required access to ammunition. Sometimes we wanted a handful of rocks and sometimes, when we really meant business, we wanted big, artillery-size rocks. You could never run out of ammunition. You always needed something to throw at the enemy, particularly if you needed to break contact. I would learn later in life that amateurs discuss tactics, professionals discuss logistics, but I already knew that principle to be true. I had learned it the hard way with my friends in Ranger, Georgia.

We needed to know where the enemy was at all times. I learned the importance of reconnaissance long before I read about it in an army field manual. If we charged the enemy's position we'd better have a weapon, a stick or a broom handle or something to swing, especially me, the youngest and smallest combatant. If our battlefield extended to the whole farm and we spread out, then we needed to find out where the enemy was, so one of us would climb a tree to get a better view of the battlefield. Over time we learned which positions were best used for observation, which gave us the best cover, and which provided good escape routes in case we found ourselves in a tight spot. Perhaps most important, over time we learned the habits of our enemy; we patterned them. We knew which positions they preferred. We knew who ran the fastest, who had the strongest throwing arm, and who we never wanted to end up fighting hand-to-hand. That simple study of the enemy and the battlefield in the fields of Ranger, Georgia, is exactly what I hoped our intelligence team would do in Afghanistan.

They did not disappoint.

Within a few short weeks, Jillian's team had gained a good understanding of how the enemy operated. Her analysts studied every document on record, plotted historical fighting positions and escape routes, and pieced together their resupply routes and observation posts. One of the things I'd noticed on our site survey in 2008 was that the maps displayed on the walls of the planning rooms and command posts stopped at the Pakistan border. They simply turned black at the boundary between Afghanistan and Pakistan as if the world ended there. I assumed it was a result of the sensitivity revolving around border violations with Pakistan.

If an aircraft was reported to have penetrated the Pakistan border by so much as a foot we had to conduct an investigation to find out why. Flying into their airspace, no matter how briefly, technically violated Pakistan's sovereignty. Nevertheless, as soon as we returned from our visit I directed that all of our maps include the Federally Administered Tribal Areas (FATA) and Northwest Frontier Province (NWFP) of western Pakistan. I felt that it was impossible to understand our operational environment without acknowledging and studying how the enemy used the FATA as a means of support and security. We had studied the tactics of the mujahideen, who fought the Soviets on the same terrain. They were masters at using the Afghanistan–Pakistan border to their advantage. Our entire team clearly saw the importance of the FATA and NWFP, so they quickly began studying western Pakistan and its relationship to our operational environment.

Our intelligence team was made up of a diverse group of personalities. Walking into their work area was an interesting experience, to say the least. Clever hand-drawn cartoons were pinned to the walls. Magazines ranging from *Muscle & Fitness* to *Popular Mechanics* were strewn about their planning table. And then there were Jillian's math and statistics textbooks, each carefully marked and highlighted. There was evidence of a unique mix of intellect and fitness throughout the room. Our intelligence professionals were a rare combination of geeky analysts and brawny athletes—scholar-warriors.

Their leader, Jillian Wisniewski, was a country girl from West Virginia—a tomboy who was very competitive by nature. As a little girl she'd run through the Appalachian foothills challenging her brothers at anything from football to Ping-Pong. Extraordinarily bright and gifted, Jillian had been an inquisitive child. She had memorized her favorite book, *The Three Little Pigs*, by the time she was three and could actually read the words by the time she entered kindergarten. An honor roll student from the start, she had fallen in love with her father's poetry books at a young age. She "had no idea what any of it meant, but the words and structure fascinated me," she later recalled. Jillian thrived in both academics and sports—a scholar-athlete, with science and math being her strongest suits.

In a world where kids naturally tend to compartmentalize themselves like TV dinners, Jillian never allowed herself to identify with one specific group. She was neither jock nor geek, neither preppy nor nerdy. Jillian was comfortable with all sorts of people of varying interests, but in reality she preferred small groups, where "I could just be myself." She was a curious child and the wide-open, mountainous spaces of West Virginia became her laboratory. Looking back years later she pushed her hair out of her eyes, smiled, and said, "I examined bugs, picked plants, tried to build a mini-greenhouse, spent hours outside at night just staring at the stars and trying to figure out how I could figure out my location on earth by using angles from celestial objects to calculate it. I would envision scenarios of changing the tilt of the earth's axis and imagine what would happen. I would explore old buildings (barns and abandoned old houses) and try to imagine how the people there had lived and what happened to them. I would draw, write, and spend hours just thinking."[1]

Both she and her high school sweetheart, Isaac Wisniewski, had applied and were accepted to the United States Military Academy. Upon graduation they were married but soon thereafter geographically separated. Isaac headed to Fort Rucker, where he would learn to fly the Apache helicopter. Jillian traveled to Arizona to train as an intelligence officer. Upon completion of their initial military training courses both were assigned to the 159th Combat Aviation Brigade at Fort Campbell. Isaac served in TF Wings during our deployment, while Jillian led our intel team. Jillian's openness toward people from all walks of life made her a tremendous team builder. Despite being a diverse array of differing personalities, her team attacked every problem with unified purpose and tenacity. Each in their own unique way contributed to the larger purpose of fully understanding the enemy we faced.

Jillian's noncommissioned officer in charge was Staff Sergeant Jay Karvaski. A good-looking, stout-built, self-proclaimed "street kid," who grew up in New Jersey and Pennsylvania, Jay was tough as nails. His dad had made a living with his hands, installing floors. He taught his son from birth to "be tough" and to take care of himself.

When Jay was about twelve he met a young boy at school who was a boxer. The kid trained at a local gym that catered primarily to professional prize-fighters. Jay's dad took him to the gym to see if they would be willing to make an exception, to train Jay to fight.

"We don't train amateurs," the owner said bluntly. But Jay and his father persisted, and the owner eventually acquiesced.

"Okay, let's see what you've got, kid. Get in the ring and fight," he said.

Twelve-year-old Jay pulled a set of boxing gloves over his hands as he watched a professional fighter in his mid-twenties step into the ring. For six rounds the man beat on Jay's face and body. By the end he was a bloody mess.

"You coming back tomorrow, kid?" the owner asked with a smirk on his face.

"Do you think I took that beating for nothing?" Jay replied.

He spent countless hours training and took many more beatings, but soon he began to win. In fact, he went on to win numerous tournaments. Weighing in at 170 pounds, he was a light heavyweight. He made it to the Pennsylvania Golden Gloves State Championships, but there were no light heavyweight contenders, so Jay opted to fight in the heavyweight class and made it to the championship fight before finally losing.

"I wanted to be an airborne Ranger," Jay later told me.

But the recruiter looked his paperwork over and noticed that Jay's test scores were high. Above-average scores were required to get into the intelligence field.

The recruiter said, "You should go into military intelligence."

"I want to be an airborne Ranger," Jay said, "but before I make a decision, what is the bonus for being a Ranger?"

"Your bonus is your jump pay, one hundred dollars per month," the recruiter replied.

"One hundred dollars a month! You mean to tell me I am going to jump out of airplanes and I only get one hundred dollars per month? That's not a bonus. I'm outta here," Jay said as he started for the door. ("I was a punk kid," he later said.)

The recruiter convinced him to come back in and reconsider. "What pays the highest bonus?" Jay asked.

"Well, a tank crewman gets an eight-thousand-dollar enlistment bonus," he said.

"Now that's a bonus," Jay replied. "My grandpa was a tanker. I'll take it," and with those words Jay Karvaski joined the army.

Jay was assigned to the 1st Infantry Division and stationed in Germany. He fell in love with the army from the start. He participated in the army boxing program, winning multiple championships, and thrived as a tough, gritty soldier.

In 2003 his unit received deployment orders. They were heading to Iraq, which meant countless weeks in the field to prepare for combat, but Jay had also managed to find time to fall in love with a young woman he met in Germany. He was married in August and deployed in September.

Jay experienced horrific fighting throughout his deployment, but one event stuck with him, remains with him to this day. In May 2004 his unit came under a severe mortar attack. Mortars fell for what seemed like hours, but it was certainly no more than a few minutes. Men lay dead and wounded all over the small FOB. "There were eight or nine killed and I think forty-three wounded," he later recalled. Jay had helped to drag the wounded to cover as steel continued to fall from the sky.

One of the men killed was an infantry captain, a close friend of Jay's company commander. Jay's commander felt that their local informant, "Mr. Purple," was perhaps playing both sides.

It was time to pay Mr. Purple a visit.

Jay served as the company commander's gunner, so he traveled in the commander's truck. The first sergeant followed them to the informant's house with his team as well. They parked on the street in front of the house. Jay's commander told him to go look in the house with his night vision goggles to see how many people were inside and report whether Mr. Purple was there.

Jay knew Mr. Purple well. He had dealt with him on numerous

occasions as information was exchanged, and Jay never felt threatened by him. Jay didn't really expect anything to happen, which is why he immediately began walking toward a window.

The house sat in a small village about five kilometers outside the city of Ramadi. A full moon provided enough light so that Jay didn't have to wear his goggles to walk to the house. Jay walked softly and pulled down the night vision goggles so that he could see inside. There he saw a man and a woman asleep on a mattress on the floor.

After a good look into the house, he returned and reported that he had only seen a man and a woman sleeping—after all, it was 2:00 A.M. The company commander decided to see if Mr. Purple was at home.

They knocked on the door, and after a few minutes the informant's father answered the door. They told him that they wanted to talk to his son. At first he resisted but soon realized that he could either go get his son or the soldiers were going to enter the house and look for him. He chose to wake his son.

Mr. Purple appeared at the door and the company commander began questioning him. He seemed nervous, agitated. "Something just didn't seem right," Jay later recalled.

The company commander told him that they were going to take him back to the FOB with them. Mr. Purple asked if he could go back and get his shoes, and turned toward the house. The commander told him no, and fearing that he might try and run, or worse yet, get a weapon, he grabbed Mr. Purple and pulled him away from his home toward one of the trucks. Suddenly, Mr. Purple turned to Jay and grabbed his rifle. He struggled to pull it away from Jay, but he chose poorly.

A jolt of adrenaline shot through Sergeant Jay Karvaski's veins, and his primal instincts—fight or flee—kicked in. As smooth as glass he dropped to a knee and pulled the butt stock of the rifle back toward himself then squeezed the trigger. The round smashed into Mr. Purple's face, exploding it at point-blank range. Jay clearly saw the bullet strike him, but he shot the man again before he hit the ground. The image was permanently burned into Jay's mind like a vivid still frame. It was a horrific sight.

"Damn, did you have to shoot him again?" the first sergeant said.

Years later it still bothered him to talk about it. As he told me the story he shook his head and kept wringing his hands. "I froze and emotion suddenly flooded me. I had killed before, but this was up close and a guy I knew. I just reacted when he tried to take my weapon," he said. "Then I thought, what have I done? I killed a man."

Every soldier knows that he might have to take a life, but no amount of preparation or training can prepare someone for the feeling of having killed another human being. Jay was a good Catholic kid. He'd gone to church his entire life. He knew that he'd done what he had to do, but still he questioned. Had he just damned himself to hell at that moment? Emotion consumed him, but he kept it contained inside. He compartmentalized it.

They placed Mr. Purple's body in the first sergeant's truck and took him to the local Iraqi police station. When they arrived Jay grasped the informant's legs as he and a fellow soldier prepared to carry the body to the station. Once out of the truck the other soldier lost his grasp and Mr. Purple fell. His head hit the ground with a soft, mushy sound and his brains splattered all over Jay's boots and legs. "The sound was terrible. Awful," Jay said. It was a traumatic sight, an experience that Jay Karvaski would carry with him for the rest of his life.

When Jay returned from Iraq, he and his wife knew they needed to find a way to spend more time together. But since his unit would soon deploy again to Iraq, they spent months on end training in the field. Jay and his wife saw each other only four months during their first two years of marriage. Hoping to save his marriage, Jay searched for options.

The deployment had been very difficult on Jay. The horrific incident with Mr. Purple had been the first of numerous up-close and personal fights with the enemy. Jay had changed in many ways, particularly in how he thought of himself. He was forced to do many things that he could not have imagined himself doing prior to the war. Combat had seemed glorious and heroic in books and movies. He felt good about serving. He loved the camaraderie forged in battle, but the killing was far from glorious. It sickened him, shook him to the core, and made him question his morality. He considered that the best thing to do would be to hang up the uniform and go back to school but ultimately decided that for the sake of his wife, he needed the certainties that the army provided, including a steady paycheck and guaranteed housing.

Reluctantly, Jay remained in the army and changed his specialty to military intelligence. While he wanted to be a frontline soldier, he hoped that the change would save his marriage. He reenlisted for intelligence and was sent to Fort Huachuca, Arizona, for training, but unfortunately, not in time to save his marriage. "That year in Iraq was the worst year of my life," he said.

Jay was not the first to lose a marriage during the war. He would not be the last. By the end of our deployment my chaplain reported that he was aware of thirty-two marriages that had ended in divorce in our unit alone.

But Jay Karvaski never did anything halfheartedly. He worked hard at school and became a phenomenal military intelligence expert. His first assignment was with our unit, Task Force Pale Horse, and he was a welcome addition to the team. Jay's in-depth understanding of ground tactics and his experience fighting in Iraq made him an invaluable asset. He gave the team focus, direction, and a firm kick in the butt when they needed it.[2]

Together, Jillian Wisniewski and Jay Karvaski focused the energy of a very talented team of intel analysts on the problem at hand—the enemy writ large. One of their more popular young analysts, Specialist Jacob Andrews, worked primarily in the operations section, where he had a lot of contact with the pilots, briefing them just before they departed for missions. Andrews was an inquisitive, smart analyst with a sarcastic sense of humor that he easily weaponized, often using it against officers who were incapable of clearly understanding if they had just been insulted or not. He smoked like a chimney, was never the first pick on an athletic team, but possessed an unparalleled passion for understanding the enemy. He loved when the pilots asked him questions about the enemy. He'd beam internally, never visibly, as he went into great detail about what he'd discovered through his study of intelligence sources. Due to his sarcasm and questioning wit, he often suffered the wrath of Staff Sergeant Karvaski, but Andrews proved to be resilient. He was a gem on an all-star team. Collectively, our team knew the enemy as well as the enemy knew themselves.

The collective "enemy" within N2KL was referred to as a "syndicate" because it consisted of an extremist stew of hostile groups including al Qaeda (AQ), the Quetta Shura Taliban (QST), Jaish-e-Mohammed (JeM), Lashkar-e-Taiba (LeT), Tehrik-e-Taliban Pakistan (TTP), Tehrik-e-Nafaz-e-Shariat-e-Mohammadi (TNSM), the Salafi Taliban, Hezb-e-Islami Gulbuddin (HIG), the Haqqani Network (HQN), and others. While these groups had varying long-term aspirations, we quickly discovered that they routinely worked together against their common enemy—us. The term "Taliban" was often used as a universal label for the forces that opposed the coalition and the government of Afghanistan, but that would be disingenuous. For our purposes I will refer to those who fought against us as simply the "enemy."

The mid-to-high-level leadership and facilitators tended to move back and forth from Pakistan frequently. They collected intelligence on us through local Afghans, who were bribed or otherwise willing to observe and report our movements.

By the spring of 2009, we had observed the following about our foe: the enemy's decision-making process was driven by simple supply-and-demand and cost-benefit economic models, even though they themselves might not fully realize it. Additionally, the effects of their decisions served to fuel those same economic models. From initial analysis, it was obvious that the enemy had to perform certain tasks in order to conduct attacks on us.

Because it was the most violent area in our battle space, we focused on the Pech River Valley first. We developed a Modus Operandi Template (MOTEMP) for the enemy forces operating in the Pech, which visually portrayed the cyclic and mutually dependent relationship between logistics and direct action. (See Figure 7). The MOTEMP would help us to understand how the enemy operated within our area, thus enabling us to interdict or disrupt their process for attacks.

According to the historical data we gathered, enemy fighters in the Pech constantly monitored and reported our activity. Each day they would rise to the sound of the morning call to prayer. Following prayer they moved to their observation posts. From there they watched everything we did, every move we made, and they reported it to their superiors. As convoys departed our COPs and FOBs, enemy observers counted the number of vehicles and called their leaders. When helicopters took off they reported how many and which direction we flew. Like my cousins and me on the farm, the enemy wanted to know where their adversaries were going and what we were doing at all times. We knew they were watching us but weren't sure from what vantage points.

When the enemy found a target that they assessed to be weak and vulnerable—a soft target—they moved into a staging phase. The staging phase (green area of Figure 7) allowed the enemy to transition into the direct action phase (red area of Figure 7), which included those immediate actions leading up to and conducting an attack; then, after an attack, they shifted to post-attack planning in order to reorganize and assess their effectiveness. The direct action cells within the Pech River Valley continued this cycle as the supporting logistics cells conducted operations outside this geographic area (yellow area of Figure 7).

Each enemy cell acted according to its own timeline, depending on the type of attack that it typically conducted against our forces (i.e., hasty versus deliberate attacks). Similarly, each phase of its operation followed its own timeline based on availability of resources, external factors, and priority of effort. Pinpointing the individual timelines based on cells and phases was invaluable at the tactical level as it exposed enemy vulnerabilities for coalition forces to exploit; however, knowing the baseline for each of those cells provided insight on where to look first for vulnerabilities.

First, based on the logistics and direct action relationship, the enemy needed to import supplies, which generally came from Pakistan, where they had a base of support. From there, enemy facilitators had to cross the border into Afghanistan, use trails on the east side of the Kunar River, and then cross the river. Then they used trails and valleys on the west side of the Kunar River to get to their staging areas in the Pech River Valley, which concluded the baseline logistics phase from Pakistan to the Pech District.

As they moved into the planning phase, they traveled to the ancillary valleys of the Pech: Watapur, Shuryak, Korengal, and Waygal. These valleys provided safe havens where they maintained caches of weapons and conducted planning meetings. Their planning was done in person since they realized that their communications were compromised. They would then conduct rehearsals and subsequently transition into the execution phase of their operation.

The execution phase began with visual observations in order to choose a vulnerable target. Like a pack of lions surveying gazelles, the enemy looked for the weak and exposed. Once the enemy found the target they wanted to attack they would move to fighting positions, wait for approval from their commanders, attack, and then attempt to coordinate follow-on actions or leave the area. As enemy fighters transitioned into their post-attack phase they again called each other on walkie-talkies or cell phones to try to determine the effects of their operation on both coalition forces and themselves. The enemy needed to know how successful their attack had been and how much damage they had suffered during the attack. They would then meet again to determine any refit needs and to discuss adjustments required for future attacks.

At this point enemy fighters either determined the need for cross-border resupply, or, if the logistics flow was steady, they returned to local caches and safe havens and secured more weapons. During the cell's decision-making cycle they had to meet to conduct a cost-benefit analysis that determined their next action. For instance, they examined whether the risk of exposing their fighters in the Korengal Valley (Cost 1) and the expenditure of the newly acquired weapons (Cost 2) were worth the potential gain of shooting down a coalition force helicopter (Benefit). The cell then planned, rehearsed, and attempted to execute an ambush, tried to shoot down a helicopter, or attempted to overrun an outpost (Output).

By building an enemy MOTEMP we were able to determine potential enemy vulnerabilities. The most prominent vulnerabilities for the enemy were those locations or tasks that most exposed their fighters and created the most crippling disruption to their operations. In the logistics phase, the vulnerable points included the river crossing. The river was a natural obstacle, had limited crossing points, and flowed through open terrain, which provided excellent visibility for both our ground forces and helicopters. Another obvious vulnerability were their pre-staging locations within the area. If coalition forces exploited those locations, it forced the enemy to use more time-consuming resupply routes from Pakistan, hindering their ability to refit themselves quickly for future operations in the Pech Valley area. Analysis of reporting and focused surveillance and reconnaissance provided insight that allowed us to further refine their vulnerabilities, including time windows for enemy activities and more specific locations.

Jillian's team laid out all of their research for our pilots. I knew the scouts would love the in-depth analysis. I expected them to ask questions and provide her with a thousand what-if scenarios. I was pretty sure our Apache pilots would do the same, but I wasn't sure how the Chinook and Black Hawk crews would respond. I was pleasantly surprised. What I quickly realized was that my childhood game of Cowboys and Indians had not been confined to my grandfather's forty-acre north Georgia farm. I was pleased to discover that my soldiers naturally took to our high-stakes, life-and-death game of what we called "snooping and pooping in bad-guy country." Thus, I was left to assume that other children had grown up playing their own version of Cowboys and Indians in Midwest cornfields, Southwest deserts, suburbs, cities, and forests all over America and her territories. Soon I noticed that pilots began to drop by the intel shop to talk with analysts, see what new things they had discovered, and if there was a way to become more effective in their collection efforts. We had tapped into something very powerful.

Figure 7 is the raw product that Jillian's team produced while sitting around a table in the middle of the night. It demonstrates the creative problem-solving capacity of Jillian's team. Everyone in her shop participated and the result was perfect—problem-solving at its core.

Prior to 2009, the battalion task force responsible for the Pech River Valley also had responsibility for the central Kunar River Valley. It was a massive piece of terrain and a near-impossible task for a single battalion task force. In 2009, Camp Joyce was expanded to provide space for an additional battalion task force in the central Kunar River Valley.

In February 2009, 1-32 Infantry (Task Force Chosin) of the 10th Mountain Division occupied the newly expanded FOB Joyce and assumed responsibility for the central Kunar River Valley, including the AFPAK border. TF Chosin also occupied four other company-size outposts in the central Kunar: Goshta, Fortress, Monti, and Penich. Company outposts versus smaller outposts manned by single platoons of fifteen to twenty men enabled TF Chosin to assemble forces quickly and project them onto the battlefield.

Occupying FOB Joyce put TF Chosin right in the heart of the enemy smuggling and facilitation routes. The primary funding source for enemy fighters came from gem, opium, and timber smuggling. The most active sources of timber were the Korengal and Chowkay valleys. The timber, primarily massive cedar trees, was cut in the back of the valleys, loaded onto trucks, and then transported to a transition point where the trees were strapped to donkeys and moved across the border via trail systems. The AFPAK border was porous, making it extremely difficult to interdict smuggling activities. Afghan border police manned checkpoints at only the most heavily trafficked crossing sites.

The timber was used for expensive furniture, which was built in Pakistan. Timber smuggling resulted in a major loss to Afghanistan's economy. If managed properly, logging could benefit the Afghan economy, but in 2009, it was clear that unregulated logging would quickly result in erosion and deforestation. Left unchecked, the deforestation would have a devastating effect on the agrarian lifestyle of Afghan citizens who lived in the Kunar Province. Prior to the arrival of TF Chosin, smuggling was essentially an unencumbered practice. Troop strengths simply did not allow for interdiction of smuggling, nor did they prevent munitions from being moved into Afghanistan for enemy fighters. The same trails that were used to move timber east served as infiltration routes for rockets, RPGs, machine guns, and ammunition. The lack of troops in the central Kunar, and along the border, allowed the enemy near complete freedom of maneuver.

By April we began to see the effects of 1-32 Infantry in the central Kunar. Our focused reconnaissance, coupled with their patrols and presence, had clearly disrupted the enemy. Jillian's team used every piece of intelligence and data available to measure our effectiveness. Rocket attacks that were once prevalent throughout the Pech and Korengal were much less frequent. Outposts on the eastern side of the Kunar, however, saw an increase in rocket and mortar attacks. The enemy was forced to engage us from positions along the Pakistan border because they were unable to transport large munitions west of the Kunar River. The price of weapons had also significantly risen both in Pakistan and Afghanistan, signifying a depletion of their caches in eastern Afghanistan. The enemy no longer had weapons caches and traveling to Pakistan to get them was a difficult and dangerous task, so they tried to buy them from the locals. The locals recognized the demand so they increased the prices.

Working closely with TF Chosin, we had made a significant impact on the enemy's ability to continue attacks in the Pech and ancillary valleys; thus, we forced the enemy to make difficult choices. If they could not reopen their lines of communication in the central Kunar, they would have to push north or south to try to get around us. We saw an increase in activity and enemy movement to the south in Goshta District and in the north, through Dangam and Nari districts. Attacks against our outposts, which sat on their lines of communication, increased. Enemy forces were willing to fight to try and reopen their support routes. On April 29, Jillian's team published a 120-day intelligence assessment. In the assessment, her team stated that all intelligence indicated that the enemy would attempt to overrun a newly established outpost in northern Kunar—Bari Ali.

There is little use for the being whose tepid soul knows nothing of great and generous emotion, of the high pride, the stern belief, the lofty enthusiasm, of the men who quell the storm and ride the thunder.

—THEODORE ROOSEVELT

BARI ALI

MAY 2009

As America's sons and daughters fight battles in far-off lands, some battles make the headline news, while others fail even to merit a footnote. The battle at OP Bari Ali received very little press coverage despite its significance. Press is a double-edged sword. Coverage of battles, particularly when the enemy inflicts casualties on American forces, usually means that the military gets criticized for everything it failed to do, but a lack of coverage leaves many soldiers feeling that no one outside the war zone knows how hard they are fighting.

About ten miles south of FOB Bostic the Kunar River Valley grows narrow and deep. It travels almost due north until just before it reaches Ghaziabad District, then makes an S-turn and continues northeast. Near the Nishagam District center, in the midst of that incredibly complex terrain, three valleys converge on the Kunar River: the Helgal, Marin, and Durin. The Nishagam District center is somewhat centrally located at the convergence of the valleys. It sits on the west side of the Kunar River overlooking numerous villages stretched out along the green floors of the valleys.

The road, which follows the Kunar River through the valley, is called the Drosh–Jalalabad Road, but during the war we called it Main Supply Route (MSR) California, and it was the only way to get to FOB Bostic by land. We used a combination of coalition military vehicles and local Jingle trucks to transport supplies from Jalalabad to FOB Bostic in Nari. The Jingle trucks, named for the small pieces of colorful metal that hung from them, sounded like traveling wind chimes as they drove. Once the supplies reached FOB Bostic they were prepared, in packages, to be transported by Chinooks into OPs Fritchie, Keating, Lowell, Mace, and Hatchet. If MSR California was closed, or if the enemy interdicted our supply convoys, it isolated FOB Bostic and prevented us from delivering supplies to all the TF Raider bases in Nuristan.

Enemy leaders were well aware of how important MSR California was for our survival in Nuristan. Furthermore, they knew that we did not have permanent combat outposts stationed along the stretch of road between COP Monti and FOB Bostic. MSR California was extremely vulnerable throughout that stretch of somewhat indefensible terrain. To make matters worse, for the majority of the twenty-mile stretch, MSR California was a single-lane dirt road that plummeted off into the Kunar River on the east side and hugged a sheer cliff that climbed thousands of feet to the west. It provided numerous ideal locations for enemy forces to ambush our logistics convoys.

The Soviets had faced the same problem during their occupation of Afghanistan. As bulky trucks slowly crawled along the raggedy stretch of dirt, bumper to bumper, enemy forces shot vehicles in the front and rear of their convoys with RPGs, thus blocking the road. The only way to continue to move forward was to push the burning vehicles into the river; many of the old Soviet vehicles still remained partially submerged, slowly rusting away in a watery grave, silently screaming a warning to those who would dare to follow.

Removing burning hulks from the road took time, time conveniently exploited by the enemy. While the Soviets had tried to move disabled vehicles out of the way, mujahideen forces worked their way to the middle of their column, attacking the other vehicles trapped in the kill zone. The terrain from COP Monti to FOB Bostic was ideal for these tactics, and the enemy would soon afford us the opportunity to see how well we could deal with the same tactical problem faced by the Soviets two decades prior.

That spring TF Raider had established an outpost on a spur about halfway up the western mountain overlooking the Nishagam District center. It sat approximately nine miles south of FOB Bostic, which was almost the halfway point between Monti and Bostic. They named the outpost after an Afghan National Army (ANA) soldier who was killed in an IED blast in that area—Bari Ali. The outpost was built to help secure the critical yet vulnerable road, as well as the Nishagam District center, which housed the governor's office and the police headquarters.

The district governor asked the Afghan National Army Commander to occupy the outpost. Initially, he had assigned the police to occupy the position, but he didn't like the army performing what he felt should be police functions in the surrounding villages, specifically checkpoint operations. Checkpoints were an oft-used tool for criminal activity such as exploiting the local populace. He felt that policemen should do police functions—checkpoints—and army soldiers should perform security functions in the outpost. The army leadership argued that the police were not patrolling enough, but the governor assured the army commander that if he manned the outpost, the police would actively patrol the villages and perform law enforcement functions through-out the district.

The army commander agreed to put a company of soldiers, about seventy Afghans, on the OP. They would have an eight-to-nine-man U.S. embedded training team with them at all times. Approximately two-thirds of the company would occupy the OP, while the other third con-tinued to conduct checkpoint operations on the road adjacent to the district center itself. Unlike most other outposts in northern Kunar and Nuristan, OP Bari Ali was built on relatively high ground, with a view of the valleys below; however, the only way to reach the outpost was by using the tiny foot trail that wound its way up to the OP, or by air. The Afghan soldiers, four Latvians, and three Americans (Sergeant James Pirtle, Specialist Ryan King, and Sergeant William Vile) manned the OP on the morning of May 1.

First Lieutenant Aaron Nichols and Chief Warrant Officer 2 Mike Downing concluded a maintenance test flight just before dawn on May 1. Clouds hung low, and a light mist fell as they landed the Black Hawk helicopter at FOB Fenty. As they were preparing to shut their helicopter down, Mike and Aaron saw two Apaches take off in the direction of the Kunar River Valley, and Aaron thought he heard the battle captain say, "And there are enemy forces in the wire," over the radio.

"That's odd. Did you see anyone around the perimeter when we flew in?" Nichols asked Downing.

"No, sir. I didn't see anything," Downing said. "Let's go to the command post and find out what's up."

But before they reached the command post, Chief Warrant Officer 2 Kevin Howey called them on their handheld radio and said, "We've gotta go. Bari Ali is under attack."

Nichols and Downing looked at each other. "Let's go!" Downing said. Nichols and Downing ran back to the helicopter, cranked it, and made radio contact with the other aircraft to try and figure out what they were expected to do.

"They have reported a bunch of casualties. We may need you to reinforce the OP with more soldiers." The reply came from a voice Downing didn't immediately recognize. In nervous anticipation, they flew directly to FOB Bostic as fast as the Black Hawks would carry them.

Before daylight, over one hundred enemy fighters had crept quietly through the rocks near OP Bari Ali. They had set up a machine gun position on the high ground above the OP while other fighters moved up the ridge from below. The enemy had used the poor weather and darkness to their advantage. Once in position they opened fire with the machine gun up the ridge, which naturally drew the attention of the men in the OP to the high ground. Simultaneously, other fighters had opened fire from below the OP with a barrage of RPGs. A small coalition observation point had been established farther up the hill from Bari Ali, called OP East. It was supposed to be manned by eight or nine Afghan Uniformed Police (AUP). Their primary purpose was to watch the southeastern approach to Bari Ali. OP East was supposed to serve as Bari Ali's early warning system; however, for some reason it was not manned that morning.

Whether coincidence or otherwise we will never know, but the enemy RPGs impacted the HESCO barriers at the precise location where the 84-millimeter Carl Gustav recoil-less rifles were stored. The secondary explosion from those rifles blew a hole in OP Bari Ali's perimeter, thus opening a door for the enemy to enter.

It was a well-coordinated attack. Within minutes King, Pirtle, Vile, four Afghan soldiers, two Latvians, and an Afghan interpreter were all killed. It's hard to know exactly how many Afghan soldiers were actually in the OP at the time of the attack, due to the chaos and confusion that ensued immediately following it. Some of them ran down the hill, seeking perceived security at the district center. One soldier was later found and assumed to have been shot execution style. Ultimately, eleven Afghan soldiers and an interpreter were taken prisoner. As soon as the attack had begun the American soldiers at OP Bari Ali reported it to TF Raider's command post. TF Raider assembled a quick-reaction force to travel south by ground while they simultaneously called our command post requesting that we launch the aerial quick-reaction force and a medevac helicopter.

Despite threatening weather, a team of Apaches was airborne within minutes. Chief Warrant Officer 2 Kevin Clark, an Apache instructor pilot, was the air mission commander in charge of the flight. Kevin was crewed with Chief Warrant Officer 2 Mike Krajnik. They were teamed with Chief Warrant Officer 2 Chris Wright and First Lieutenant David Daniels. The team had no idea what they might find once they arrived in the valley. The entire crew was optimistic that the radio call was wrong, that the OP had been attacked but hadn't been overrun. We had received reports like that in the past. Eight out of ten times our ground forces could pound the enemy with artillery, and the attack would soon stop. That's what Chris Wright was thinking when he broke the silence in the helicopters. "I'm sure they'll have it all under control by the time we get there."

As they flew past COP Monti they climbed to a slightly higher altitude so they could establish line-of-sight radio communications with the OP.

"OP Bari Ali, this is Weapons 1-5, over," Chris calmly called, using his tactical call sign.

After a long silent pause, he repeated, "OP Bari Ali, Weapons 1-5, over."

Nothing. Silence prevailed on the radio. It wasn't uncommon to have difficulty reaching the OPs in the mountainous terrain, but by May we had flown the valleys so much that we knew exactly at what point we should be able to reach them. Given the situation, the silence concerned the Apache crews.

They were getting close. There was one final hill where the valley made an S-turn and then they would be able to see Bari Ali. Everyone remained quiet in anticipation. They continued to gain altitude, crested the hill, and then they saw it. The OP was burning. A swirling plume of dark, black smoke ascended into a ceiling of gray clouds. It was as if the sky were connected to the OP through a churning tube of smoke—consuming everything in waving red flames, then sucking it, black and burned, into the heavens above.

Chris continued to try and make radio contact with the men on the OP, but it was clear that no one was going to answer. Our Apache pilots had fought in and around OP Bari Ali numerous times in the past. They knew where the enemy liked to hide, so they immediately oriented on the most often used fighting positions in the mountains surrounding the OP and searched for enemy fighters.

"I see some guys down there moving around. I'm moving in closer to take a look. Cover me," Kevin Clark told Wright and Daniels. He saw several Afghan soldiers on the east side of the OP. "That's one of the Latvian soldiers. He's dragging soldiers out of the OP."

The reality of the moment struck the pilots with disbelief. What they were seeing was not normal, everyday enemy contact. The soldiers on the ground ducked and flinched as ammunition began to explode randomly in the OP due to the fire—distinct pops in the midst of a raging blaze.

Clark made contact with Crazy Horse 6. "Crazy Horse 6, I see several men moving around. I can identify one of the Latvian soldiers but no Americans. The Latvian is moving the dead and wounded out of the OP. We need to establish communications with the OP. If you have a radio I will land and pick it up."

Crazy Horse 6 found a handheld radio to send up the mountain.

"I have a radio ready. Land to the district center and I'll give it to you." Clark landed his Apache at the district center, picked up the radio, and flew it up to the OP. The landing zone at Bari Ali was very small and sat on a thin saddle between the mountain, which continues to climb to the west, and a spur upon which the OP sat.

As the helicopter approached, the Latvian realized that they were trying to get his attention. Kevin brought the Apache to a hover right over him while Mike Krajnik dropped the radio down to him. "Shit. It rolled down the hill. I don't know if he knows where it went,"

Krajnik said. "He just ran back to the OP. He doesn't get what we're trying to do."

"Okay. Let's get another one and we'll land in the LZ and hand it to him," Clark said. Krajnik didn't respond. The mountain was still crawling with enemy. Bullets were zinging by them. Landing in the middle of the engagement area didn't sound smart, but Krajnik knew that's what they needed to do, so he kept his comments to himself.

"Okay, I'm going to land this time and have Krajnik hand him the radio. Cover me going in," he told Wright and Daniels, whose responsibility it was to protect him as he approached the OP.

"Roger, we've got you covered," Wright replied.

Clark circled around and lined up for the approach to the LZ. He wanted to keep his speed up as long as possible, yet he had to slow down in enough time so as not to overshoot the LZ. Speed was critical to our safety in Afghanistan. In discussions with our pilots, I often used a dove hunting analogy. The faster a dove flies and the more he darts and dives in flight, the more difficult it is to hit him. It was no different in a helicopter. Keeping our speed up and constantly changing direction and altitude would make for a difficult shot.

Clark slowed down significantly as he neared the small LZ. Chris Wright suddenly caught movement out of the corner of his eye.

"RPG! RPG! Break off, break off!" Wright yelled over the radio. Kevin snapped the cyclic left, diving the helicopter away as an RPG passed by the Apache and exploded into the ridge on the other side of the valley. An enemy fighter had stepped out from behind a huge boulder with an RPG as Clark slowed to land. Chris Wright and Dave Daniels were perfectly positioned to cover Clark's break. As soon as Wright saw the enemy fighter he pointed the nose of the helicopter directly at him. As they dove at the fighter, and the mountain, Daniels asked, "Where is he?"

Wright squeezed the trigger, sending a salvo of rockets at the enemy fighter. Daniels answered his own question. "Right there," he said in a calm voice, seeing that the enemy fighter had been killed.

Clark circled back around for another approach. Wright and Daniels moved into position to cover him once again. This time Kevin landed at the LZ and Krajnik quickly tossed the Latvian a radio, but he did not appear to know how to use it. It was painfully clear at that point that we had to reinforce the OP with more soldiers, American soldiers, and quickly.

Meanwhile, back at FOB Fenty, our team of planners was busy coordinating reinforcements and additional assets to help in the fight. Jack and I began working with TF Duke, Special Forces, TF Raider, and TF Thunder to ensure we had enough aviation resources to keep Apaches and Kiowas over the OP throughout the day and lift helicopters to move reinforcements around the battlefield. Jack and I determined that we would, once again, need help from TF Eagle Lift, so I called Colonel Ron Lewis. I told him everything we knew about the situation at that point, then I told him I thought we'd need at least one more Chinook, along with a team of Apaches, to help out. He agreed and directed that TF Eagle Lift provide the aircraft and crews to support us.

Jack worked with Major Keith Rautter, the TF Duke chief of operations, to ensure we were operating within Colonel Spiszer's intent. We wanted to make sure we were handling the situation the way he wanted us to, before we began moving helicopters around RC-East.

Major Tom Sarrouf, the Special Forces advanced operating base (AOB) commander, ran over to our command post to keep abreast of the situation and to think through what his forces might be able to do in response to the attack. He had only one Operational Detachment—Alpha (ODA) at FOB Fenty. This small elite team was responsible for training Afghan commandos. They were truly the only reserve force Colonel John Spiszer had at his disposal. His infantry battalions were spread very thin throughout N2KL. He could use his forces to regain control of Bari Ali, but if he wanted to conduct a follow-on operation to go after those responsible for the attack he'd have to coordinate through the Special Forces command structure to gain approval to employ them. Approval was normally a given, but they were not under his direct control. As it turned out, Lieutenant Colonel Jim Markert had already been pulling what forces he had together to go to Bari Ali. Colonel Spiszer called Lieutenant Colonel Mark O'Donnell and told him to plan to go and assist as well.

I decided to send Captain Steve Souza, one of our planners, and Chief Warrant Officer 3 Gary Parsons, our tactical operations officer and personnel recovery expert, forward to FOB Bostic to work with Jim Markert's TF Raider. The two men would serve as aviation planners for Jim Markert's team. Kevin Clark's Apache team had been on duty throughout the night. They were already committed to the fight, but they were nearing the end of their duty day. We needed to get the next shift of Apache pilots into the fight, but we could not afford for Clark's team to fly all the way back to FOB Fenty to switch out the crews. That would take Apaches off of Bari Ali for way too long.

Limited resources became the challenge. I needed to get the day crews into the Apaches that were already being flown by Clark and Wright. We simply didn't have enough Apaches for the day and night crews to each have their own helicopters. As we discussed the situation in the command post, Chief Warrant Officer 2 Fred Taroli, the air mission commander of the Apache team needing to get into the fight, recommended that they fly to FOB Bostic in a Black Hawk and then swap out in the FARP.

"Perfect. That works. Let's do it," I said. The pilots strapped themselves into a Black Hawk, along with Captain Souza and Gary Parsons, and they flew with a medevac helicopter up to FOB Bostic.

Chief Warrant Officer 3 Warren Brown and Chief Warrant Officer 2 Ray Andrel flew the Black Hawk. Sergeant Jeremy Arend served as the crew chief and Sergeant Lindsey Andrews served as the door gunner. Warren Brown was the pilot in command of the aircraft. Warren departed FOB Fenty thinking that his team was just going to fly the Apache crews forward to the fight, but they would soon discover that they would play an integral role in moving and resupplying forces throughout northern Kunar all day. Their call sign was Flawless 0-8.

Warren Brown was a freckle-faced, rosy-cheeked Southerner with strawberry blond hair and a thick drawl. He was from Alabama and his full name was Warren H. Brown IV, which sounded quite sophisticated to me. Being from rural north Georgia myself, I had a lot in common with Warren, but I often reminded him that he was not cut from the same wood as I. With a name like that he had to be Southern aristocracy. "My people worked the ground that your people owned," I kidded him.

Warren was a happy-go-lucky guy in whom I had great confidence. He was an utterly competent and fearless pilot whom I knew I could always count on in a tight spot.

The Apache crews that Warren flew to the fight consisted of Chief Warrant Officer 2 Gary Wingert and Capt. Matthew Kaplan, who would fly in the lead aircraft, while Chief Warrant Officer 2 Jesse Powell and Chief Warrant Officer 3 Fred Taroli flew trail.

Warren, along with the medevac bird, departed FOB Fenty at 9:30 A.M. As they neared COP Monti, Warren called Kevin Clark on the radio. "How do you want us to pass by Bari Ali?" he asked Clark.

It was a tight valley and Warren wanted to stay out of the way as he passed to the north. The low-hanging ceiling, made up of a layer of thick gray clouds, prevented them from climbing up over the mountains. They had to make a run through the narrow valley, which would put them between the burning outpost and the eastern wall of the valley.

When Warren called Kevin on the radio the ground forces at the Nishagam District center and the forces on the OP were still taking machine gun fire from literally every cardinal direction. "Fly fast and keep to the east side of the valley," Clark told Warren, which he did and made it through the valley unscathed. Once on the ground at FOB Bostic, the battle captain at TF Raider told Warren that he needed him to air-assault an infantry squad to the OP. He said Lieutenant Colonel Jim Markert would be on the aircraft to lead the team.

Not expecting to be used in the actual fight, Warren called back to the Pale Horse command post and asked to speak to me. "Sir, they want us to take a squad, maybe two, up to Bari Ali. I'm not briefed for that. What do you want me to do?" Warren asked.

"There is no telling what you may be asked to do today, Warren. I would rather use you right now, in a single Black Hawk, to get folks in. A Chinook would be slower getting in and out and it's a bigger target. You're going to have to make the calls on this. Fly the reinforcements in, but as they ask you to do more, do what you think you can do. You don't have to call me for approval on everything unless you don't think you can do what they are asking. If that's the case, then call me and we'll find another way to get it done. I trust you to make the calls," I told him.

"Roger that, sir," he said and hung up.

Because of the inherent risks associated with aviation operations, each crew received a specified mission. The pilots then conducted a risk assessment for those particular tasks they were to accomplish. If there were deviations, they were required to get approval to amend the plan, particularly when the deviation increased the risk. However,

in a situation such as Bari Ali, I liked to speak to the air mission commander and tell him that I trusted him to make the right decisions. I
could not, and would not, try and quarterback every move from my
command post at FOB Fenty.

We desperately needed to get U.S. soldiers on the OP, but only the
guys there, in the fight, knew when the time was right to do it with
the least likelihood of getting a helicopter shot down. I was confident
that we had the right guys in the right place to make the best on-the-
spot decisions.

Warren loaded eleven soldiers in the back of his Black Hawk. Then
his copilot, Ray Andrel, called Clark.

"We've got a squad on board, and we need to get them into the
OP. Can you cover us as we land?" he asked.

Clark told him where he thought the enemy was located, but the
situation was still pretty chaotic at that point. Ray acknowledged as
they departed FOB Bostic for the OP. Clark's team of Apaches flew
north and met Warren and Ray to escort them into the OP. Ray ran
the systems inside the cockpit while Warren concentrated on flying
the helicopter, focusing his attention outside. They had to get in as
quickly as possible, offload the troops, and get out. They knew that
from the time they began slowing to land until they were clear of the
OP they would be a target. As they approached the LZ, dust, smoke,
and debris flew into the air, swirling around the rotors and envelop-
ing the helicopter. It was difficult to see, but Warren landed safely in
the LZ. Bodies lay all around the OP, both wounded and dead. As
soon as the wheels touched down, the squad exited the helicopter.

"Clear!" Sergeant Arend announced in back of the aircraft, and
Warren pulled in power and took off, circling around and heading
back north to FOB Bostic.

TF Raider wanted to continue to reinforce the OP with more soldiers, and they wanted more men at the district center as well. A
ground quick-reaction force drove from FOB Bostic south to the
Nishagam District center and set up a tactical command post to help
control all the soldiers that we planned to move into the area. Due to
the terrain, our line-of-sight radios were spotty at best, so the tactical
command post was needed to coordinate and give clear direction to
all the soldiers in the valley and up on the OP.

Back at FOB Fenty, we called for a Chinook crew and two Kiowa crews to report to the command post. The battle captain instructed them to fly to COP Monti and pick up a third platoon, Charlie Company, TF Chosin. Colonel John Spiszer had decided to commit the entire company to the fight, but we had room in the Chinook to carry only twenty-five soldiers at a time, so it would take multiple turns with the Chinook in order to get them all to Bari Ali. He had told us to fly them to the district center, and from there they would attack up the hill to reestablish the OP.

Lieutenants lead platoons; however, Charlie Company was short one lieutenant, so the platoon sergeant, Sergeant First Class Richard Tacia, led the third platoon. Tacia and most everyone else in Kunar Province had been glued to their radios throughout the morning, trying to gain a better understanding of what was going on at Bari Ali by piecing together random radio calls. When Colonel Spiszer decided to send the third platoon to Bari Ali they were given thirty minutes to prepare themselves and assemble in the pickup zone. They were further instructed to take provisions to sustain themselves for three days. The situation was tense. Their fellow soldiers at Bari Ali were in trouble, and they were going to help, but flying into the middle of a firefight with limited information was always nerve-racking.

Jeff Dorsey and Adam McCullough flew the Chinook. They departed FOB Fenty with a bit of apprehension themselves. Dorsey knew that a significant battle had been raging for hours by that point, and he would potentially be delivering infantrymen into the middle of the shooting. That was enough to make anyone uneasy, particularly in the largest helicopter in the fleet. Jeff had flown to Bari Ali countless times. He knew that he'd have to slow way down to land on the LZ, and in that tight valley he would quickly become the focus for all enemy fire.

The crew remained relatively quiet and focused as they flew up the Kunar Valley. As they approached COP Monti, Dorsey and copilot Adam McCullough could see Sergeant First Class Tacia's men standing by, waiting to be picked up. Dorsey set the helicopter down in the LZ, and Sergeant First Class Tacia counted his men onto the bird. Within two minutes they were back in the air, headed for the fight.

Sergeant First Class Daniel Glick served as the flight evaluator on the Chinook. He was the senior crew member in charge of everything in the back of the helicopter. Dan operated the ramp on the back of the aircraft, gave instructions to the passengers, and gave direction to the other crew members in the back, which consisted of crew chief Sergeant Antonio Lewis and the door gunner, Specialist Kenneth Williams.

Jeff Dorsey was our Chinook maintenance test pilot. His primary job in the task force was to conduct maintenance test flights after major repairs or services had been completed on the Chinooks. We had put all of our most experienced mission pilots on the night shift to conduct night resupply missions in the Kamdesh. We put Jeff—a very strong mission pilot as well—on the day shift, so he could conduct test flights in order to ensure that the helicopters were ready for the night missions. May 1, 2009, would turn out to be a day Jeff Dorsey and the crew of Flex 6-3 would never forget.

We sent a team of Kiowas up with Jeff. Their job was to escort the Chinook into the valley, then remain there to help the Apaches find and kill enemy forces. Chief Warrant Officer 2 Kris Klusacek and former Navy SEAL Chief Warrant Officer 2 Don Cunningham flew in the lead helicopter. Their trail aircraft was flown by Chief Warrant Officers 2 Jason Aldins and Ray Illman. Kris Klusacek was a gifted Kiowa pilot who seemed to thrive in chaos. He was younger than many of our other air mission commanders, but Kris was a natural cavalryman.

Just as not every athlete has the ability to perform at the professional level, not every pilot is born with the instincts to be a good air mission commander. Air mission commanders are not designated based on rank; instead, and because they represent the unit commander, they are chosen based on their demonstrated maturity, flight proficiency, and, perhaps most important, their ability to make the very best decisions with the information they have on hand. They are problem-solvers, responsible for safely and smartly employing all aerial assets on any given mission. Generally, the most seasoned, senior pilot in the flight serves as the air mission commander; however, the most senior aviator is not always the best choice. In the army we often confuse rank and experience with innate talent. An air force officer once asked me, "Jimmy, do you know what's wrong with the army?" Not knowing exactly where to begin, he bailed me out by answering his own question: "The army thinks that the smartest captain is just a little bit dumber than the dumbest major."

Guilty as charged. My observations since that time, with few exceptions, have proved his theory true. Without consideration of talent, we tend to think that an operation is inherently safer and will go more smoothly with a chief warrant officer 4 serving as the air mission commander versus a chief warrant officer 2 or a lieutenant. Certainly, experience makes us wiser and more proficient, but superior instincts seem to be a natural gift that no amount of experience makes up for. Not everyone can play quarterback—see the receivers, feel the blockers, sense the rush, and make the pass under pressure—nor do all pilots have good air sense. Through practice we can certainly improve, but some people are born with a natural knack for managing complexity. It is a leader's responsibility to identify those who possess those skills and exploit their talents. As author and scholar Jim Collins might say, "Put the right pilot in the right seat on the bus."

Kris Klusacek was one of those gifted junior air mission commanders who could instinctively visualize the battlefield. Like Michael Jordan on the basketball court, Kris intuitively knew where his teammates were at all times. He could make the pass to a spot blindly because he knew his teammate would be there. He was not the only junior officer with superior air sense. Shane Burkhart, Ryan Neal, Matt Fix, and many others fell into that category. They could see multiple gun target lines—the path that a mortar or artillery round must travel from the gun to the target—in their mind. They were able to remain clear of danger while continuing the fight.

I have personally been the air mission commander in the Watapur Valley when we were shooting 155-mm howitzers from FOB Wright, 120-mm mortars from COP Honaker-Miracle, 105-mm artillery from FOB Blessing, dropping bombs from air force jets, and employing our attack helicopters simultaneously. It is a very complex situation that demands an air mission commander who can visualize all of those gun target lines in order to continue attacking the enemy. In 2009 we placed a tremendous amount of focus on air mission commander training before we deployed, despite hurting the feelings of several senior aviators. I put the right pilot in charge of the right mission without regard for rank, and Kris Klusacek was one of the best.

Rolling vortices, visible in the dust, swirled off the rotor blades as the Chinook lifted up off the ground. Once airborne, Dorsey immediately contacted the tactical command post that was then operational at the district center, just down the hill from Bari Ali. Crazy Horse 6 told Jeff to proceed directly to the OP, "not the district center." Dorsey passed the word to Sergeant First Class Glick, who in turn told Tacia. "We're going to land on the OP," he shouted.

The soldiers passed the information man to man down the row of red nylon seats, screaming to one another over the roar of the turbine engines. As they approached Bari Ali, Sergeant Glick began lowering the ramp in preparation for their exit. As the ramp slowly lowered, everyone stared out the back of the helicopter, trying to get a glimpse of the unknown. Dorsey kept his speed up as long as possible, flared at the bottom to slow the aircraft, then planted it on the LZ. Tacia's soldiers exploded out of the Chinook, not knowing if they would take immediate fire or if other friendly forces were already there. They immediately laid down behind whatever cover they could find in a 360-degree circle around the OP and scanned the mountains around them for enemy fighters.

With all the air assets in place—fresh Apache and Kiowa teams, a Chinook, a Black Hawk, and a medevac bird—we began reinforcing the OP and evacuating the casualties. Jim Markert controlled the operations on the ground, while our command posts collaboratively planned for the days ahead. While Taroli's Apache team and Klusacek's scouts searched for enemy forces still hiding in the boulders, Warren Brown and Jeff Dorsey flew their helicopters back and forth among the outpost, the district center, and FOB Bostic, moving men and supplies into the valley.

As Jim Markert and his men tried to make sense of what had happened at the OP, it became evident that there were some Afghan soldiers missing, along with one of the Latvians.

Taroli called Klusacek: "Hey, they are missing some Afghan soldiers and a Latvian. We need to start looking for them."

"Roger," Klusacek replied and the search began.

Within a few hours, intelligence sources indicated that the enemy had indeed captured eleven Afghan soldiers and a Latvian, and that they were moving them into the neighboring Helgal Valley. Within minutes other intel sources confirmed the initial report. We immediately sent Klusacek's scouts into the Helgal Valley to try and find them.

Warren Brown landed at FOB Bostic to pick up another load of soldiers, but this time they loaded his helicopter with body bags. "We need you to deliver these speedballs to the East OP," the soldier on the ground told him. The "speedballs" were the black body bags, filled with water bottles, ammunition, grenades, and MREs.

"Roger," Warren said, and gave him a thumbs-up.

The East OP sat up the hill from Bari Ali on a very steep slope. We needed to supply the post with enough ammunition, water, and MRE-FOOD=FOOD READY TO EAT to last several days. It was uncertain how long the soldiers might be there, and whether the enemy would attack again at dusk, but if they did, we wanted to make sure that the men at that small OP were adequately supplied. Due to the steep slope of the mountain, the Chinook was too large to hover close to the mountain and drop the speedballs to the soldiers below, so Warren had volunteered his crew for that mission.

"Crap. Look at the slope of that thing," he said as they approached. The East OP was literally built into the side of a vertical ridge. The crew would have to kick the speedballs out the door with extreme precision because they could not hover directly over the OP without their rotor blades striking the side of the mountain. It would be a very tricky maneuver. Warren slowed to a hover off the side of the ridge, then slid the helicopter over as close as possible to the mountain. Sergeant Andrews, the crew chief in the back, told him how close his rotor was to the terrain. "Five feet, four feet, three feet, hold," Sergeant Andrews relayed.

Warren held the Black Hawk steady and Andrews kicked the first speedball out. It hit the ground and immediately rolled down the mountain. The men on the OP could not believe what they were seeing. They stared in disbelief as Warren hovered dangerously close to the side of the mountain. One of the soldiers on the OP snapped a quick picture. Five years later, when I called to interview him, that was the first thing he mentioned. He still had the picture and later sent it to me.

Sergeant Andrews saw the small trail that the men used to walk from Bari Ali to the East OP. It was a well-worn path with a lip on the downhill side. He thought if he could get the speedball to land on the trail it might hold.

"Come back five," he told Warren. "Now up ten," he said. "Hold." He kicked the next one out. It landed squarely on the trail and stuck. He kicked out several more along the trail and then told Warren "mission complete." Warren flew away from the mountain and headed back to FOB Bostic.

On Jeff Dorsey's second turn into OP Bari Ali, nine Heroes (soldiers killed in action) were loaded onto the back of the Chinook. We had decided not to use the medevac aircraft because its only use was to remove the wounded from the battlefield. At each turn the helicopters received machine gun fire, so we needed to maximize the use of the cargo aircraft. Therefore, we used the Chinook to drop off reinforcements and supplies, and removed the dead and wounded on the way out.

After the fifth trip to Bari Ali it was sufficiently secured with a combination of American and Afghan soldiers. With the OP secure and enemy fire becoming more sporadic, our full attention turned to the missing soldiers.

TF Raider sent forces by vehicle to the entrance of the Helgal Valley to prevent the enemy from escaping out of the mouth of the valley with the prisoners. Fred Taroli's Apaches continued to search for enemy fighters who remained hidden in caves and rocks on the ridges. The enemy knew that if they moved, if they were seen, death was imminent. Once the Apache pilots found them and locked on to their heat signature, running did very little good. Under the thermal sight, running only made them glow brighter.

But the enemy we fought were disciplined. In fact, the biggest difference I had noticed between enemy fighters in Iraq and the enemy we fought in Afghanistan was their disparate levels of discipline. In Iraq, once the enemy fighters knew we had them, they often gave up or threw their weapons down and pretended to be innocent of any wrongdoing. Enemy fighters in Afghanistan, on the other hand, would lie for hours in the cracks between boulders with a wet blanket draped over them to try and dissipate their heat signatures—trick our thermal sights. They'd wait for the perfect shot, the one they thought they could get off undetected, and when the opportunity presented itself they would seize it. There were days that I flew over the same area for five or six hours, not realizing that the enemy were close by, and then suddenly they were there—shooting at me from below. Fred Taroli and his team knew that there were still enemy fighters hiding in the rocks, watching, listening, hoping for a good shot, and Fred was determined to find them.

Knowing that the enemy could not have gone far on foot with a dozen hostages in tow, Klusacek took his team deeper and deeper into the Helgal Valley, looking for them and searching for a landing zone so that we could quickly move forces into the valley to isolate the enemy once we found them. Most villages in the mountains of eastern Afghanistan looked like beehives from the air—houses and terraces were connected by a maze of rock walls—but the Helgal was different. The Helgal Valley, and the soaring ridges surrounding it, was filled with trees and gnarly scrub that seemingly grew out of the rocks—a hard place, both figuratively and literally. The houses were squeezed into the trees with the occasional terrace, which we conveniently used for landing zones when we were able. The Helgal was so deep and narrow that a well-placed cloud could constitute a sky, so deep that only a few hours of sunlight actually reached the valley floor on a cloudless day.

We had to find a place to land the Chinooks near the back of the valley, because if the prisoners were indeed being held there, we would need to trap them. We would do that by occupying the high ground and preventing anyone from leaving or entering the valley. Klusacek eventually found an area that he thought might work for an LZ. He took pictures of it and flew back to FOB Bostic.

"Sir, that's about the best I can find. There just aren't many places to land," Klusacek told Jack Murphy over the phone after sending the jpeg.

"Okay, go back to the valley and keep pressure on the enemy. We are going to put an air assault together. We just need to keep them in the valley. Don't let them get out," Jack said.

"Roger, sir."

Colonel John Spiszer told us to work with Major Tom Sarrouf, the Special Forces AOB 9210 commander. He wanted us to air-assault the Special Forces and their Afghan commando partners into the Helgal. Quiet and unassuming, Tom Sarrouf sported a thick black beard with a hint of gray on either side of his chin. Lean and wiry with a Roman nose, Tom fit the Special Forces stereotype to a tee. He just looked like a warrior. Tom had enlisted in the army in 1988, as an infantryman. He later attended officer candidate school and was commissioned a lieutenant in the infantry. In 1999, he became a Special Forces officer. He'd previously deployed to Kosovo, Bosnia,

Algeria, Kuwait, Iraq, and, of course, Afghanistan. Tom was a fine man—a total team player. He was there with genuine intent to help in any way he and his men could.

Jack, Tom, and I pored over the pictures, maps, and imagery in disbelief. There were few if any decent places to land a Chinook in the Helgal Valley. It was going to be very difficult to get Tom's men in. The best options we identified would allow only a two-wheel landing. On a positive note, once Tom's men were in the valley the terrain would be helpful in containing the enemy that hid within. Tom's men would have excellent observation of the entire valley from the ridgeline.

Ultimately we picked two landing zones and decided we'd give them a try and count on the Chinook pilots to get Tom's men in somehow.

I decided to fly the mission in a Kiowa. I chose Chief Warrant Officer 3 Scott Stradley to fly as my lead. Scott Stradley was a military policeman turned Kiowa Warrior standardization instructor pilot, who seemed to get into a fight almost every time he flew. Scott could make something out of nothing, or maybe he just provoked the possible. Whatever it was, when he flew, the enemy just seemed to be unable to contain themselves. It was like they could sense it was him and had to know, had to find out, if they could take a shot at him and survive. I'd seen other teams fly over a ground force, providing security for them, in a valley for hours and never was a shot fired in anger. Scott would show up to relieve the team on station, and before the relieved team could get to the FARP they'd hear Scott on the radio—in a gunfight. I told him that the enemy usually sought out soft targets to attack, so that should tell him something. He wasn't amused.

On one end of the spectrum was Mike Woodhouse, whom we called the White Dove because wherever he flew, peace broke out. He was almost never shot at. Scott Stradley was the antithesis of Mike Woodhouse, so everyone who flew with him knew that they'd better be ready for a fight. An emblem of strength to the young pilots in his troop, Scott had been in the unit longer than anyone. In fact, his entire career as a warrant officer was spent in the squadron. He had cut his teeth and gained extensive combat experience in Iraq, but the Iraqi fights paled in comparison to the battles he found himself fighting during our 2009 deployment.

With thin blond hair and a slightly crooked smile that drew a bit further back on the right side of his mouth, Scott was easygoing and fun, somewhat quiet, but prone to laugh out loud. He was the guy everyone loved to see at a party, but for the enemy forces we faced, he was truly a dangerous man, tough as nails in a fight—the one they didn't want to show up. Once he latched on to them he would not let go. Getting shot at really pissed Scott off. He took it personally.

Once, he flew lead for me on a mission deep in the Watapur Valley. We had been receiving sporadic machine gun fire for quite a while, and with each pass I noticed that Scott's helicopter crept lower and lower to the ground. Finally, I sarcastically transmitted over the radio, "Scott, are you trying to get shot down?"

"No, sir," he replied, "but I've just about figured out where they are, and when I find 'em I'm gonna kill 'em."

Scott was precisely the guy I wanted on my team going into the Helgal. If we ended up in a fight I could count on him unleashing hell on the enemy.

We planned to use a team of Apaches to clear the high mountaintops that surrounded the valley while my team of scouts escorted the Chinooks into the landing zones. Captain William Gargone was the Special Forces team leader. His detachment and their Afghan commando partners would serve as the ground force in the Helgal.

Just as the flight crews began to assemble to begin planning, we heard the muffled thump of a Chinook's rotors in the distance. It was the TF Eagle Lift team from Bagram that we had requested several hours earlier. The pilot in command of the Chinook was Chief Warrant Officer 4 Stacy Owens. Stacy and I had served together previously, flying UH-1 Hueys around Washington, D.C. Stacy was a small, fit, prior infantryman with a Ranger tab and a fire in his belly. A true mission pilot with a can-do attitude, Stacy served as the TF Eagle Lift's battalion safety officer. Before the rotor blades stopped turning he jogged from his Chinook to our command post and found me.

"Sir, we're ready to go. What do you need me to do?" he asked.

I briefly described the situation to him. I told him there were very few good landing zones, so we'd have to make do with what we had found. "We'll get 'em in, sir," he said matter-of-factly.

I told him to go link up with the other crews and help them finish planning the mission. I turned to walk away, but he stopped me. "Hey, sir, just so you know, at some point between Bagram and here a panel on the aft pylon of the Chinook came off," he said.

We had to have that Chinook for the air assault. My heart dropped, thinking we would have to try and get another Chinook flown to Fenty. "Is it okay to fly it with the panel missing? Will it safely fly this mission, Stacy?" I asked.

"Absolutely, sir," he replied. "I just wanted you to know that when you look at the helicopter you are going to see a big panel obviously missing."

"Okay, then let's get to planning," I said.

The Helgal Valley ran east to west. At its eastern terminus the Helgal opened into the Kunar Valley. From there it snaked west for about ten kilometers. It was a narrow valley with ridgelines on either side climbing to altitudes of over ten thousand feet. While the steep, rocky, heavily vegetated terrain was extremely challenging to operate in, in reality it was a huge box, which proved to be beneficial to us. The valley ended in the western end at a wall of a mountain. We clearly saw that if we could control the high ground and keep pressure on the enemy it would be extremely difficult, if not impossible, for them to get the prisoners out of the valley without us seeing them. The valley in which the enemy sought refuge had essentially become their prison.

Back at Bari Ali, Warren Brown conducted the final resupply run to the East OP and returned to FOB Bostic to link up with Jeff Dorsey. We told them to return to FOB Fenty after they were done so they could get a quick briefing, then turn around and fly as part of the air assault into the Helgal.

"Land but do not shut down. We'll send an ATV to pick you up. You'll get the briefing and then we'll drive you back to the helicopter and you can go," Jack Murphy told Dorsey.

"Roger that, sir."

It had already been a long, tough day of flying and fighting. I knew Warren's and Jeff's crews were tired, but as I spoke to them on the radio it was clear that they were focused and prepared to do whatever was necessary to help the men on the ground. When they arrived we rushed them into the planning room and quickly brought them up to speed. Then, after a back brief to ensure they had a firm understanding of what we were telling them to do, they headed back out to their aircraft to brief the other crew members.

Colonel Spiszer, along with Tom Sarrouf, myself, and Colonel Lewis, spoke with Brigadier General Mark Milley, the deputy commanding general for operations, CJTF-101, and explained our plan. Normally, major operations such as this required a thorough concept of operations (CONOP) briefing for his approval, but considering the situation he took a verbal brief and approved the mission.

I had full confidence in our crews, but I knew that this was going to be an extremely challenging mission. We had pounded the enemy pretty well throughout the day, but I wasn't sure how many fighters were still hiding in the rocks waiting to take a shot at us. I also knew that it would take a few minutes to get Tom's men, along with their gear and crates of water and ammunition, off the Chinooks. The offload concerned me most. Stacy and Jeff would have to hold the Chinooks steady at a hover with only two wheels touching the ground while everyone and everything was offloaded—a very vulnerable position during daylight hours. My Kiowa team would fly close, right around the Chinooks, to cover them while the Apaches would scan the high ground in case anyone popped up with a rifle or RPG.

Colonel Lewis called me just before I headed out to my aircraft and asked, "Jimmy, can we get these guys in there?" he asked.

"It's sporty, but—yes, sir—we can. We'll figure it out. I think we've got the right crews to get it done."

"Okay, be safe and give me a call when you get back. We'll talk about what we're going to need tomorrow."

"Yes, sir."

There was never a guarantee that we would not get an aircraft shot down. That was always a possibility, but I felt that we had mitigated every risk we possibly could with every asset available in theater. It was now up to us. The mission had to be executed, and I was confident we'd make it happen, one way or the other.

We lugged our gear out to the helicopters and suited up for the mission. I knew it would be cold in the Helgal, so I added a layer of wool under my flight jacket. I then buckled and Velcroed my body armor on, like an exoskeleton. We carried everything we'd need if we ended up on the ground and had to fight or evade and escape. I wore a bib attached to my body armor with pouches on it. In the pouches I carried a survival kit with a signaling mirror, whistle, first aid kit, tourniquet, medicine, and survival knife. In ammunition pouches I carried six thirty-round magazines of 5.56-mm ammunition for my rifle, and four magazines of 9-mm ammunition for my pistol. I attached a Garmin Foretrex 201 GPS to my bib with all of the locations of U.S. outposts in our area. I zip-tied my 9-mm holster to the center of my chest, and my M4 rifle snapped into the dash of the Kiowa. In a small "go bag" (backpack) I carried water, food, a British Special Forces sleeping bag that was no larger than a volleyball, and several more magazines of ammunition. I weighed 165 pounds at the time, but with all of my gear on I weighed 210.

We flew up the Kunar River Valley in silence. I don't recall a single radio call other than the check-in calls at each FOB. There was no need for talk. I often wondered what others thought about on those long flights to an objective or to and from a fight. I suppose some experienced fear and anxiety. Others probably rehearsed what they had to do once we got there over and over in their heads. I often thought about my wife and kids. I know that's what I thought about on the way to the Helgal. I didn't want the mission to go badly because I had a lot of things I still wanted to do with my wife and kids. That motivated me to get it right.

A biting wind whipped through the doorless Kiowa cockpit. The thin mountain air grew colder the farther north we flew, stinging a little as I drew in a deep breath. The Apaches flew as high as the clouds allowed, which was no more than five hundred feet above the ground.

The Special Forces and Commandos rode along in silence in the back of the Chinooks. Once in place at the LZs we had selected, high on the northern ridgeline, they would set up their sniper teams, and any enemy they observed would be shot. If the enemy were out of range, or if there were a lot of enemy forces moving together, they would either use jets to drop bombs or they would hand the target off to our Apaches to attack.

Back at the airfield, Jack devised a plan for continuous, 24/7 air coverage over the valley.

"They are in that valley," Jillian had told him. "I've got multiple sources of intelligence confirming that they are there."

"Then all we have to do is keep them from moving them until we can negotiate their release or go in and take them back."

Once we had them trapped in the valley, Colonel Spiszer and General Milley would work with the provincial governor to demand that the prisoners be turned over. We hoped that they would see that it would be their only option, that there was no other way out alive, so they'd turn them over to us.

The afternoon shadows grew long as the light of day faded. *We'll get them in just before dark,* I thought to myself as we rounded the S-turn and saw OP Bari Ali. Then we made a sharp left turn into the valley. The Apaches led with the Chinooks closely behind them. I flanked the Chinooks in my Kiowa. We were conducting the most rapidly planned, briefed, and executed air assault to date, and it was being flown in the most challenging terrain one could imagine. Nevertheless, our crews were focused, confident, and comfortable with our plan. Jeff Dorsey and Stacy Owens identified their LZs right away and flew straight to them. I followed Stradley low over the small village to keep anyone peeking out of their houses focused on us versus the Chinooks.

With the Chinooks in the LZs, soldiers began pouring out of the backs of the helicopters. It was already drizzling rain and promised to be a miserable night, but as I watched insanely fit, bearded men armed to the teeth explode off of the Chinooks, I was confident that they would be just fine. Stacy's aircraft emptied first, so he called clear of the LZ and headed back toward the Kunar. We flew in beside him and escorted him to the mouth of the valley.

The first man off Jeff's aircraft was Sergeant Azad "Oz" Ebrahimzadeh. He ran straight up the side of the mountain, about fifty meters from the bird, and stood watch. He scanned the ridges with his rifle at the ready. Everything about him said, *I'm ready. If you feel froggy, jump.*

While he was Persian, his olive skin, coal black hair, and thick beard reminded me of the Spartan king Leonidas, but it wasn't just his skin color and beard that held my attention, it was his stature. Standing six-four and weighing 270 pounds, his mere presence was intimidating. He was a Special Forces medic. *A Persian lion,* I thought to myself the first time I saw him. Tattoos decorated skin that was stretched thinly over massive muscles. His appearance alone sent the message, *I mean business!*

Oz was born in Iran during the Iranian revolution. His father, a no-nonsense scientist/mathematician/engineer, was abroad when Ayatollah Khomeini closed the Iranian gates to the free world. I guess you could say Oz was born for the military, having accompanied his mother on his first life-and-death escape and evasion mission at the tender age of two.

Born the only girl in a family of seven siblings, Shahla Ebrahimzadeh was a scrapper. She was tough as nails, a trait she would need later in life. She was a nurse when the revolution began. Shahla sold everything their family had, including her wedding ring, to secure enough money to smuggle her two-year-old son out of Iran. By her account, they almost died numerous times along the way. Often the only thing that kept them alive was the kindness of strangers. Ultimately finding her way to West Frankfurt, Germany, she made it to freedom.

Oz's father, Mohsen Ebrahimzadeh, had desperately tried to return to Iran to help his family escape. "On one of his final attempts soldiers caught him, beat him, and put him on his knees to execute him— the soldiers put a pistol to his head and pulled the trigger. The pistol malfunctioned. The soldier recocked the weapon and again placed it to [his] head—*click*—again it did not fire. Frustrated, the soldiers beat him nearly to death,"[1] Oz told me.

Eventually Mohsen joined Shahla and Azad in Germany. In 1988 they migrated to California.

Oz grew up there and fell in love with the army. He liked guns, grenades, and things that exploded, so as soon as he graduated high school he enlisted as an infantryman in the army. In 2003, he favorably assessed with the Special Forces and became a medic. Oz spoke English, Dari, and Farsi. As intimidating a figure as he was, when clean-shaven and dressed for town he looked like someone you'd see posing on the cover of *GQ* magazine. Standing tall and lean, with his square jaw and olive skin, his jet black hair slicked back with product—he was a model. Those two contradictions said it all. If you read his palms you'd see it written plainly in ink: on his left hand the medics' emblem and the words *To Give*. In the palm of his right hand a sickle and the words *To Take*.

As I watched Oz standing there, surveying the ridges like a sentinel, I suddenly wished I were there. I desperately wanted to be on the ground with the troops. I felt great pride just being a soldier at that moment, being a part of an amazing operation that most nations could not imagine executing.

With all of the men unloaded, Jeff Dorsey pulled in power and followed us out of the valley. Once we were out of the Helgal, ODA 9212 began setting up positions to observe the valley, particularly the small village where we suspected that the prisoners were being held. Our Apaches remained in the valley to support the ground forces as they set up their positions, beginning a rotation of teams that would cover the ground force day and night until we succeeded in getting the prisoners back.

As darkness fell on May 1, TF Raider and elements of TF Chosin had regained control of OP Bari Ali and the East OP. They had sealed off the mouth of the Helgal Valley and occupied several other positions on the high ground near the entrance to the valley. ODA 9212 and the Afghan commandos had established two positions on the northern ridge of the Helgal. Our Apaches covered the valley from the air, along with continuous close air support (CAS) and unmanned aerial vehicles (UAVs). Jaguar 1-3, the Special Forces joint tactical air controller (JTAC), wrapped a poncho around his shoulder, pulled a black balaclava over his head, leaned back against a gnarly tree in the rocks, and prepared for a long wet night. He was responsible for coordinating and sequencing everything flying in support of their mission. He was an air force airman specially trained to call for attacks from close air support, including fighters, bombers, and, of course, our helicopters.

It had been a very busy day for everyone involved. Some of our crews had flown for over ten long, stressful hours. The complexity of the terrain, coupled with heavy fighting and terrible weather, made May 1, 2009, a day that many of our pilots would later say was the most difficult flying they had ever done. The crews had demonstrated tremendous flexibility to meet the needs of both Task Force Duke and our Special Forces brothers.

According to our operating procedures a pilot could fly for eight hours during the day. If some of the time was flown during the day and a portion using night vision goggles, then we were limited to seven hours of flight time. If the entire flight was flown using night vision goggles, then the limit was six hours. Colonel Lewis and I could grant extensions to the flight time if necessary, but only when it was absolutely necessary—on days like May 1, 2009. To put the day into perspective, Jeff Dorsey's crew flew twelve and a half hours. Warren Brown and his Flawless 0-8 crew flew just over nine hours. Collectively, TF Pale Horse aircraft flew 157 flight hours that day alone, a day that had been supported by a cast of men and women who fueled our helicopters and armed them, soldiers who planned landing zones, coordinated with other units, shared intelligence reports, and did a thousand other things that had to be done to help the team successfully complete the mission.

Colonel Lewis had watched our helicopters on Blue Force Tracker (BFT), a battle tracking system, which enabled us to see the aircraft depicted virtually on a digital map as we executed the mission in real time. He called me that evening.

I saw that it was him on the caller ID. "Sir, it's Jimmy."

"Hey, Jimmy. Good job today. Well done."

"Thanks, sir. It was a busy one but the boys did great," I said.

"Yes, they did. Tell them I'm proud of them. What now? What do you think?"

"Well, our plan is to keep Apaches and Kiowas over the valley round the clock in order to keep the enemy from moving the prisoners. I didn't have enough Apaches to cover the Helgal Valley and to be prepared to respond to TICs [troops in contact] in other places. You know we're going to have a fight somewhere else tomorrow, so I need an additional Apache team every day until we get them out of there," I said.

"Okay, I'll talk to Rob Dickerson and tell him to send them your way. Clearly, you guys are the main effort until we get these prisoners back."

"I appreciate it, sir."

"Well done today," he repeated, and we agreed to talk again in the morning to discuss long-term plans.

Back in the Helgal, ODA 9212 settled in for a miserable night. They took shifts pulling security and watching the village for activity. Just after midnight one of our Apaches spotted three men with weapons moving in the rocks on the south ridge, across the Helgal Valley from ODA 9212. The Apache pilots were in the process of reporting what they saw to Jaguar 1-3, who sat leaning against a big tree, when the men across the valley took up fighting positions in the rocks and began shooting across the valley. Our Apache crews immediately shot the men with 30-mm rounds. As the rounds impacted the rocks, ten armed men, previously undetected, suddenly leapt up out of the boulders and began running. The Apache crews killed eight of them. A couple of the fighters dove into crevasses in the rocks and small caves, not to be seen again throughout the night. We were unsure if they were mortally wounded, or if they knew that to move would mean certain death.

In the weeks preceding the May 1 attack on Bari Ali, TF Raider had established a vehicle patrol base (VPB) at the mouth of the Tsunel Valley, just north of OP Bari Ali. Like the Helgal, the Tsunel was an east-west-running valley that emptied into the north-south-running Kunar, but the Tsunel lay a couple of miles to the north of the Helgal. Also, like the Helgal, the Tsunel was a narrow, steep valley. Just across the Kunar River from Tsunel was the Saw Valley. The Saw Valley quickly rose to the high ridge, upon which sat the Pakistan border. We knew this valley was used routinely for cross-border movement into the Nari District; however, a small, steep, rocky road provided the only access to the valley.

TF Raider knew that if the enemy wanted to get the prisoners out of the Helgal they would most likely make a run for Pakistan. It was the best chance, and shortest distance, the enemy had to move the prisoners north of the Helgal, then down through the Tsunel. They could then cross the Kunar River and travel up through the Saw Valley and into Pakistan. Our hope was that the Tsunel VPB would deny the enemy that option.

The following morning, a fresh team of two Apaches, Weapon 1-6 and Weapon 2-0, relieved the night team at 7:30 A.M. When they arrived in the Helgal, the Apache pilots checked in with Jaguar 1-3 and asked if there was anything he needed them to look at specifically before they began a thorough reconnaissance of the entire valley from west to east. Jaguar 1-3 told them that he had observed a man moving back and forth from a log cabin to a waterfall on the south side of the valley since daylight. He asked them to take a look and see what he was doing.

The pilots took a look and actually saw several men. For over almost two hours the Apache pilots watched from a distance as the men moved nervously in and out of the cabin. From time to time they stole a glance at the helicopter but were careful not to look overly suspicious. They were clearly up to something, but they did not appear to be armed.

After a couple of hours the Apache pilots left the valley to go to FOB Bostic and fuel their helicopters. When they returned from the FARP, Jaguar 1-3 asked them to take a close look at the southeastern end of the village in the bottom of the valley. "See if you can see anyone moving around. Let me know if you see women and children out," Jaguar 1-3 requested. "I'll keep an eye on the men at the cabin," he said, then placed binoculars up to his eyes to look.

As soon as the Apaches began flying east, Jaguar 1-3 saw movement at a cabin just up the trail from the waterfall. A close look through his binoculars revealed three men with weapons. They appeared to be stacking something adjacent to the cabin. He was pretty sure they were moving weapons, perhaps a cache. *They've got a weapons cache by the cabin, and they are getting weapons out of it right now,* he thought to himself.

"Weapon 1-6, Jaguar 1-3," he called the Apache over the radio.

"Roger, send it," Weapon 1-6 replied.

"I've got three men with weapons and what appears to be a cache." He gave Weapon 1-6 the grid coordinates to the location. "Request you engage with Hellfire missile."

"Three men with weapons and a cache. Engage with Hellfire, over," Weapon 1-6 repeated back to ensure that he had copied the report correctly.

"Affirmative," Jaguar confirmed.

The missile hit a small shed adjacent to the cabin, between the cabin and the cache. There was an initial explosion closely followed by a much larger, secondary explosion, indicative of a large cache of munitions. Birds exploded from trees, monkeys scattered, and three men ran from the cabin, disappearing into the woods. A UAV, which had also been orbiting overhead searching for the prisoners, spotted the men as they ran but lost them once they hid in the woods. Anticipating the need for big bombs, Jaguar 1-3 coordinated with a jet that had been orbiting overhead to drop a bomb on the cabin. He wanted to make sure that the cache was completely destroyed.

"Weapons, move your team to the north side of the valley. I'm about to drop a bomb on the cache," Jaguar 1-3 said.

"Roger." Within minutes an explosion echoed throughout the valley, and a black mushroom cloud rose into the air. The cabin was gone.

Weapon 1-6 took a good long look through its sight before flying across the valley to take a closer look at the cabin. The pilots saw a bunker under the cabin, which had been reinforced with lumber and sandbags. It appeared as though the secondary explosion was generated from whatever they had stored inside the bunker.

"1-6, this is 2-0," the lead Apache called to his trail aircraft. "I've got five males on a trail headed for the waterfall."

Clearly, the five men had either run from the cabin after the first shot or they had been in the woods hiding all along. Their walk turned into a run once they realized the helicopters were coming closer. They ran into a large cave behind the waterfall, and Weapon 2-0 lost sight of them. A few minutes later one of the men came out of the cave and began walking, running, and randomly hiding behind trees, but he was not armed, so the pilots kept an eye on him and reported what they saw to Jaguar 1-3, who also watched through his binoculars from across the valley. While they knew with relative certainty that he was an enemy fighter, the rules of engagement required that he demonstrate a hostile act or hostile intent before they could shoot him, so the Apache pilots kept an eye on him as he moved along the trail system.

That night the men tried to sleep, but sleep came hard. It rained all night. Most of the men had ponchos, and a few had rain jackets, but "there was no level ground, and we were attempting to sleep in animal feces,"[2] Sergeant First Class Russell Klika, the combat cameraman, later told me.

The local farmers grazed their goat herds all along the mountain. The ground was covered with feces. Each man found a spot to lean against a tree, and tried to remain as dry as possible. Every time they would doze off our Apaches would shoot or the air force jets would drop a bomb. It was a tough night with very little rest.

The next morning they built a fire, and everyone gathered around it to try and dry their clothes. They had told the Afghan soldiers to pack enough food for three days, but they ate all of their food the first day and were now hungry. From the time the men had arrived a small goat had taken up with them. It followed them everywhere. It even squeezed in between the men to warm itself at the fire that morning. "My initial thought was that the commandos would have a good meal of goat that first day, but they didn't kill the goat,"[3] Klika said.

But they were certainly hungry and wanted to go in search of food on the mountain.

The Afghan commandos had noticed a family living just up the mountain from their position. They decided to see if the family had any food they could spare, or perhaps they could buy an animal to slaughter.

Oz, Sergeant First Class Russell Klika, a couple of their teammates, interpreters, and a few Afghans walked along a small goat trail to reach the family. Upon seeing the soldiers, a woman who appeared to be the matriarch of the family did not appear frightened at all. "She stood up and put her hands on her hips,"[4] Klika said.

Typically, Afghan women covered their faces and ran for the house when we approached, but the Helgal encounter turned out to be quite different. Instead of the husband coming forward and greeting Oz, the woman coldly greeted him. She stared at him through dark brown eyes that sat deep in hollow sockets, eyes that had clearly witnessed hardship and pain. "Are you Russian?" she asked in a strange dialect.

Oz could not understand her. The interpreters later said that she spoke a dialect of Dari that is not officially recognized. The isolated people in that region of Afghanistan had developed their own unique dialect over time.

Caught off guard, Oz responded through the interpreter, "No. We represent your government. We are here to help you."

She stared off into the distance and considered his response. A black scarf covered her long, straight black hair. Her leathery skin was deep golden brown and her thin face had a line in it for every hard year of life she had lived. She looked to be at least sixty but was certainly no more than forty. A tiny silver stud in the right side of her nose caught sunlight and sparkled. Oz was perhaps the first American to have ever entered the Helgal. "What government?" she asked, still staring out across the valley.

"The Afghan government. We are here at the request of your president, Hamid Karzai," he answered.

"We have a president?" she asked, casting her eyes back to Oz.

Oz confirmed that President Karzai was leading the Afghan government in Kabul.

Meanwhile, the Afghan soldiers had approached the husband to ask for food. Klika noticed that the old woman kept pulling at a purple rag wrapped around her hand. Flies swarmed her hand as she raised it to her mouth. She used her teeth to hold the end of the material as she wrapped it more tightly around her hand, which was clearly hurting.

Klika turned to Oz. "Do you have any aspirin you can give her?" he asked.

Oz looked back at the old lady. "Can I take a look at your hand? I am a medic," he said.

"No man has touched me since they killed my sons," she said.

"Who killed your sons?" Oz asked.

"The Taliban. Are you Taliban?" she asked.

"No," he replied.

"The Taliban came and told my sons they must fight for them. My sons refused, and they cut their heads off," she explained with clear mistrust in her voice.

"How many sons?" the interpreter asked.

"Two," she said sadly.

And then the old woman looked up at Oz and said, "If you are going to kill me, do it fast."

"We're not going to kill you," Oz assured her.

Meanwhile, the Afghan soldiers had convinced the old man to sell them a cow. He led them to a pitiful-looking creature about the size of a Great Dane, except skinnier. He pointed to it and the haggling began. In the end they gave him one hundred dollars for the old bag of bones. They paid him, bid them all farewell, and began dragging the puny animal back down the mountain.[5]

Seeing they were ready to depart, Oz gave the woman aspirin and told her to swallow the pills.

"It will help with the pain," he said, then turned and walked away.

While the soldiers had bartered with the husband, Sergeant First Class Klika had noticed an old rusty knife lying beside the man and a sharp stick that he had whittled. As he walked by the man, Klika took his Gerber multitool out and handed it to him. Tears ran down the old man's face, and in perfect English, he said, "Thank you."[6]

The conversation with the old lady confirmed our opinion that progress in the remote mountain regions would be difficult if not impossible in the short term. To those people Kabul may as well have been a different country. Their concerns in life lay within their valley. They argued and fought over grazing and water rights with neighboring clans. They did not see how Kabul could positively influence their lives in a meaningful way, and it would be difficult to convince them otherwise.

As for me, I secretly wondered if we had a right to try and drag them into the future. They lived, by our standards, a difficult but simple existence. They were trapped between radicals that would enslave them and Westerners that wanted to drag them into the future—both would significantly change their way of life. The thought troubled me as I flew into the back of the valley on the second day of our standoff. A cool wind whipped through the cockpit as my eyes focused on crevasses, caves, any potential hiding spots for enemy forces. We circled a small hut where monkeys, the only wild animals I had seen in Afghanistan, leapt from the roof into the nearby trees. I had been told that there were ibex and bears in Afghanistan, but despite covering a lot of ground from the air, I never saw them.

A woman stopped hanging clothes on a line and stared up at us as we flew over. I thought of my own simple north Georgia childhood. In the 1970s I didn't know much about the world outside of Ranger, Georgia. It wasn't until I was swept away with the army that I was exposed to other cultures. I thought how strange it would have felt for outsiders to have invaded my way of life.

I saw a young boy sitting on a log high up on the ridge. He was alone and peering out into the valley—a valley that defined his world. I wondered if he knew what life was like outside the Helgal. He knew sheep, goats, his family, his village, and the Helgal Valley. He'd probably been to Nari but not much farther. The tribes of the Hindu Kush had been influenced by outsiders many times throughout history, and I knew that their way of life was being transformed yet again. I also knew that they had very little power to resist it. I clearly recognized the alternative, but I questioned if it was the right thing to do. Did we truly know what was best for them?

Later that evening, just after dark, in a land with a view of a million stars, I climbed up on a deck at FOB Fenty. It was an elevated wooden structure with a worn-out parachute for a roof and a few plastic yard chairs. The soldiers had built it for one purpose—cigars and relaxation. Alone, I sat down and looked out across the airfield toward the Kunar River Valley. Heat lightning flashed cloud to cloud out over the valley. My thoughts returned to the boy I'd seen earlier that day. We represented the establishment of a democratic society that idealistically brought with it freedom, individual rights, and equality.

I wondered where the line between forceful establishment of democracy and freedom to choose democracy lay. For me, there was no questioning the necessity of our mission in Afghanistan. Vividly, I recalled the day that over three thousand people were butchered. I remember how it felt when I found out that people I knew had died in the Pentagon. We would bring justice to those who were responsible for the attacks of September 11, 2001, but I also knew that we could not leave Afghanistan a failed state. What troubled me was how we could convince isolated tribesmen like those in the Helgal to embrace our vision of their future. It must have seemed like such a foreign concept to them, like my grandmother trying to convince me that caster oil was good for me as a child. I figured that it would take longer than the American people were willing to give us.

The reality was that we were in Afghanistan. The Taliban had been removed. A government was in place, and we had an obligation to ensure that the people of Afghanistan were afforded the opportunity to govern their country and to protect their people, many of whom didn't even know that they had a government. That meant development, both physical infrastructure and systems of government, and the removal of extremist groups that would do harm to Afghanistan and its citizens. I returned to my room, thanked my Heavenly Father for another day alive, and laid down for a few hours of sleep.

We kept continuous pressure on the enemy throughout the next two days and nights with only light contact with them, but during the evening of the third day enemy forces attempted a decisive move. The Tsunel Vehicle Patrol base took machine gun fire throughout midday, but as soon as TF Raider fired 155-mm artillery shells at them the enemy sought cover and stopped shooting. It seemed like normal daily contact to us, but later that evening, at 8:30 P.M., they attacked in force.

It was like someone flipped a switch. Suddenly the VPB was hit with heavy machine gun, RPG, and mortar fire from the high ground to their west. The standard procedure of firing artillery was applied, but this time the enemy kept coming. They were making a significant attempt to overrun the VPB, as well as the OP higher up on the ridge.

Enemy forces quickly closed the gap, sprinting forward between artillery impacts, then diving for cover as the shells rained down from above. Major Matt Fox, my executive officer, was the air mission commander of the Kiowa team that responded. When they arrived the men on the OP could literally see the enemy crawling, trying to get inside the barbwire that surrounded the American position. The soldiers manning the OP had fired all of their weapons, had expended all of their ammunition, and were throwing hand grenades at the enemy when the Kiowas arrived. Matt and his team fired everything they had at very close range to our own men. The team made multiple turns into the FARP at FOB Bostic to get more ammunition and rockets. Each time the team departed to rearm, the enemy resumed the attack.

Finally, after several hours of heavy fighting, the valley suddenly went silent but for the sound of rotors. It was like someone had flipped the switch off, and they were gone. We resupplied the VPB and OP as quickly as possible and prepared for another attack, but it never came. The enemy simply disappeared with their dead and wounded. The only trace of the enemy the following morning was blood on the rocks. In the days that followed they continued sporadic attacks, but nothing significant ever came.

Meanwhile, Jim Markert, Colonel John Spiszer, and Brigadier General Mark Milley worked with local leaders to try and persuade them to facilitate the return of the captives. At FOB Fenty we planned another large air assault, this time to conduct a valley-wide clearing operation. The assault force would be Green Berets from the 3rd Special Forces Group along with their commando partners. As we supported the men in the Helgal we had continued to search for better landing zones. We found two places in the valley floor that were perfect. They were at the very back of the valley, which is where we wanted to put the ground force. Once on the ground, the soldiers would move from the back of the valley to the mouth, clearing every house, building, shed, and barn along the way. Tom Sarrouf's men, up on the high ground, would cover them as they maneuvered through the valley.

Before dawn on May 6, two Chinooks, escorted by a team of Kiowas and a team of Apaches, inserted the air assault force with no enemy resistance at all. Afghan soldiers, along with Jim Markert's men, blocked the mouth of the valley. They were there to ensure that no one got out of the valley. Colonel Spiszer told the village elders, the district governor, and the police chief that we were going to attack throughout the valley. If they would facilitate the release of the prisoners then he would call off the attack. If not, we would find them by force.

The commandos led down the valley, and soon thereafter a couple of small pickup trucks came racing out of the valley. Riding in the back of the trucks were twelve weary men. The prisoners were liberated, at least physically. What scars remained, ghosts in their dreams, from six days in captivity I do not know.

There are events in life that never leave us, events that serve as a barometer for future life challenges. For every soldier who has completed Ranger school, it is an experience that we look back on; when things are tough we know that we have endured tougher trials in life. It seems to provide some level of comfort and confidence that "you can do this." Bari Ali was one of those events for Task Force Pale Horse. Later in the deployment, when the enemy was attacking, the terrain was foreboding, and the weather threatened, we would recall Bari Ali and suddenly things didn't seem so bad.

The morning after the operation I received the following emails:

> Sir,
>
> On behalf of SOTF-92 [Special Operations Task Force], we would like to thank you and your staff for the planning and remarkable execution of OPN Open Toe. Also, the CCA [Close Combat Attack] coverage could not have been supported any better last night. For these insurgents, they now know Death does ride a Pale Horse, and so do our men on the ground. Thank you.
> Very respectfully,
> CPT, AVSOTF-92
>
> I wanted to take a minute of your time this morning to thank you all for the commendable performance on OPN Open

Toe. Your mission support and dedication to excellence truly set the example for fellow comrades and units on the battlefield. I speak for the entire CJSOTF—A/SOTF-92 [Combined Joint Special Operations Task Force—Afghanistan] Element when I say, without your detailed planning on such a collapsed timeline and actions on the objective in light of such harsh weather and threat, the operation would have surely failed.
Warrant Officer 3rd Special Forces Group (Airborne)

Lieutenant Colonel Jim Markert shared the following sentiments with the families of his squadron in their unit newsletter.

TF Pale Horse pilots have done more to keep our soldiers alive than perhaps anyone else outside the TF and the bravest of them remain the OH-58 pilots who routinely fly into enemy fire to support us during firefights. We will never be able to thank them enough for their excellent support.
James C. Markert

I had told our troopers all along that our measure of success would be the value that our ground brothers placed on our contribution to the fight. These notes were proof that we were on the right track.

MOUNTAIN WARRIOR

In early spring, Colonel Randy George, the commander of 4th Brigade, 4th Infantry Division "Mountain Warrior," conducted his site survey. His brigade would be replacing Task Force Duke in the summer. I'd known Colonel George for several years. He had commanded an infantry battalion in the 101st Airborne Division during our 2005 to 2006 deployment to Iraq. Standing six-three, weighing two hundred pounds, and sporting a perfectly level, tightly cut flattop, the square-jawed infantryman was an imposing figure in full combat equipment, but he had a warm smile. Randy George was a caring leader who was unflappable under pressure—a quality I appreciated. He would face some incredibly challenging situations—stress beyond measure—in 2009, yet I never once saw him lose his cool. He was a genuinely positive leader whom I was very excited to serve with again.

George had established a reputation as a fierce war-fighter in Iraq, but he was revered as a man who passionately cared for his soldiers and their families. There are leaders in our army who venture down into their soldiers' workplace, shake their hands, and ask them how they are doing. Genuine, authentic leaders truly want to know the answer to that question. But there are some leaders who seem to feel an obligation to go pat a few backs, shake a few hands, and ask, "How you doing, soldier?" I suppose circulating among soldiers and asking how they are doing makes them feel somewhat better about themselves, as if they are doing what they know is expected of them. Yet what they don't seem to understand is that the second they ask the question—How are you doing?—their soldiers know if they really want to know the answer to the question, if they genuinely care what the answer is. "He knew his soldiers by name, and always took the time to learn something about their lives,"[1] Maj. Rodney Dycus, George's battalion doctor, told me.

Randy George was a leader who looked his soldiers in the eye, and asked them with complete sincerity how they were doing, and cared what the answer was. I admired Randy George.

During his visit to FOB Fenty, Colonel George and I had dinner together. We caught up on old times, then we moved to my office to discuss his vision for N2KL in the coming year. He spoke with visible excitement about realigning the region. The primary mission for the soldiers in N2KL was to provide security within the major population bases—the cities (Jalalabad, Asadabad, and Mehtar Lam)—and to ensure the security of Highway 7, which was the primary road traveling from Peshawar, Pakistan, northwest through the Khyber Pass, and through Nangarhar and Laghman provinces, before exiting our area of responsibility on its way to Kabul.

Task Force Mountain Warrior's mission in N2KL was a supporting effort within Afghanistan, just as TF Duke's had been. It was not the main effort. The main effort was RC-South (Kandahar and the surrounding area), a difficult dose of medicine for our soldiers to swallow, in light of the fact that they were engaged in more deadly fighting than anyone else in Afghanistan. That fact alone supported Colonel George's campaign plan for N2KL.

His plan was to close the combat outposts in the Kamdesh Valley, which included OP Fritsche, COP Keating, and COP Lowell. We literally fought the enemy every day in those locations, assumed tremendous risk, and the gains were negligible at best. Colonel George felt that the soldiers living and operating out of those outposts would be better employed in Nari District, thus focusing our manpower on the larger Afghan population base in the central Kunar River Valley. Once the outposts in the Kamdesh were closed, we would close all of the outposts in the Korengal Valley as well. Those forces would be transferred to the central Pech River Valley. The shift in forces would also allow us to put more troops in the vicinity of Torkham Gate, where Highway 7 enters Afghanistan through the Khyber Pass.

No one was more excited about Colonel George's plan than my soldiers. We had believed all along that we were assuming too much risk in Nuristan and in the Korengal Valley for the very limited progress we were making. I told Colonel George about Flex 6-4 getting shot down in the Korengal and explained how that event drove us to conduct resupply missions only during "red illumination" periods. Moving all of the men, equipment, and infrastructure out of the Kamdesh Valley would be an extensive operation. It would require our Chinooks to make multiple turns throughout the night for at least a week. A high-risk and complex mission to be sure, but if we were given the priority for close air support, artillery, and UAVs, we felt that we would be able to mitigate the risk. Colonel George acknowledged my concerns, sort of smiled, then told me to begin planning.

I called Jack over, and we looked at the moon cycles for the remainder of the year. Colonel George pointed to July. "Our transfer of authority is June twenty-sixth. I want to begin coming out of the Kamdesh during the first red-illumination cycle after we take over. Plan for July," he said.

Colonel George had already presented his plan to Major General Curtis Scaparrotti, who would be deploying with the 82nd Airborne Division to assume command of RC-East on June 3. Major General Scaparrotti had agreed with his plan, so it would be up to us to figure out how to most effectively and efficiently execute the mission. Planning began that night.

By early June the snow line had crept high up on the mountaintops, leaving only the peaks capped in white. The sun bore down on us, forcing our crew chiefs to build makeshift shade to work under. Ponchos stretched overhead with bungee cords gave some relief, but the humidity penetrated the shade. Wrenches were so hot crewchiefs had to douse them in water in order to pick them up. Yet soldiers flew in from Bagram still bundled up in thick clothes, only to find us in short sleeves. Nangarhar, sitting at only 1,800 feet above sea level, never got overly cold. We ran in shorts and T-shirts most days throughout the winter, but when our missions took us up the Kunar or into Nuristan, we'd learned from painful experience to bundle up before departing.

The nights remained much cooler than the days, but the heat in the asphalt runway lingered for hours after sundown. That's when I ran across my first cobra, warming on the asphalt after dark. The Kiowas were parked on the east side of the runway. My headquarters was on the west side. We used a red light, operated by the air traffic controllers in the control tower, to cross the runway.

I wore a Petzl headlamp to see at night. That Petzl had been with me in the Balkans, two tours in Iraq, and then Afghanistan, and on that cool June night it probably saved my life. I waited for a green light, flight gear draped over my shoulder, at midfield. Finally, the light turned green and I began to cross. I just happened to have my eyes down looking at the ground when I saw a long, green cobra. It was about five feet long and was stretched out and lying flat, absorbing warmth from the asphalt, which had not yet cooled.

In June, Randy George's Mountain Warriors began flowing into Afghanistan. Like all units in RC-East they initially flew into Bagram Airbase. Some of them were then flown to FOB Fenty by fixed-wing airplanes (C-130), but we flew the majority of their soldiers to the FOBs and COPs using our Chinooks and Black Hawks. Our focus throughout June was to move Mountain Warrior into FOBs and COPs and transport TF Duke soldiers out.

My old friend Lieutenant Colonel Brian Pearl commanded 2-12 Infantry, the battalion replacing Brett Jenkinson's Blue Spaders in the Pech and Korengal valleys. Brian and I had served as operations officers together during Operation Iraqi Freedom. Following that job, Brian became the secretary of the general staff (SGS) of the 101st Airborne Division. I followed Brian as the SGS. Brian and I were close friends, had been for years, and it was good to be fighting with someone I knew personally.

An incredibly talented armor officer, Lieutenant Colonel Brad Brown, commanded 3rd Squadron, 61st Cavalry Regiment. Brad and I shared a cavalry background—his on the ground and mine in the air. We had both served in the 3rd Armored Cavalry Regiment "Brave Rifles." Brad's squadron would replace Jim Markert's team in northern Kunar and Nuristan, with his headquarters based at FOB Bostic.

During the first week of July, all of the battalion commanders serving under Colonel George met at FOB Fenty. We discussed the plan for the future, then we flew them back to their headquarters locations. Both Brian and Brad departed FOB Fenty excited to begin the work of shaping the environment for closing outposts and realigning forces—or so they thought they would be doing.

THE PLAN BEGINS TO UNRAVEL

In August 1847, General Winfield Scott went to speak to the men of the 3rd U.S. Cavalry, the same unit in which Brad and I later served. They had fought valiantly at the Battle of Contreras in the Mexican War. General Scott went there to tell them that their work was not yet complete. He went there to order them on to a new battle. The men were fatigued and bloodied—war weary. Their uniforms were dirty and worn, yet as the general approached they tucked their shirts in to try and look the best they could, given the circumstances. They stood proudly at attention as General Scott walked to the front of their formation. As he looked at the men who stood before him, he was overcome by emotion as he said, "You have been baptized in fire and blood and came out steel."[1]

Task Force Mountain Warrior arrived in Afghanistan at the beginning of the summer fighting season. They brought in fresh new soldiers who were excited to tackle a very challenging mission. They had not yet fought, but like the Brave Rifles of the 3rd Cavalry, they would quickly become baptized in fire and blood.

On June 16, I got up and ran a lap around FOB Fenty. I finished on the flight line and walked into my office to cool off. I grabbed a bottle of water from the refrigerator and sat down to catch up on emails and read the news. I subscribed to the online edition of *The Washington Post*, so all I had to do was click on the headlines. As soon as the *Post* opened I saw the headline GEN. MCCHRYSTAL, NEW AFGHANISTAN COMMANDER, WILL REVIEW TROOP PLACEMENTS. It was our new commander's first interview since arriving in theater, and it dealt directly with our plan—redistribution of forces in N2KL.

With great interest I began reading the article. On June 15, Greg Jaffe of *The Washington Post* had interviewed General Stanley Mc-Chrystal, as well as Colonel John Spiszer. In the interview General McChrystal rather strongly hinted at our restructuring plan. He noted that we had to focus on the large population centers and not the isolated areas deep within the mountains. Specifically, both Spiszer and McChrystal mentioned the Korengal Valley.[2] We took that as a clear indicator that General McChrystal was on board with Colonel George's strategy to get out of the Kamdesh and Korengal valleys. After reading the article I thought for sure that our plan was going to work, but I had no idea at that time what fate had in store for us.

The first unforeseen event of the summer occurred on June 30. We received a message that a soldier was missing. A Duty Status—Whereabouts Unknown (DUSTWUN) had been declared for Private First Class Bowe Robert Bergdahl. Private Bergdahl had been in Paktika Province when he was reported missing. We assumed that his captors would try and get him into Pakistan as quickly as possible, so time was of the essence. We had to follow all leads, and flood the area with soldiers to prevent the enemy from moving him until we could figure out where he was being held.

Task Force Attack, our sister battalion, was responsible for aviation operations in that area. The composition of their task force was roughly the same as ours. They had a few more Apaches than us, and we had a few more Kiowas than they did, but both of us could have used more Chinooks.

They had just enough helicopters to do their mission, but they did not have enough crews or helicopters to sustain operations day and night for a prolonged period of time. We, along with all of the other aviation task forces, sent helicopters and pilots to aid in the search for Private Bergdahl. Task Force Attack rapidly began air-assaulting special operations and conventional forces alike into locations in which emerging intelligence gave even the slightest of hints that Bergdahl might be there. It was like a game of leap frog all over the province, day and night. All other missions in TF Attack's area of operations remained on hold as U.S. forces conducted the search. TF Attack also received priority for all fixed-wing and UAV enablers that could assist in finding Bergdahl. Already scarce, aerial resources were suddenly shifted to that region. Private Berghdal was the main effort in Afghanistan, and rightfully so.

Meanwhile, in N2KL, it had already been difficult to balance our heavy mission load in support of TF Mountain Warrior with the limited number of Chinooks and Apaches we had, but giving up helicopters and crews to help in the search for Bergdahl made operations exponentially more difficult. We simply could not do everything that was required; therefore, prioritization of missions became critical. One afternoon Jack Murphy came to my office and plopped down in a chair, exhausted. He'd been trying to figure out how to get everything done without dropping a mission, like juggling crystal balls with one hand tied behind his back.

"Sir," he said.

Then his eyebrows rose, and he matter-of-factly said, "If they don't find Bergdahl soon we're not closing Lowell and Keating in July."

"Yep. I know. We could really use another company of Apaches and a company of Chinooks."

"You're not kidding."

"Well, while I'm on midtour leave you see if you can get us some more airplanes," I said.

Jack smiled. "Yeah, right. So what's the plan on midtour?" Jack asked in a warm tone. The very hint of time spent with family changed Jack's entire demeanor.

"As soon as I get home we're going to hit the road for Gulf Shores, Alabama. We've gone down there several years in a row now. Lisa's sister, Leigh Anne, her husband, Craig, and their kids always go with us. The kids love it down there."

"How long will you stay?"

"We'll spend a week at the beach then a week at home, just hanging out, and then I'll head back over here."

Jack smiled. "Sounds like a great time."

I departed for midtour leave in late June. I traveled through Kuwait and on to Nashville. Lisa, the kids, and I spent two great weeks together, then I boarded a plane back to Afghanistan. Again, I was routed through Kuwait, but once I got to Kuwait I was told that I would be delayed for a few days. I found a secure phone so I could call Jack and tell him that I was stuck. He delivered alarming news.

"CJTF-82 told us that some senior Afghan official in Kabul told General McChrystal that enemy forces have taken over Barg-e Matal," he said. "They want us to go up there and take it back."

Barg-e Matal is a small, remote village in Nuristan Province. I had flown there in January to provide the locals with a hydroelectric generator and several hundred pounds of grain. It had been one of the highlights of my year in Afghanistan. At that time the village was completely snowed under. It was the closest thing I'd ever seen to the alpine images I had formed in my mind while reading books about Everest and Greg Mortenson's *Three Cups of Tea*. As we rounded the bend at COP Keating and headed north on that January morning, snow-covered peaks pointed heavenward for as far as the eye could see. I began snapping pictures over and over. It was beautiful.

From high above, we could see a small dirt road and a snaky, green river lying like a ribbon in the gap between the massive mountains—the Ketegal Valley, which leads to Barg-e Matal and the hinterlands beyond. Houses built out of huge timber were clustered close together on both sides of the strikingly clear river that spewed out of a choked-up glacier to the north.

As we began our approach into Barg-e Matal I saw that the river ran through the middle of the village. A single, centrally located wooden bridge connected the village across the water. Because of the heavy snowfall and year-round runoff, the icy water, compressed between two mountains, flowed with a roaring current. The hydroelectric generator would use the powerful current to produce electricity for the village.

Nuristan literally means the "Land of Light," which is ironic, since before it was forcibly converted to Islam, Nuristan was called Kafiristan, or "Land of the Unbelievers." The Kafirs were polytheists, but in the late 1890s they were conquered and forcibly converted under the direction of Afghan Emir Abdur Rahman Khan. The Nuristanis are an ancient people living in tiny villages sparsely scattered throughout valleys that pierce their beautiful mountainous homeland.

Getting to Barg-e Matal was no easy feat. Afghans had to navigate the towering rugged mountains using tiny trails that wound their way through them. Due to the altitude, we were forced to fly north from

FOB Bostic, up the Kamdesh Valley, past COPs Lowell and Keating, then turn due north and follow the river valley into the heart of Nuristan—a forty-minute flight from Bostic. Deviating from the valleys would have required supplemental oxygen for our crews due to the altitude.

"We are going to commit a ton of firepower, troops, and enablers to a remote-ass village dozens of miles from anywhere—just to reinstate the mayor and Afghan National Police. It makes no sense at all," Jack said. "I can't believe we're actually planning to do this. We're at the top of our game right now. We've got a plan to get out of the Kamdesh, and we are attacking the enemy in the Pech every few nights, making huge gains."

"Do we really know that it has been taken over? Or could it be a false report?" I asked.

"We flew a team of Apaches up there to look around, but they couldn't really tell. Then Division sent a UAV and it looks like it's true, but still, in the big scheme of things, what does it matter?"

We were told that Nuristan's governor, Mohammad Tamim Nuristani, had urged General McChrystal, the newly appointed commander of the International Security Assistance Force, to send troops to protect the people of Barg-e Matal and to eradicate the enemy, who had taken control of the village. To me the situation mirrored that of Afghanistan writ large. We went to Afghanistan to hold those responsible for the attacks of 9/11, accountable, but once they were removed, the true work began. The challenge now was helping Afghanistan prevent extremist groups from returning and regaining control of the country. The answer to that question would be predicated upon conditions, not timelines. Similarly, we knew that we could go to Barg-e Matal and remove the enemy there, but no one truly knew what it would require, or how long it would take, to help the people of Barg-e Matal and neighboring villages to develop the armed capacity to keep the enemy out of their village after we left. We could potentially get stuck there, isolated in extremely challenging terrain, for a very long time, requiring a tremendous amount of resources to sustain the force. It's easy to send troops to a location, but history has taught us that it's much more difficult to get them out.

"How long do they think we'll be there?" I asked Jack.

"They are saying ninety-six hours, but you know the deal, sir. We may get stuck up there. Jillian is on fire. She's pissed off. She told me, 'You have to convince them not to do this!'" Jack said. "I told her that no one wants to go, but we're going. You can imagine how she took that," he said and chuckled.

I couldn't help but laugh. When I was there I shared her infrequent but intense outbursts of fury, but with me being gone, poor old Jack had to take it all. Of course, she was almost always right, but there were forces at work well above us that we could not fully understand because we were not privy to those discussions in their entirety. Jack and I loved her passion for the mission.

"We're going to try and convince them not to go, but this is way above our head and you don't know what pressures the Afghans are putting on General McChrystal," Jack had told her.

"I get it but it's a huge mistake," Jillian had said. "We are going to lose all of our gains in Kunar and accomplish very little at Barg-e Matal. We know their logistics routes. We're interdicting them. We understand their direct-action cells in the Pech and we are slowly killing them. It took us months to figure out the northern end of the Watapur and now we are going to throw all of that away by overextending ourselves."

She'd been red-faced and angry. She and her team had poured their heart and soul into this problem and we'd been making tremendous headway. It enraged her to think that it might all unravel. Jillian and her team's emotion made me proud. It meant that they truly cared.

"By going up there Chosin will have to come off of key areas in the Kunar, and it's going to open the floodgates from the FATA. They will move logistics freely into the Pech again, and the foreign fighters are going to come pouring in. We've been able to predict almost every move they make in the Pech and Kunar. If we go to Barg-e Matal that will end and they *will* surprise us," she'd added.

While Jack agreed with her, he had heard enough to know that we were most likely going to be told to go to Barg-e Matal. We'd just have to do the best we could.

"Colonel George will be honest in his assessment. You know that, but in the end this decision is not going to be his to make," Jack had replied.

"It's a mistake," she'd said, and walked out.

When Jack told me about their conversation I smiled to myself.

I could see her walking out the door, storming off. She was passionate about our mission, and I loved that. From an intelligence perspective she owned our area of operations. I felt like she understood the
enemy as well if not better than anyone in N2KL. She studied everything collected on the enemy, from every intelligence-collection asset
in RC-E. Eighteen to twenty hours a day most days, she worked to
understand the enemy.

The UAV Jack had mentioned filmed a video that clearly revealed
an enemy presence, and later, other intelligence reporting confirmed
that enemy forces had indeed taken control of the Afghan Border
Police's (ABP) weapons and stockpiles of ammunition.

Colonel George, a few key members of his staff, and Jack conducted
a video teleconference with Major General Scaparotti. Colonel George
intended to advise him that, simply put, he did not want to send forces
to Barg-e Matal. From our perspective, it was a remote location of
little strategic value. The one certainty that we were painfully aware
of was that it would derail our larger plan for closing bases in the
Kamdesh. Everything was going to be delayed due to the missing soldier anyway, but if we became decisively engaged at Barg-e Matal,
we thought we might never get to close the outposts in the Kamdesh
at all. General Scaparotti acknowledged Colonel George's concerns,
but it appeared that there was much more at stake politically in
Kabul. We simply weren't privy to that information. Ultimately, we
were told to execute the plan, and that's what we did.

Colonel George chose to send a portion of Lieutenant Colonel Mark
O'Donnell's TF Chosin and the 2nd Afghan Kandak Company to regain control of Barg-e Matal. As quickly as possible, they would train
Afghan security forces and local volunteers to maintain long-term control of their village. The decision to go to Barg-e Matal meant that we
could not begin realignment of forces in the Kamdesh until we were
out of there. Due to the long distance and the high altitudes, only
Chinooks and Apaches would be able to operate at Barg-e Matal.
Those same Chinooks and Apaches were required to close the Kamdesh outposts, so realignment was officially put on hold.

The mission was called Operation Mountain Fire, and when all
was said and done, the task force consisted of 220 soldiers. Mark
O'Donnell sent one of his infantry companies, Attack Company, which
Captain Mike Harrison commanded. Initially, TF Chosin expected to

take the Afghans with whom they had been partnered, men they knew personally and trusted. But at the last minute they received word that the 2nd Afghan Kandak and their U.S. Marine and Latvian advisers would be going with them instead. Lieutenant Colonel Mark O'Donnell was very concerned with this change of plans and did not receive an answer as to why the decision had been made. "We didn't know them, and they didn't know us,"[3] O'Donnell later said.

"There was no trust because we had never operated with them. It was very difficult to plan and rehearse the mission because we had differences of opinion about how to conduct it. We had no relationship and that made it tough,"[4] he added.

Nevertheless, they did eventually agree on a plan and prepared for what they expected to be a very difficult fight. The two landing zones were on the north side of the village, one on either side of the river. Mark O'Donnell didn't like that at all, but his new partners wanted to use those two LZs. "The Afghan soldiers were landing on the opposite side of the river from us. We would be separated by a major terrain feature that we knew divided us, one that could not be crossed. If either of us got into significant contact with the enemy, we could assist with direct and indirect fires, but we could not maneuver to help each other. We knew there was no way to cross the river from the direction we were heading into the village," he said. "I thought it was a bad plan,"[5] he added.

Most concerning for me and my aviators was the fact that the approach and departure paths to the LZs gave us no other alternative but to follow the narrow valley to the village itself, then fly right over the top of it to get to the LZs. If the enemy was paying attention, if they expected us to come, then they knew how we would approach the village. There was only one way in and one way out.

Due to the long distance from FOB Bostic to Barg-e Matal we decided to move two Apaches and a medevac helicopter to Bostic. We would rotate them daily, but we would keep Apaches and a medevac bird there for as long as we had soldiers in Barg-e Matal. Through Colonel Lewis, Jack requested support from TF Eagle Lift. Lieutenant Colonel Rob Dickerson's Eagle Lift aircrews were already stretched thin with their mission at Bagram and helping TF Attack search for Private Bergdahl, but once again they helped us out.

It was difficult for our team to hide their disappointment. Only a couple of weeks earlier we had briefed a very sound plan to realign forces in N2KL. TF Chosin had made a tremendous impact on enemy operations in the central Kunar, and we felt like we had the enemy on his heels. We were clearly making progress. Now, our forces in the central Kunar were once again stretched thin and the Kamdesh realignment was on hold. Our Apaches were completely focused on Barg-e Matal, our Chinooks continued to resupply the Kamdesh Valley outposts, and now we would move troops and equipment in and out of Barg-e Matal.

Jack flew in the jump seat of a Chinook. He planned to go in on the lead assault bird. Twenty-first-century technology had changed warfare in a multitude of ways. One of those ways was the ability to remain in contact with home while fighting a war. It seemed strange to go out and fight a battle all day and then return to the FOB and Skype your family. One minute you were fighting for your life and the next you were talking to your loved ones via video teleconference.

Jack had established a pattern. When he was going out on a mission he would Skype J, his wife, just before he departed. He never told her what he was doing, but she learned that if he was wearing his army combat shirt (ACS) it meant that he was about to depart for a mission. "I was concerned about that one [Barg-e Matal]," he later told me. "It was a bad place to go. I told her that I loved her. She could tell I was going out because of the shirt, but she could also see a look of worry and concern. She asked, and I let her know this was a dangerous mission to a remote and bad place. I didn't want to scare her; I just wanted her to know that I was going out, and I quietly tried to hold back some tears. When we were done, I went back to the TOC for a final conditions check and then grabbed my weapons and gear. To this day J hates the army combat shirt."

In the early, predawn hours of July 12, four Chinooks and four Apaches departed FOB Fenty. They flew to FOB Joyce and then FOB Bostic, where they picked up 220 warriors awaiting transport to the remote mountain village of Barg-e Matal. We had previously flown a large portion of the ground forces to FOB Bostic, in order to minimize the time it took to make trips back and forth between Bostic and Barg-e Matal. It would require two turns of the four Chinooks to get all of them into the valley, and we wanted to build as much combat power as we could as quickly as we could. If our arrival was opposed by an enemy force from the high ground, which we expected, we at least wanted overmatch in terms of numbers and firepower. The Apaches topped off their fuel tanks at FOB Bostic in order to maximize the time they would be able to remain overhead once they got into the valley. Operation Mountain Fire was under way.

We had to climb over a ten-thousand-foot mountain pass to get to Barg-e Matal. We called it the BK pass, and the Apaches struggled to keep up with the more powerful Chinooks as they climbed. "We were only flying about eighty knots because that's all the Apaches could do and climb," Jack said. Once we cleared the BK pass I called Ross Lewallen, the Apache air mission commander, and told him to push forward, ahead of us.

UAVs had been orbiting high above the valley for forty-eight hours prior to our arrival. A DShK heavy machine gun, mounted in the back of a pickup truck, had been seen in the village, so we told our Apache pilots to focus on finding and destroying that weapon system. It was the weapon that concerned us most.

There was only a sliver of a moon, but it was bright out. The light from the moon was reflecting off of the sheer granite rock faces. It was too bright. "I thought the enemy might be able to see us as we flew over the Kamdesh," Jack said. Jillian had been talking about all of the enemy gathering in the Kamdesh, so the Apaches had been picking fights up there as they supported the resupply missions. It was easy to provoke a fight if you hung around a few minutes. If the pilots saw something that looked just a little bit suspicious they would circle it a few times and sure enough they'd get shot at, then they'd kill the guy and more would come and they'd kill them, which was fine, they were killing bad guys, but as our crews flew over the valley for this mission I really didn't want them to start shooting at them.

"I called the joint terminal attack controller (JTAC) as we flew over COP Keating and checked in with him. He said everything was quiet. Then we turned up the valley toward Barg-e Matal. We didn't descend below two thousand feet until we passed Papwrok village, then we began to descend. I had horrible communications up there. Even the satellite radio was intermittent. I finally got the B-1 bomber and told him to go ahead and drop his bombs. I really appreciated that General

McChrystal had approved the pre-assault fires," Jack later recalled. Jillian had plotted the likely location of DShKs, so we decided to bomb those spots. "The blue silver flashes of three bombs exploding was beautiful and reassuring as we approached the LZs," Jack said.

"When we were about two kilometers out I suddenly heard Ross Lewallen shooting his thirty-millimeter. My heart stopped. I called him on the radio. 'Ross, what are you shooting at?' " Jack asked.

Silence.

"Ross, what are you shooting at?" Jack called again.

"Uh, nothing. I thought we were supposed to suppress the treeline as we went in," he said.

"I pulled the seat out of my ass and we continued inbound," Jack said.

As the first lift went in, the Apache crews did not find the DShK they were looking for, but they did see men with machine guns and RPGs, clearly alarmed by the echoing sound of rotors in the valley, run from the girls' school and Afghan National Police (ANP) station. Forty to fifty men burst out of the buildings and sprinted for the mountains. It was obvious that they did not expect us—we had achieved surprise.

A large group of men clustered together under a tree up on the side of the mountain, as if it were a pre-planned meeting location. The men were not in a position where they could affect our assault at that point, and they were running away from the village, so the Apache crews kept them in their sights until our forces were safely on the ground. The pilots were ready to shoot if the men appeared to be preparing to engage our soldiers, but they preferred to wait until we landed and everyone was safely on the ground before they started a fight. The Chinooks were most vulnerable just before they touched down, as they slowed for landing.

Inside the Chinooks tensions were high, both in the cockpit and among the infantrymen in the back of the aircraft. Throughout the week preceding the operation, the Afghan soldiers had shared not only their knowledge of the terrain in Barg-e Matal but also their open fear of the enemy. "The fighters in those mountains at Barg-e Matal are tough. They are experienced fighters with good training," they told TF Chosin soldiers.

The general feeling among our men was that the enemy knew we would eventually go to Barg-e Matal, and they would already be in tactically advantageous positions awaiting our arrival when we got there.[6] It was the field of dreams. They built it, and they knew we would eventually come. The pilots dreaded landing in a deep valley surrounded by mountains, potentially crawling with enemy forces. To make matters worse, the only available landing areas were north of the village, and we would have to approach from the south. The pilots would have to fly over the village as they slowed for landing. It would be very easy for an enemy fighter to step outside of a house and shoot at the Chinooks as they slowly passed overhead, when they were most vulnerable. The greatest advantage we had was darkness.

The Chinook is a big aircraft and when you fly it into an LZ, thinking you may be shot at any moment, it seems to slow to a pace that is nerve-racking—a crawl. The anticipation of being shot down coupled with the urgent desire to get on the ground is gut-wrenching at best.

Mark O'Donnell surveyed the men inside the Chinook as they flew north. He later told me, "I remember thinking, as a Ranger I've done so many air assaults, and now I am doing the most difficult and dangerous one of my life, and I have no idea what these Afghan security forces are capable of once we hit the ground. With my experience in the Rangers, I knew that you exit the back of the aircraft thinking you could tackle any foe and be successful. I was on the back of the aircraft wondering if our Afghan police forces would know how to unbuckle themselves to exit the aircraft."[7]

"Two minutes!" the crew chief yelled to the men, who then passed the word down the line.

The pilots had hit the release point on their route and initiated their approach in the thin, black Nuristani air at 3:58 A.M., two Chinooks on the east side of the river and two on approach to the west. The only thing that connected the east and west sides of the village, across the cold raging river water, was the single wooden bridge that would soon become key terrain. The river flowed dangerously fast. It was impossible to cross it in combat gear without the bridge—we knew it, and the enemy knew it as well.

The Chinooks touched down in the LZs at 4:00 A.M. Soldiers, relieved to be on the ground at last, and seemingly in control of their own destiny, poured off the helicopters into a very uncertain situation.

The task force executive officer, Major Pete Granger, along with the Afghan soldiers and the marine trainers, landed on the west side of the river. Their mission was to move to the district center and set up a command post. Lieutenant Colonel O'Donnell, Captain Harrison, and the other American soldiers landed on the east side of the river. They were to begin clearing houses and buildings as they moved south to the center of the village.[8]

Captain Mike Harrison was no stranger to the mountains of eastern Afghanistan. In 2006 he had deployed for a sixteen-month tour in the Pech River Valley. He had served as a platoon leader in 1-32 Infantry. He lost two very close friends on that deployment, and on the day he flew to Barg-e Matal he had flown over the outposts named in their honor. First Lieutenant Ben Keating and Sergeant First Class Jared Monti had deployed with Mike in 2006. He had thought about both of them a lot as he fought to survive yet another challenging deployment in Kunar and Nuristan in 2009.

As soon as the Chinooks cleared the village to the south, the Apaches called Mike Harrison on the radio to get clearance to shoot the enemy fighters who were by then scrambling along spider trails to go and occupy fighting positions. "Roger, you're cleared to engage," Harrison said, authorizing the start of a struggle that would last for months.

All the Apache pilots needed was the go-ahead. They already had their crosshairs on the fighters. As soon as the words "cleared to engage" left Harrison's lips, the pilot squeezed the trigger on his 30-mm cannon, killing two enemy fighters.

It was as if the enemy, hiding in the rocks, was also waiting for a trigger to initiate the fight. The burst of 30-mm did the trick. Suddenly, the Apaches took a barrage of machine gun fire from the ridgeline above them, at over nine thousand feet. The bullets missed the Apaches, due in large part to the darkness, but the muzzle flashes, sparking in the night, gave the enemy's positions away. The Apaches went to work.

It was just beginning to get light enough to see when Lieutenant Colonel O'Donnell and his men began their movement south. "My fears were eased within a few minutes of landing," O'Donnell later told me. "They didn't hit us hard right after we landed, so I figured it was not as bad as everyone had predicted."[9]

As the *thump, thump, thump* of rotors beating the air into submission echoed through the valley, O'Donnell's men moved cautiously toward almost certain enemy contact. They used an army movement technique called "bounding overwatch," in which one portion of the force moves to a position with protection while the other soldiers cover them, ready to return fire if fired upon. They alternated covering each other and moving forward as they worked their way, bounding and overwatching, bounding and overwatching, to the south. As they approached the first group of buildings, one group of soldiers provided overwatch while others began entering and clearing buildings.

Suddenly, they saw movement in the village. Families, anticipating a hateful battle, began pouring out of Barg-e Matal. Upon hearing our helicopters land, they had immediately gathered all of their most precious belongings and nervously fled their homes—some to the north, some to the south. They passed Mike Harrison and his men in a solemn, lifeless procession, their heads down and their eyes fixed on the ground, some visibly shaking. They were scared and knew that battle was imminent in their village, among their homes. These were people who had been pro-Afghan government. They were people whom we had helped prepare for winter, providing them with thousands of pounds of grain and power generation. The fact that they would not look at or speak to our soldiers meant they were afraid that they would be harmed if they helped us. It was not a good sign.

As the valley grew brighter, the sun shone on the snowcapped peaks above. To Mike Harrison it looked like Colorado but felt like a crypt, a strange juxtaposition of beauty and danger. One of Harrison's platoon leaders found the first enemy cache—RPGs, ammunition for several types of machine guns, including DsHKs, and a large stack of voter registration forms to be used in the upcoming presidential election.

Everyone looked to the south as the faint yet distinctive sound of massive Chinook rotors echoed up the valley. The second lift of soldiers approached. Sporadic shooting between the Apaches and enemy soldiers in the ridges high above continued to echo in the valley, but none of the men in the valley had been shot at. Ultimately, all of the ground forces made it into the valley unscathed and began moving to their planned objectives. Along the way three more caches of weapons and ammunition were found in homes. The Chosin soldiers moved fairly quickly but with extreme caution. The anticipation of

an attack was stressful for the men; still, they had not yet been attacked. They knew it was coming but from where and when? The
anticipation is worse than the actual fight, Harrison thought.

On the opposite side of the river, Major Granger led his men south
toward the district center. O'Donnell thought it was selfless of Granger
to volunteer to accompany the Afghans. He didn't know them, had
never worked with them, but was willing to put his life in their hands.

The district center and the sawmill were located on the west side
of the river. Vast cornfields hugged the road that led to the south out
of town toward Paprowk—a known enemy safe haven. The sawmill
marked the center of town and served as the gathering place—the
social hub—of the village. It provided income for a significant portion of the residents of Barg-e Matal. It was important to their small
economy as well as a place of social significance, like a small-town
barbershop in America, where old men gather to discuss politics and
the weather.

On the east side of the river, Captain Harrison's men continued
clearing buildings to the south. The girls' school, a labyrinth of log
houses, and the Afghan Border and National Police headquarters all
sat on the east side of the river. Numerous spider trails wound their
way from the village up the steep eastern ridge, which ultimately led
into Pakistan.

When conducting combat operations, we always try and remain
within artillery range. Barg-e Matal was well beyond artillery range,
so the men relied on their 81-mm mortars for indirect fires, but the
mortar system itself and the rounds were incredibly heavy, making
transport difficult. The mortar sergeant, Staff Sergeant Metcalf, and
his men used a Skedco litter to drag the mortar system and ammo.
The Skedco is a hard yet flexible piece of plastic, slightly longer than
a grown man, and is used to transport wounded soldiers. It looks like
a sled but folds up around the soldier like a canoe. The men strapped
the mortar and ammunition to the Skedco and dragged it behind them
as they moved.

Major Granger and his team made it to the district center unscathed
and set up a command post. He erected an antenna and established
communications with his command post back in the Kunar. His men
then began trying to locate the national police, army, and border
police commanders. They half expected to be met by at least one or

two of the police, but no one appeared. They needed to discuss the situation with them, determine how to regain full control of the valley, and set up a defensive perimeter in case the enemy attacked.

Eventually, the men found the police leaders in a building on the south end of the village. Afghans never discuss business before hot tea, so Pete sat down for a cup of piping hot green chai first, then began discussing a plan. As they sat drinking chai and considering options, they suddenly heard a commotion outside the district center. The men rose from the floor and went to investigate.

Just outside, numerous local villagers gathered around two dead men. The villagers had walked up the mountain and recovered the bodies of the men our Apaches had killed when the shooting first began. The two men had long black unkempt hair and beards. They wore militant-style clothing and tennis shoes as opposed to the traditional Afghan dress. The men looked out of place. The locals did not want to bury their bodies, which clearly indicated that the men were not from the region, or even Afghanistan. However, as a matter of Islamic necessity the dead must be buried within twenty-four hours of death. To deny even the enemy a proper burial was uncommon. It took some convincing, but eventually our soldiers got the locals to bury the bodies.

By 2:00 P.M. the command post was operational and initial security positions were in place. The mortars were set up and prepared to fire should they be needed. The shooting between the Apaches and enemy forces in the mountains had stopped. It was very quiet. O'Donnell picked up no radio chatter—either there were no enemy forces in the mountains or they were using disciplined radio silence. The latter would prove to be the case.

By 4:00 P.M Granger and his team were out of water. They were preparing a group of men to go get some when all hell broke loose. The first RPG impacted fifty meters south of their southernmost position. Instantly, the once quiet valley exploded in a rattle of gunfire and pounding explosions. The enemy opened fire from literally every direction. Their dispersion along the ridges made it difficult for the men to gain fire superiority by concentrating their fire on one general location. Suddenly, the enemy broke radio silence, making it clear that they had planned a well-coordinated attack, and now it was game on.

First Lieutenant Jake Miraldi and Staff Sergeant Eric Lindstrom, the weapons squad leader and acting senior noncommissioned officer, ran toward their commander's location. They needed to speak with Mike Harrison to decide where to place their machine guns to try and repel the enemy. Lieutenant Colonel Mark O'Donnell was crouching beside a long rock wall. He saw Miraldi and Lindstrom hunker down and run along the wall. He saw the explosion as an RPG hit the wall right between the two men.

"I wasn't sure who it was running, but both of them fell when the RPG struck. There was a huge plume of smoke and debris. I thought both of them were dead, but they both got up and kept running. I couldn't believe it,"[10] O'Donnell later told me.

Miraldi and Lindstrom made it a little farther, then sought cover. Both were injured.

"Medic!" Harrison yelled. Two medics ran from cover to treat the men.

Jake Miraldi had shrapnel in his legs, but he refused to stop fighting. Eric Lindstrom had small shrapnel holes in his abdomen, below the waist, and in his thighs. The medics called for Captain Ryan Smith, the battalion surgeon, who quickly made his way to Lindstrom. They moved him into a small thatch hut and began treating his wounds.

Meanwhile Harrison made a dash for his radio to send up a medevac request, and to tell Mark O'Donnell that they had two wounded men. Having watched the two men get up and keep running, O'Donnell assumed that they were not injured too badly.

Where are the Afghans? Harrison wondered. He didn't see any of them fighting the enemy. He began trying to find out where they had gone. After a few broken radio calls, he was told that they had fled south to the police station as soon as the shooting started. Two of the Afghan National Policemen had sustained head injuries that needed immediate attention. Without hesitation Harrison's two medics ran through machine gun fire and a barrage of RPGs to their location to treat the wounded policemen.

Meanwhile, across the river, Major Granger and the Afghan Army contingent found themselves in a difficult fight of their own. When the enemy opened fire, it was from directly above them. It was almost impossible to find sufficient cover and impossible to maneuver. If the importance of the bridge was not previously apparent to everyone, it certainly was by then. Chosin's forces were separated by the river.

Without the bridge each force would be completely isolated and unable to reinforce one another. Fortunately, they slowly began to identify enemy fighters who were dug into the mountain like ticks, and focus all of their firepower on them, one position at a time. With the help of our Apaches and jet fighters they slowly regained the initiative.

In the meantime, Staff Sergeant Lindstrom's condition began to deteriorate. Mark O'Donnell received a call that Lindstrom was fading, then he was stable, then fading again. It seemed as though the medevac would never get there. The men hung on to every beat of Lindstrom's heart. O'Donnell ran to see for himself.

It hit him like a ton of bricks when he saw Lindstrom. He was stripped down and the surgeon was working feverishly to keep him stable. Lindstrom was unconscious. Mark O'Donnell's first thought was of Eric Lindstrom's family.

Lindstrom's wife, Tara, had just given birth to twin girls in January. He had not yet been able to go home and see them since the birth. Eric was a twenty-seven-year-old former policeman from Flagstaff, Arizona. Referred to as "Leonidas," he was "the living and breathing epitome of 'the standard' for a soldier,"[11] Mark O'Donnell said.

"We all loved him. However, Command Sergeant Major Carabello, our battalion command sergeant major, especially loved him. Command Sergeant Major Carabello, easily the most caring, competent, and demanding NCO I have ever served with, thought the world of Staff Sergeant Lindstrom. Anytime we were going to conduct a big mission, and it required a superior junior noncommissioned officer, Staff Sergeant Lindstrom was generally who Command Sergeant Major Carabello counted on,"[12] O'Donnell said.

In spite of shrapnel wounds to his legs, Jake Miraldi, a former full-back on the army football team, continued to lead his platoon. Another one of Mike Harrison's noncommissioned officers suffered shrapnel wounds to his hand, yet he too was able to continue to fight. They were fighting from the inside of a fishbowl. The enemy had the high ground, and there was nothing they could do about that. They were surrounded, but they were determined to turn the tide of the battle.

They directed the Apaches onto targets and used their mortars to destroy enemy positions as they identified them throughout the day. When they found an enemy position they focused their fires until the enemy was gone. The medevac helicopter was on its way from FOB Bostic, flying into a "hot" landing zone, which concerned them, but they had to get Lindstrom out of the valley and to a forward surgical team. They moved him, under fire, to the evacuation LZ "Rattlesnake" on the east side of the valley. Everyone there was very concerned, but "the wounds didn't look that bad on the outside. I felt pretty sure he'd make it,"[13] Mike Harrison said.

Finally, they heard the faint sound of rotor blades in the valley to the south. Slowly, the sound grew until the sound was a dot in the valley with two slightly smaller dots flanking it—the Apache escort. The medevac bird came in hot and fast, flared at the end, and planted on LZ Rattlesnake. The men loaded Staff Sergeant Lindstrom quickly and moved back to their positions. The medevac was off the ground in seconds. The pilots flew the skin off the bird to get him to the surgeon at FOB Bostic.

Task Force Chosin had lost twenty-one men on their previous deployment to Kunar Province. Eric Lindstrom was the first casualty of their 2009 deployment, and his loss invoked pain beyond description for the men who served with him, who loved him. He was the first soldier to die at Barg-e Matal. He would not be the last.

By 8:00 P.M. the enemy appeared to be pushed to the south of the village and had had enough fighting for the day. As darkness fell like a blanket over the deep valley, Task Force Chosin felt like they had the initiative; still, three Chosin soldiers had been wounded and one killed. Two Afghan border police had been wounded, and one Afghan army soldier had been killed.

They tried to determine how many enemy they had fought. The intelligence estimates had predicted around one hundred enemy fighters, but it was difficult to figure out how many enemy forces were hidden in the mountains. They had taken fire from every direction, and once the shooting started the echo of machine gun fire and RPGs made it impossible to tell where the shots were coming from and how many there were. It was just as hard to determine if they had achieved any success: if they had killed any of the men trying to kill them, or if they had just shot rocks all day.

It was too dangerous to walk up into the mountains to look around; besides, it was already dark, and the enemy usually dragged their dead off for burial without being seen. That evening Mark O'Donnell, Mike Harrison, and several other leaders huddled together to discuss what had happened and to plan for the next day. Through a series of radio intercepts they were able to determine that they faced at least fifty enemy fighters that day. They were made up of a combination of foreign fighters, speaking Arabic, Nuristani, Dari, and Chechen. As best as Mark and Mike could figure, they had killed about nineteen of them.

While it was good to know that they inflicted casualties on the enemy, everyone knew that they could never kill their way to victory in a war like this. It would be very easy for the enemy to recruit fighters to come shoot down on the Americans from the towering cliffs that dominated the tiny village. O'Donnell and his men knew that it would take enduring Afghan capacity to secure Barg-e Matal.[14] That's what Mark O'Donnell's men set out to do, create a community-based security plan with local villagers and Afghan security forces. It would take time, and they would have to do it while constantly fighting the enemy, but it was certainly the best chance they had for a ticket out of the valley.

Throughout July, TF Chosin taught and trained Afghans. We resupplied them every night or two, Apaches raced to the valley every time they fought, and they did the best they could to teach the locals how to secure their village with the help of Afghan National Security Forces (ANSF). It was a herculean task executed in very challenging terrain.

The base of the valley was just over six thousand feet above sea level. The ridgeline to the west rose to a snowcapped peak of seventeen thousand feet, and the eastern ridge crested at fourteen thousand feet. The distance across the valley was a mere 1,500 meters at the valley floor. From the valley floor the terrain climbed almost straight up to the towering mountains above. Goat trails zigzagged along the gentlest sections of the terrain. Caves dotted the cliffs like black dots on an otherwise gray, rocky landscape. TF Chosin, working in the valley below, was under the constant observation from enemy forces in the caves and crevasses above. Theirs was a difficult task, but the only way for TF Chosin to return to their bases in the central Kunar was for the people of Barg-e Matal to be able to adequately secure and defend themselves.

Lieutenant Colonel Mark O'Donnell met with local village elders and explained that his men would train them if they would provide volunteers. Meanwhile, Colonel Randy George's staff went to work procuring uniforms, weapons, and ammunition. We flew the equipment to Barg-e Matal, and Mark's team, between fights with the enemy, began training the locals. Mark's men taught the Afghans basic soldier tasks like how to stand in formation, how to salute, and how to march in order to instill discipline in their ranks. With the approval of village elders, they chose those who demonstrated the aptitude to lead their fellow Afghans as squad and platoon leaders. They taught them marksmanship, how to clear and clean their weapons, how to fix malfunctions, and how to throw grenades.

They even taught them how to establish a personnel management system complete with a payroll tracker. The Nuristan Provincial Reconstruction Team (PRT) came up with the money to pay the new recruits, which boosted morale. Within weeks they saw definite progress, but the harder questions remained: How good is good enough, and how could Mark's team convince leaders in Kabul that the Afghans were ready to secure the village on their own? It was certain to be a long and difficult summer at Barg-e Matal.

Out of every one hundred men, ten shouldn't even be there, eighty are just targets, nine are the real fighters, and we are lucky to have them, for they make the battle. Ah, but the one, one is a warrior, and he will bring the others back.

—HERACLITUS

THE WATAPUR

In 1898, Congress authorized the raising of the 1st United States Volunteer Cavalry. Teddy Roosevelt was pivotal in securing the authorization; thus he was offered a commission and subsequent appointment to colonel in order to command one of the three regiments. Having no previous military experience he deferred the command to his friend Dr. Leonard Wood, who had gained a substantial amount of experience fighting the Apaches, during which time he earned the Medal of Honor. Roosevelt was appointed a lieutenant colonel and assigned under Wood's command.

The cavalry force was to be raised from the "wild riders and riflemen of the Rockies and the Great Plains."[1] Roosevelt and Wood selected scholar-athletes from Yale, Princeton, and Harvard. They chose an adventuresome lot of Native Americans, riflemen, and cowboys, men who were shrewd tactically and fierce in battle. He wanted problem solvers who thrived in chaotic situations.

In present-day Afghanistan, those same qualities appealed to Colonel Ron Lewis, having served in numerous cavalry units himself. He commonly referred to our brigade as a "cavalry organization." The only cavalry organization by lineage, of course, was our very own 7th Squadron, 17th U.S. Cavalry, but Colonel Lewis knew that. It was the character, the attitude, that he was after, that he wanted to permeate throughout the brigade. He wanted a cavalry state of mind. He knew that agile, flexible units that could rapidly respond to the ever-changing complexities and ambiguities of the modern battlefield would carry the day. He wanted tireless leaders who were tactically savvy yet fearless in battle. On one scorching hot mid-July morning, just five days after we began operations at Barg-e Matal, our cavalry agility was put to the test.

Our focus during the first half of July, particularly for the Chinooks, Apaches, and medevac, had been on Barg-e Matal. We still held out hope of closing the bases in the Kamdesh, but those operations were certainly on hold for the time being. Meanwhile, it was fighting season, and Brian Pearl's men were finding themselves tangled up with the enemy left and right in the Pech River Valley—the enemy's way of welcoming them to Kunar Province.

Sergeant First Class Henriques Ventura was the platoon sergeant, the senior noncommissioned officer, of 3rd Platoon, Charlie Company, 2-12 Infantry, located at FOB Honaker-Miracle. Early on Friday morning, July 17, he led a patrol into the Watapur Valley.[2]

As Sergeant First Class Ventura and his men stepped off on the small dusty trail leading into the Watapur on July 17, a fierce enemy, an enemy that had walked those mountains since birth, an enemy that was acclimated far better than any U.S. force could ever hope to be, watched and waited. Lean, bearded men with leathery, brown skin crawled slowly through the rocks and settled into crags and crevasses along the eastern wall of the Watapur. Once in place, only the muzzles of their rifles were visible. They knew the valley; they understood how to use the terrain. They knew that our helicopters would come, and within a matter of hours, they would try to kill Sergeant First Class Ventura and his men.

COP Honaker-Miracle sat in the Pech River Valley, at the mouth of the Watapur Valley. The Watapur marks the crossroads of enemy lines of communication from the north and east, supplying weapons and fighters to other infamous valleys in the area such as the Korengal, Waygal, and Shuryak. We had previously fought three significant battles in the Watapur. The battle of July 17 would dwarf all others.

Sergeant First Class Ventura departed the FOB with fifteen soldiers and an interpreter. Their mission was to conduct an area reconnaissance around the Pun Sahr peak on the eastern ridge of the Watapur. They wanted to find enemy mortar and fighting positions. In another time and place it could have been a walk in the Colorado Rocky

Mountains. In fact, it looked like a Colorado summer day as they filed out of the gate at Honaker-Miracle, but it wasn't, not even close. Enemy spotters, men who always watched our movements, began calling their leaders on handheld radios as Ventura and his men departed the gate and entered the valley. Ventura's men moved with discipline. They were alert and maintained a good interval between them. If the enemy attacked, they wanted to be dispersed. If they were bunched up several could be killed or wounded with a single burst of machine gun fire.

From above, the men looked like ants on a brown path. They paralleled carefully tended farmers' fields—a precious possession that sustained life in the valley. The men wiped sweat from their faces and swatted at flies as they pressed on into the valley.

High above them enemy fighters patiently observed. "They are coming. Move to your positions," they chattered on their radios.

Most of the enemy fighters came from the houses high up on the ridge, well above the valley floor. Spider trails led from the heavily wooded ridge where the enemy fighters lived down to the valley floor. About two-thirds of the way down the ridge the trees ended abruptly, and the terrain turned to rock and dirt. Their fighting positions were in the rocks and cliffs. Boulders the size of VW Bugs protected them from machine gun and rocket fire. We were better trained, better equipped, and better led, but the terrain negated many of our advantages, and the enemy knew it. Pikes Peak was conveniently close to his home base at Fort Carson, Colorado, so Sergeant First Class Ventura had prepared his men for eastern Afghanistan by having them hike up and down the mountain countless times in the months prior to their deployment.

"We're as fit and ready for these mountains as we can be," Brian Pearl told me when he arrived in country. They had done everything humanly possible to replicate the environment in which they would fight. Truthfully, their work in the Colorado Rockies was valiant, but environmental training can take you only so far.

Less than a half mile into the valley, intelligence intercepts began to detect enemy conversations. Enemy fighters were watching the patrol, and they were discussing what to do. The thought of being watched, the anticipation of an attack, brought an uneasy, stressful feeling to all of Ventura's men. In some respects it's easier to be surprised and react rather than to know they are watching, planning to attack, yet not knowing where or when.

Most patrols in the Watapur traveled to the small village about halfway into the valley and conducted meetings with the local elders. Very few if any patrols ventured out of the valley, up onto the ridge, but that was where Ventura was headed.

Back at Honaker-Miracle the men had found the radio frequency the enemy was using to talk to each other. They used a simple two-way radio, so the men at the company command post sat with an interpreter listening and relaying what they were hearing to our helicopters and Sergeant First Class Ventura. The enemy forces soon came to a consensus.

"Get closer. Move down the hill and get one of them. Capture an American," was the order, and it struck fear in every man listening to the radio. While relatively common, these intercepts were disturbing and increased the anxiety in the patrol. Having only arrived a few days prior, Ventura's men were not yet used to these reports.

Sergeant First Class Ventura's men had worked their way to the east side of the valley. Once they got to the finger that they planned to use to walk up the ridge, they turned east and began to climb using a small trail. "Stay alert. Keep your heads on a swivel," Ventura told his men.

It was just a few minutes before 9:00 A.M. The men tried to remain ready for an attack as they labored to climb under the searing July sun. It was eerily quiet.

Then the world exploded.

As the enemy initiated the attack with RPGs, AK-47 machine guns, PKM and DShK machine guns, Ventura's men dove for cover and immediately began returning fire into the rocks above them. It is difficult to figure out where the shots are coming from in the valleys of eastern Afghanistan. The rocky, mountainous terrain causes the sound to echo, and the enemy is very good at using the terrain. They are nearly impossible to find if they remain still and do not move. If you are lucky enough to see muzzle flashes or movement, then they can be targeted. Otherwise, the best course of action is to narrow down their location as best as you can, then overwhelm them with superior firepower. That is exactly what Sergeant First Class Ventura's patrol did. Once they sensed a slight lull in the enemy fire, they increased their own rate of fire where they thought the enemy was hiding, and ran to the south in an attempt to get out of the enemy engagement area. The enemy had caught them in the open. They had to find better cover.

Private Joshua Dow had just joined Charlie Company that week; prior to that he had served on Colonel Randy George's personal security detachment. Dow laid down suppressive fire with his rifle in an attempt to force the enemy to keep their heads down, then he got up and ran for cover, but before he could find it he was struck by a bullet that passed through his belly.

Private First Class Eli Casas also made a run for a better position, but before he got there he was hit in the right hip. Despite a perfect tactical movement while in contact with the enemy, the men were being accurately engaged from the high ground to their west. Staff Sergeant Jonathan Wedemeyer, a squad leader, fractured his ankle while running for cover. Three of Ventura's men were quickly unable to move without assistance. It was clear that the patrol faced a significant enemy force. Walking out was no longer an option without help. They needed air support, quick. Sergeant First Class Ventura called COP Honaker-Miracle and asked for a medevac and close air support.

We numbered our scout weapons teams by their sequence of duty throughout the day. Our first up on that Friday morning was Scout Weapons Team 1 (SWT 1), a flight of two Kiowas. They responded first to Sergeant First Class Ventura's request for help. Constantly manipulating the controls so as not to present an easy target, they entered the valley darting and diving at 9:20 A.M. Chief Warrant Officer 2 Don Cunningham and First Lieutenant Chad Marzec flew flight lead, with First Lieutenant Brandon Jackson and Chief Warrant Officer 2 Chuck Folk in trail. Folk served as the air mission commander.

Chuck Folk was what we referred to as a "high school to flight school pilot." He had submitted a warrant officer packet when he was seventeen years old—a junior in high school. As a senior he was notified that he had been accepted. After graduation he would first attend basic training at Fort Sill, Oklahoma, and then travel to Fort Rucker, Alabama, where he would attend warrant officer candidate school and finally flight training.

Chuck's grandfather had been career army, having fought in both Korea and Vietnam. His father retired from the air force after twenty years as an investigator in the Office of Special Investigations. Upon completion of the initial flight training phase, Chuck was selected to fly the OH-58D Kiowa Warrior. Chuck's tall, lean physique made him a natural athlete. He excelled at everything from horseshoes to football. He was smart and fit—an excellent soldier and aviator. He had earned the respect of his fellow warrants through his maturity and a natural affinity to fly the Kiowa. He had been awarded the Distinguished Flying Cross for his actions in a tough fight in Iraq. Chuck was only twenty-five years old in 2009, yet he was a mature air mission commander, who now led his team into a very complex and uncertain situation.

The team was originally tasked to conduct a routine reconnaissance mission in the Pech River Valley, so as soon as they heard the call for help over the radio, Folk told Marzec and Cunningham to lead the team into the Watapur.

When they arrived, enemy fighters were engaging the patrol with RPGs and machine guns from multiple locations. Two A-10s (call sign "Hawg") had just completed a gun run with their 30-mm canons, which still echoed in the valley as the A-10s pulled up and climbed back into the blue summer sky. Marzec called the patrol to check in.

"Charlie 9-3, Pale 5-2, over."

"Charlie 9-3, over."

"Charlie 9-3, Pale 5-2, team of two Kiowas. I have six hundred rounds of fifty cal. and fourteen rockets on board, one and a half hours of station time. SITREP [Situation Report], over," Marzec transmitted over the radio.

He spoke with Sergeant Claude Hodge (Charlie 9-3), the patrol's forward observer, on the radio. Sergeant Hodge, who explained the patrol's situation to Folk, would remain a very busy man throughout the rest of the day.

For obvious reasons, the most important thing attack helicopters must do before shooting at the enemy is to find all the friendly forces. Folk's team located the patrol rather quickly and with the help of Hawg began trying to find the enemy. They marked several areas by shooting white phosphorous rockets while Hawg used their sensors to search for enemy movement in the rocks. Folk sensed that this might be a significant fight, so while Marzec spoke with Hawg and Charlie 9-3, Folk coordinated with SWT 2 and 3, both of whom were conducting other missions in a nearby area. He explained to them what was going on in the Watapur and told them to be prepared to come to the Watapur and join the fight if they were needed. Folk foresaw this as a protracted fight, and he didn't want to have to leave Ventura's men with no cover when his team eventually had to go to the FARP for gas and more bullets, so he wisely planned to rotate the other SWTs into the fight. They would then establish a cycle that would provide constant coverage for the patrol.

It was not the first time Folk had fought in the Watapur Valley, and he knew that if the fighting escalated it would take at least three teams, constantly rotating, to maintain pressure on the enemy.[3] It would take approximately thirty-five minutes to fly from the Watapur to FOB Wright, fill up with gas, load more ammunition, and return to the fight. One team would not be enough if the fight progressed.

The battle did progress. The intelligence intercepts proved accurate. Enemy forces wanted to get close and capture an American soldier. Uncharacteristically, they maneuvered down the mountain, carefully using the terrain to mask their movement, and began trying to surround the patrol. It was extremely hard to see them as they blended into the terrain, but they spoke freely on their radios and that helped our pilots know what they were attempting to do.

As Ventura's patrol took fire from the enemy they began telling Folk's team where the enemy was located. After multiple engagements, Folk took a close look around Charlie 9-3's position to ensure that no enemy forces were attempting to move around their flank. As they made a low pass, Marzec and Cunningham heard a "slow, low repetitive thud . . . a baritone thump"[4] that seemed to be inside the cockpit with them.

"That's a DShK," Marzec said.

Both of the pilots recognized the frightful sound of the DShK, but before they had a chance to react to it, or feel that cold burning in their chest, Cunningham saw a puff of smoke at Marzec's chest, and he was suddenly lifted up in his seat. He lurched up and forward until the shoulder restraint system locked and caught him. The first round entered the aircraft underneath Marzac's seat and, fortunately, deflected forward into the flight controls, making the aircraft difficult to control but manageable. The second round entered the back of the fuselage and blew a hole the size of a grown man's thumb clean through the aircraft.

"We're hit!" Marzec announced on the team internal radio as he simultaneously dove the helicopter down and left to try and avoid being hit again with a sustained burst.

"Will it fly?" Folk asked.

"Yeah, but I'm getting a lot of feedback in the flight controls. We need to get to Abad now,"[5] replied Marzec.

"Are you hit?" Cunningham asked Marzec, concerned that a bullet had actually hit him.

"I don't think so, but I don't know. It knocked the crap out of me."

"I have the controls," Cunningham said and began flying so Marzec could check himself out to make sure he wasn't shot.[6]

Folk contacted SWT 2 and told them that his lead aircraft had been hit. "We need immediate relief on station," he told Scott Stradley, the air mission commander of SWT 2.

Scott Stradley, who previously had flown lead for me into the Helgal Valley, answered with excitement in his voice, "We're on the way!"

Chief Warrant Officers 2 Ryan Neal and Mike McClain flew lead in Stradley's team. Chief Warrant Officer 3 Scott "Scotty" Hill, a maintenance test pilot who wore his cavalry Stetson like Gabby Hayes with the brim pinned straight up, flew with Stradley. Scotty Hill was born with a smile and lived in happiness. Never has there been a more pleasant maintenance pilot to hold a wrench in his hand. A constant cutup, Scotty Hill carried a big toothy smile with him everywhere he went. He was a small man with a big grin. What he lacked in stature, he made up for in personality. Easy to laugh and loud when he did it, Scotty never met a stranger, and I never met a man that knew him and did not like him.

Hill and Stradley had begun their day with somewhat of a religious debate. Stradley, a devout Catholic, had strapped into the Kiowa and opened his laminated checklist to a weathered, yellow card. He began to read.

"Oh, Saint Joseph, whose protection is so great—"

Scotty Hill interrupted, his brow furrowed. "What are you doing?"

"I'm praying. Now let me finish," Stradley said.

"Praying? I'm Christian, and we don't pray to a saint. We pray to God," Hill said with his ever-present smile.

"Well, I'm Catholic, and we pray intercessory prayers. I always say this prayer before a fight," Stradley said.

Hill considered it for a minute then spoke. "Well, if that's how you vehicle your faith, okay, but I'll pray to God," Hill said, then paused again as he thought to himself. "You sure do get into a lot of bad fights to say that prayer every time," he added.

"Yep. You're right. I've been in a lot of bad fights. That's a fact. But I've returned unharmed from every single one of them. Look, the pope gave this prayer to Emperor Charles when he was going into battle. It protects me in battle, protects me from drowning, keeps me from falling into the hands of the enemy, and protects me from fire, and you are flying with me today, so do you want to let me finish or not?" he asked.

Scotty Hill thought about it for a minute. "You've got a point," he said. "Go ahead, and I'll say mine too."

"O, Saint Joseph, whose protection is so great, so strong, so prompt before the throne of God, I place in you all my interests and desires. O, Saint Joseph, do assist me by your powerful intercession, and obtain for me from your divine Son all spiritual blessings, through Jesus Christ our Lord. So that, having engaged here below your heavenly power, I may offer my thanksgiving and homage to the most loving of Fathers. O, Saint Joseph, I never weary contemplating you, and Jesus asleep in your arms; I dare not approach while He reposes near your heart. Press Him in my name and kiss His fine head for me and ask Him to return the Kiss when I draw my dying breath. Saint Joseph, patron of departing souls— pray for me."[7]

When Folk asked Stradley to move his team to the Watapur they had already been on a mission with troops in contact [TIC] to the north. Their initial mission was in northern Kunar. It was supposed to be a mission to conduct reconnaissance around the outposts in that area, looking for enemy fighters, but after test-firing their weapons and entering the Kunar River Valley, they received an urgent text message in the cockpit: *Change of mission. OP Bari Ali is in contact. They are receiving small arms fire, sniper fire, and B-10. Move there now, and contact them inbound for a situation report.*

Stradley acknowledged the change of mission, and they flew their helicopters as fast as they could—ninety knots (approximately 104

mph). Due to the rising terrain they began climbing after passing FOB
Monti. Once they made contact with the men at OP Bari Ali they
asked them where the enemy was located. As previously mentioned,
it is extremely difficult to locate the enemy in the rocky, cavernous
Afghan terrain. Enemy fighters sneak undetected into fighting
positions that have been used for years, in this case many of the
same fighting positions they had used on May 1, when they over-
ran Bari Ali.

The crevasses in the rocks provide terrific protection and conceal-
ment. Once in position they lie down and wait until they are ready to
attack. One time I was fighting in the Watapur Valley, and one of the
ground soldiers told me he had found the frequency the enemy was
using to talk.

"You have their radio frequency?" I asked.

"Sure. My interpreter is listening to them and telling me what they
are saying," he replied. He had used a simple scanner to find their
frequency and listen to them.

"What's the frequency?" I asked him. It was a VHF frequency, which
I quickly dialed up in my Kiowa. I could hear them talking. It sent
chills up my spine, and a lump formed in my throat when I heard my
own rotors in the background as they spoke. They were directly under
me, in the rocks below, yet I could not see them. I had been flying
over them for hours. They were disciplined. They only took the shots
they wanted to take.

If signal intelligence was available, which was the case at Bari Ali
that day with Stradley's team, the enemy often provided good targeting information. They would check on each other, asking by name if
each fighter was still alive. Sometimes the fighter would answer by
saying that we had shot just below or above them, which was very
useful information.

The soldiers at Bari Ali told Stradley's team that the enemy
was higher up the ridge that day. The team ultimately shot all of
their ammunition, so they flew to FOB Bostic to get fuel and more
ammunition.

Determining if we killed or injured the enemy in the Afghan mountains reminded me of stories I'd read about hunting grizzly bears in
the western States. Even with a good blood trail you dare not follow

a wounded bear too closely into thick cover. Stradley's team, like all of our teams, wanted to know if they had been successful in killing the enemy, so after returning to Bari Ali they began carefully to look for bodies in the rocks. They didn't want to leave the men at Bari Ali, only to get called back because the fighters had crawled out of their holes and resumed their attack.

Stradley's team tried to remain outside of small-arms range and use the mast-mounted sight as much as possible. The sight gave them a day sensor and thermal capability, both of which could zoom in, but it was still very difficult. An enemy fighter, hidden in the rocks, with the discipline to remain perfectly still, was almost impossible to find. For Kiowa pilots, the best way to look was to move in closely. Like trailing the wounded bear, it was tempting but risky.

The team worked with the men at Bari Ali for another hour. While keeping their speed up they took a good look into every known and suspected enemy fighting position but didn't find anything. Finally, they decided to go to the FARP again, but this time they flew south to FOB Wright to get fuel. As they passed the entrance to the Pech Valley, Folk contacted them on the radio to fill them in on the ongoing situation in the Watapur. Stradley acknowledged and continued to FOB Wright.

After taking on a full tank of gas, rockets, and .50-caliber ammunition, the team departed to the north with a plan to return back to OP Bari Ali. Then, suddenly, Marzec and Cunningham's aircraft was hit.

"Pale 2-2, this is Pale 2-5, over," Folk called to Stradley.

"This is Pale 2-2, go."

"Roger, our lead aircraft has been hit. Charlie 9-3 is pinned down on the east side of the valley with three casualties. We need immediate relief-on-station."

"Roger, we're on our way," Stradley replied, almost giddy.

After a quick battle handover in which Folk passed the most current information about friendly and enemy forces to Stradley, SWT 1 departed the valley. They then called the Pale Horse command post to request that a maintenance team meet them at FOB Wright, so they could try and get their aircraft fixed and back in the fight.[8]

Mike McClain sat in the left seat of the lead aircraft in Stradley's team. It was Mike's responsibility to talk to the ground unit, in this case

Charlie 9-3, so while Stradley relayed information and coordinated with the higher headquarters, McClain contacted Charlie 9-3 and asked for a situation report.

Charlie 9-3 reported, "Pale 2-2, we are on the ridge to your twelve o'clock. Our position is marked by a VS-17 panel [large orange marking panel]. We have three men wounded. One has a gunshot wound to the abdomen, one is shot in the hip, and one of my men has a broken foot. Hawg is overhead. We are receiving accurate small-arms fire from the north, east, and west. Request you attack all locations beginning as close as you can to our location, over."[9]

McClain acknowledged the information and identified the VS-17 panel marking the patrol's location.

"Charlie 9-3, confirm that all of your men are within fifty meters of the VS-17 panel," McClain asked, to ensure that he knew exactly where everyone in the patrol was located before the Kiowas began shooting in close proximity to the men on the ground.

"Roger that," Charlie 9-3 confirmed.

With that, the team turned inbound and prepared to shoot where they thought the enemy was located. Then, suddenly, it felt as if every enemy weapon in the valley turned on the Kiowas and began shooting all at once. Bullets zinged by the aircraft, their *pop* breaking the squelch on the intercom system as they passed dangerously close. As bullets zinged by, Ryan Neal gripped the cyclic tight. Mike squinted his eyes and clenched his teeth as he prepared for Ryan to shoot. Ryan picked a spot and pressed down on the fire button with his thumb. Just thirty-six inches from Mike's head, .50-caliber rounds began to spew from the gun's barrel to the tune of nine hundred rounds per minute, sending a salvo of steel toward enemy fighters just a few hundred meters in front of Charlie 9-3 and his men. Just before he broke right, Ryan again used his thumb, this time to switch to rockets, and sent two 2.75-inch-high explosive rockets crashing into the mountainside. As he heard the *whoosh* of the rockets leaving the tubes on his side of the helicopter, he banked hard right, and Stradley went to work.

Stradley pressed the trigger on his gun, shooting the same location Ryan had shot. McClain told Hawg to use his sight to try and see if he could find any enemy fighters higher up on the ridge. Stradley knew they had to quickly find a suitable landing zone for the medevac. With three men wounded it would be impossible for Charlie 9-3 to move very far. They had to find a spot where the medevac could land close to their position. Ryan Neal flew the aircraft while McClain worked the radios. Ryan flew them right over Charlie 9-3 to try and find a spot. Suddenly, muzzle flashes erupted all over the ridge to their front.

"I think we're hit," Ryan said. He heard a distinct change in the sound of the rotors. He banked the aircraft and turned sharp, which caused the enemy to shift their focus to Stradley's aircraft. Stradley immediately received a high volume of fire, so he broke off the attack. He had found what he needed anyway—a potential LZ for the medevac. Hawg asked if McClain could mark the spot where he thought the enemy forces were located. Charlie 9-3 also needed them to mark the LZ so he would know where to try to move.

Ryan and McClain were out of smoke grenades, but Stradley and Hill had several with them, so the team executed a quick lead change. With Stradley and Hill now in the lead, they turned back inbound. Scotty Hill took a smoke grenade in his hand and pulled the pin. They flew directly over the LZ, and he dropped it out of the door. Stradley then shot a single rocket to the area where he thought enemy fighters were located. He banked hard right and called Hawg on the radio. "You're clear to drop," he told him, and within seconds Hawg dropped two bombs and followed the bombs up with two 30-mm gun runs, silencing the enemy, at least for a few minutes.

Stradley's team circled back around and prepared to shoot everything they had left to try and keep the enemy's heads down while Sergeant Ventura moved his patrol to the LZ. With McClain and Neal back in the lead they turned in for a gun run. A plume of dust and smoke extended like a mushroom cloud above the impact points of Hawg's bombs. Neal saw enemy fighters moving in the rocks. "I see them. I see them! Follow me in and shoot where I do!" he told Stradley as he flew directly at the enemy.

He fired at the fighters with his fifty-caliber and described to Stradley what he was seeing as he did it. Neal broke right and Stradley opened fire with his fifty-caliber. Hawg came over the radio and said he could see the enemy, who were shooting at Stradley. Stradley also saw them. He sprayed them with machine gun fire, but before Stradley broke off the engagement he and Hill felt a jolt in the helicopter, followed by a loud bang and the sudden rush of wind in the cockpit.

"Lead, this is trail. We're hit!" Stradley reported.

"You okay?" Neal asked.

"I think so. Everything is still working, and we're still flying," Stradley said with a nervous laugh.

"We're out of ammo," Neal reported on the internal team radio.

"We're not. I've got lead," Stradley said, in typical Stradley fashion. With wind blowing through the huge hole at Hill's feet, Stradley whipped the Kiowa around and flew straight back at the enemy. As Stradley engaged, Ventura's patrol took up fighting positions near the LZ.

After Stradley had shot every bullet he had, he contacted SWT 3, who was holding south of COP Honaker-Miracle and escorting the medevac helicopter. They had been waiting for Stradley to bring them into the valley. He gave them a thorough battle handover, then he flew back over Charlie 9-3's position one more time and marked the LZ again with a yellow smoke grenade so that SWT 3 and the medevac bird could clearly see it. With the battle handover complete, Stradley's team headed to FOB Wright to rearm, refuel, and assess the damage to their aircraft.

When Operation Mountain Fire began at Barg-e Matal, we positioned an Apache team and a medevac helicopter forward at FOB Bostic so that they could respond as quickly as possible should they be needed at Barg-e Matal—a daily occurrence. We rotated the crews in shifts. Dustoff 2-4, which was our medevac bird, had just finished its shift at FOB Bostic. It had already been a very busy night with missions to Barg-e Matal. They were returning to FOB Fenty for a down day when the medevac request for the wounded men in the Watapur came into the Pale Horse command post. The battle captain immediately diverted Dustoff 2-4 to the Watapur to conduct the mission. The crew consisted of Chief Warrant Officer 4 Brandon Erdmann, Chief Warrant Officer 2 Scott St. Aubin, Staff Sergeant Tom Gifford, and Staff Sergeant Emmett Spraktes. They entered the Pech just as SWT 3 was preparing to take control of the fight from Stradley's team.

SWT 3 was originally tasked to be the day quick-reaction force, but with Chuck Folk's assessment that the fight in the Watapur would be an all-day affair, it was clear that we needed to move them forward to enter into the battle.

SWT 3 consisted of Captain Brian Patterson and Chief Warrant Officer 2 Adam Stead, in flight lead. Stead was a graduate of North

Georgia College, my alma mater. He was commissioned as an infantry officer but later wanted to become a Kiowa Warrior pilot, so he applied for a branch transfer from infantry to aviation. His request was denied, so he resigned his commission and went to warrant officer candidate school, after which he attended flight school.

Adam had been married for less than a year when we deployed. He had met his wife, Carrie, through mutual friends. They were married in April 2008, Carrie became pregnant in October, and Adam deployed in December. For the birth of their son, Cohen, we had been able to time Adam's midtour leave perfectly. He arrived home on May 16 and Carrie's water broke that night. Adam got to spend two full weeks with his wife and son before returning to Afghanistan.

Adam Stead was an incredibly competent officer and pilot. He could have assumed command of a cavalry troop with ease. He was a quiet professional who was extremely mature and insanely fit. He had been selected to assess for a special mission unit in October, but, as we would later find out, that was not to be.

Flying trail in SWT 3 was Chief Warrant Officer 3 Henry Quiles, an outstanding maintenance test pilot, and Captain Tim Harloff. Tim was a gifted officer who served as the air mission commander of SWT 3.

As they flew north, up the Kunar, Harloff received a SATCOM (satellite communication) call from Pale Horse command post. "Fly to Asadabad and link up with Dustoff 2-4. They will be traveling south from Bostic. Escort them into the Watapur for a medevac mission in the valley," the battle captain directed.

Harloff linked up with Dustoff 2-4 and led them to the Watapur, where they held, waiting for Stradley to rotate them into the fight. They flew lazy circles south of Honaker-Miracle. Looking in from the mouth of the valley, in all of its enormity—a snowcapped massif in the back, rock wall ridges running for five miles on either side of a green strip of a valley—the Kiowa team, already in the valley, flew in mad circles like tiny yellow jackets in the distance. Smoke trails emanated from their rocket pods and terminated with dust clouds in the mountainside. From time to time a jet would dart in from high above—heaven sent. From a brilliant blue sky the A-10 Thunderbolt would dive down with fury, unleashing its ordnance, until it was no more than a few hundred feet above the narrow valley floor, then level off for just a split second before pitching straight back up and climbing vertically, disappearing into the heavens from which it came. Lagging several seconds behind, racing to catch up, came the deafening sound of its jet engines, concluding with the distinctive *GRRrrrrrrrrr* of its 20-mm cannon.

Then, once rearmed and refueled, the scout weapons team would swap out, putting a new team with a full load of gas and ammunition back into the fight while the other team raced back to the FARP for more gas and bullets. From that perspective, from afar, it was hard to imagine that a small group of men were sprawled behind rocks fighting for their lives. Back home, thousands of miles away from that place, their families watched television, read books, played video games, watched movies, and otherwise lived their lives, completely unaware that their father, brother, son, husband, lay in a valley battling to remain alive, praying to return home in one piece.

One of my son's high school teachers would later tell him that the war we were fighting was not really a "big war" like World War I or II. Compared holistically, I guess he was right, but I can't help wondering how his views on what counts as "big" or not might have changed had he been struggling to stay alive with Sergeant Ventura's men in the Watapur Valley on that hot July day in 2009.

Brian Patterson was responsible for the air-to-ground communication, so once Harloff received the battle handover from Stradley, Brian contacted the ground patrol for an update. Sergeant First Class Ventura answered the radio.

"We need a medevac now," Ventura said. "We can't control the bleeding. Dow is not stable!" he reported.

Patterson called Dustoff 2-4 and spoke with Erdmann. "Their patient is bleeding out, but the LZ is hot," he said.

As Patterson spoke, everyone on Dustoff 2-4 could hear the chaos, the *cack cack cack* of gunfire in the background. Erdmann told the medic, Staff Sergeant Emmett Spraktes, that he would most likely have to hoist in, so ultimately it was up to him. Spraktes felt the weight of the decision; he also felt a cold knot in his throat, a strange feeling. He was scared.

Emmett Spraktes was not your typical young army medic. Emmett was a forty-eight-year-old California National Guardsman who came to us as a part of C Company, 1-168th General Support Aviation

Battalion. He had served for ten years with the Navy Reserves in a Special Boat Unit before joining the California National Guard as a flight medic. In civilian life he was a paramedic with a SWAT team in the California Highway Patrol. Emmett Spraktes was a technical expert as a paramedic. Strong as an ox, he was in better physical shape than most soldiers half his age.

Numerous mornings I'd walk out of my room onto the flight line and hear the pounding of feet and the quick, short breaths of Emmett Spraktes coming up the long stretch from the medevac birds to the Apaches. With a pained grimace on his face and sweat popping off his body, he'd fly down the flight line to end a morning run.

Often there would be a victim in tow, some soldier half his age whom he'd convinced to run the 3.4-mile loop around Fenty with him. "We'll go easy," he'd assure them. "You can set the pace."

And then, when they were over halfway around the loop, and fully committed, he'd start cranking up the pace, hoping to hear that high-pitched grunt of pain. He fed off knowing that he still had it, that he could still make them hurt. "It builds character," he'd say.

He'd run just fast enough to push them to the redline, but allow them to stay right off his shoulder until they entered the flight line, and then he'd kick for all he was worth.

"Pride is a terrible thing," I'd tell him, laughing.

"I know, sir, but we've got to keep these young guys in their place."

Passionate and fearless, Emmett found himself filled with strange emotions when Brandon Erdmann asked if he wanted to hoist in the middle of the fight. He had never truly felt fear like that before.

Emmett loved God but did not practice religion. He felt that as an adult you should pray for others, certainly not for yourself. To Emmett that was a selfish thing to do. He had uttered brief prayers here and there as he had worked on wounded soldiers, but they weren't really for him. He had asked God to help guide him to help others, but he had never really prayed for himself.

"Ask them if there's a place to land," he told Erdmann.

After a short pause the answer came, "No, it has to be a hoist," and Emmett Spraktes prayed. He asked God to help them find a place to land. He didn't want to hoist into the jaws of hell. The air was filled with bullets, and despite how much he didn't want to admit it to himself, there was no other way to explain it: he knew he was going to die on the cable, and he was not ready to die. The whole idea made him sick. He felt nauseated. He wanted to throw up.

"Well, Emmett, what do you think?" Erdmann asked again.

"Let's do it!"[10]

The Lord didn't provide an LZ that hot July day; He sent Kiowas instead. Emmett gained confidence as he listened to Tim Harloff orchestrate the fight, pounding the enemy with his own Kiowa team and directing Hawg where to conduct gun runs and drop bombs. He knew everything flying in that valley was going to unleash its fury on the enemy as he hoisted in.

Spraktes attached himself to the cable and began to lean out of the door. A thousand things were going through his mind. He could hear the horrendous amount of machine gun fire in the valley below, and he was certain, at that point, he would not live through this. He thought about his daughter, then his mind flashed to medical protocols, only to be interrupted by the sound of gunfire over the deafening rotors. Emmett Spraktes had been in tough spots before. He had been under fire many times, but at that time, in that valley, it took everything he had to focus on what he had to do, what he must do.

Gifford manned the hoist. Erdmann turned the helicopter toward the plume of yellow smoke marking the spot to which he was to deliver Spraktes. The Kiowas made two gun runs, then circled around and picked up Dustoff 2-4. With a Kiowa Warrior on either side they headed for the yellow smoke, and Spraktes began to descend below the helicopter on a wire the size of his pinky. Gifford watched Spraktes closely as he lowered him, calling his height above the ground over the headset to Erdmann, who flew the helicopter. Bullets flew all around them from the ridge to the east. Just prior to the LZ they slowed. For the first time Spraktes saw the men he was going to save. They were fighting but stopped and looked up to see him riding a cable into the fury. He saw their faces. Thirty feet to go and the cable stopped. He bounced a bit and just hung there.

"Several seconds went by and I thought Gifford must have been hit. I imagined that Gifford was up there on the deck of the bird with a big hole in him, his life leaking out of him. Shit! With all of the bullets striking the ground, the wall of the ravine looked like a range with a line of soldiers shooting all they had into the dirt,"[11] Spraktes recalled. Finally, he couldn't stand it any longer. He screamed into his radio, "Get me on the ground now! I'm like a freaking piñata down here!"[12]

Suddenly the descent continued, and he hit the ground hard. Dazed, he unhooked the cable and looked around to see all eyes on him. *They are bewildered at how I made it to the ground alive,* Spraktes thought, and that made him smile. He wondered the same thing: *How did I make it to the ground alive?*

Men were crammed into tiny cracks between small rocks trying to get any protection they could from the continuous fire from above. He asked who needed help, and they pointed to Dow. Emmett sprinted over to Joshua Dow just as a Kiowa flew over them and opened up on the ridge. Fifty-caliber casings rained down on them, making a tinkling sound as the expended rounds bounced off rocks.

Spraktes placed himself between the enemy fire and Dow while administering treatment to control the bleeding. Like heavy raindrops falling on calm water, dirt flew up all around Spraktes as he prepared Dow for extraction. Suddenly, Sergeant First Class Ventura called out to Spraktes, "I know you!"

"What's your name?" Spraktes yelled back.

"Ventura."

"I know you!" Spraktes yelled back over the sound of the Kiowas engaging the enemy right over their heads. Spraktes had medevaced Ventura himself on a previous mission.

"I was both relieved to see that Ventura was okay, but also pissed that I knew someone in that shit-storm," Spraktes said.[13]

"This ain't like our last one, is it?" Spraktes yelled to Ventura. Both men smiled at each other and went back to work.

RPGs exploded between each helicopter gun run. Spraktes realized that he couldn't do much for Dow in that environment. Dow needed a surgeon, so Emmett stabilized him, strapped him to a litter, and called Erdmann in for the pickup. It would be a dangerous hoist, not only for the patient but also for Spraktes, who would have to expose himself while holding the tagline in order to reduce oscillation and spinning as Dow was winched up into the helicopter.

Gifford would lower the cable to the ground. Spraktes would attach Dow to the cable and hold on to a tagline as Gifford pulled Dow up to the helicopter using the hoist. Erdmann had to hold the helicopter steady, under enemy gunfire, while Gifford and Spraktes worked to get Dow into the medevac. The vulnerable helicopter, and Dow, would become a lucrative target. Erdmann acknowledged that Spraktes was ready, but Harloff's team was on a gun run. The fighting was too intense for Erdmann to come in at that moment. They'd have to wait.

Back at the FARP, Stradley's team shut down to inspect their helicopters. Chuck Folk's team, SWT 1, stood around discussing the fight. Due to the damage to Marzec's aircraft they were out of the fight. McClain and Neal examined their Kiowa closely but could not find any damage. Stradley and Hill's left side chin bubble was shot completely out, but the bullet did not appear to have damaged any important systems. The only issue would be the difficulty communicating with the rushing wind blowing through the chin bubble, between Hill's feet, and into the cockpit. Recognizing the dire situation on the ground they decided to rearm, refuel, and get back into the fight.

Stradley checked with Neal. "You good to go?" he asked.

"Yeah, we're good," Neal replied. "You gonna fly it with no chin bubble?" he asked with a cheesy smile on his face.

"Yeah, we're good. Let's get back in the fight. I'll meet you on the radio," Stradley said, and walked off toward his helicopter.

Ryan Neal, the little, tattooed man from the mountains of western Maine, took the last long drag of a Marlboro, flicked what was left into a butt can, and blew smoke out the side of his mouth as he turned and walked toward his own helicopter. Ryan Neal was one of those lucky few who get to see their childhood dreams come to fruition. He had always been fascinated with flight. As a child he'd lie in bed and stare at posters of airplanes taped to his bedroom walls. He'd stand under the stars at night and watch blinking lights cross the Maine sky. They were specks on a tapestry of black. They seemed so far away, so distant, like his dream, but that didn't stop him from dreaming about what it would be like up there in the cockpit, flying to some exotic destination. When asked the age-old question, what do you want to be when you grow up? he never faltered. The answer was always emphatically "a pilot." He recorded every episode of the hit TV show *Wings,* and watched them over and over until the VCR tape finally gave out. It was a pretty lofty goal for a kid who grew up in an old farmhouse in rural Maine, who spent his days fishing in creeks, hiking in the mountains, swimming in the Sandy River, and tending a farm full of chickens, pigs, and turkeys, but he was an American and becoming a pilot was his dream.

By the time Ryan was a senior in high school he had decided he wanted to fly the Apache helicopter instead of jets. He chose to write his final high school English paper on the Apache. His research led him to discover the army warrant officer program. He decided that would be the quickest way to fulfill his dream, to get into a cockpit. He visited the local army recruiter and explained what he wanted to do. The recruiter told him that the easiest way to get his foot in the door was to enlist as a Black Hawk crew chief, then apply for the warrant officer flight program. Ryan jumped at the opportunity.

Following basic and advanced individual training, Ryan was assigned to Aviano, Italy, and soon thereafter he deployed to Iraq. As a Black Hawk crew member Ryan spent over one thousand hours crewing in the back of the helicopter, but he still wanted to become a pilot. While in Iraq he saw the Kiowa Warriors out conducting reconnaissance and security missions. He was drawn to the cavalry mission, so while he was deployed he submitted his warrant officer application. Ryan Neal's dream came true. He was selected for the program. He traveled to Fort Rucker, Alabama, where he completed warrant officer candidate school and flight school, and received his aircraft of choice, the Kiowa Warrior. In 2006, Ryan was assigned to 7th Squadron, 17th Cavalry Regiment at Fort Campbell, Kentucky, and we were lucky to have him.

Ryan's childhood dream seemed a lifetime ago, a distant memory. He'd had so many experiences in such a short period of time. The little boy who once stood in awe watching jets paint the blue Maine sky with streaks of white pulled in power and departed FOB Wright. He led his flight back to the Watapur, where the enemy awaited them, not knowing if this would be just another hairy flight or perhaps his last flight.

As they entered the Pech River Valley, a team of Apaches—call sign "Overdrive"—arrived to join in the fight. The air mission commander of the Apaches was Chief Warrant Officer 5 John Jones, a maintenance examiner assigned to our aviation support battalion who flew with TF Eagle Lift out of Bagram. John had flown with our task force on numerous missions. He was not only a great maintenance test pilot but also a first-rate tactical pilot.

Stradley gave Jones his team-internal radio frequency and told him to fly his team at seven thousand feet and above. He told him that he would keep the Kiowas at five thousand feet and below. That would provide separation and keep them safe in the airspace. The last thing we needed was a midair collision. He told Dustoff 2-4 to tune to their FM radio to his team frequency as well, making it a common frequency for all helicopters operating in the valley.

Stradley called Harloff and conducted a battle handover. He told Harloff to fly west and circle around them on the way out. With Private Dow now ready for hoist, Stradley's Kiowa team and the Apaches escorted Dustoff 2-4 back into the valley for the extraction.

Staff Sergeant Gifford lowered the cable as Erdmann flew inbound. As they slowed for the hookup, muzzle flashes erupted all over the ridgeline in front of them. Neal began engaging while Stradley identified targets for Overdrive to shoot.

"I've got muzzle flashes, two o'clock, and four hundred meters by that dark boulder!" Stradley reported.

"Tally [code word meaning target is visually sighted], engaging with thirty-millimeter," replied Overdrive.

A young redheaded soldier, Sergeant Jensen, helped Spraktes prepare Dow for the hoist. Spraktes told Jensen not to touch the cable before it hit the ground: "It will shock the piss out of you if you grab it," he screamed over the deafening sounds of the battle.

Nevertheless, when the cable was about head high, Sergeant Jensen reached up and grabbed it—static electricity shot through his body like a lightning bolt, but amazingly he held on. He did it for his buddy. He just wanted to get Dow out of trouble—to save him. Spraktes admired Jensen, he understood him.

Spraktes hooked Dow up to the cable and told Gifford to hoist him up at full speed. At full speed the tagline rope would rip through Spraktes's gloved hands. It was certain to burn them, leave blisters, but it was the best bet at getting Dow out safely. Bullets filled the air as Dow ascended. Spraktes screamed out in pain as the tagline ripped through his hands, but Dow made it to the helicopter without getting hit. As Dow neared the helicopter, Gifford reached out and grabbed him. He spun the Skedco around and pulled him into the helicopter.

With Dow safely on board, Erdmann banked hard left and sped out of the area. Erdmann flew as fast as he could to FOB Wright while Spraktes, remaining on the ground, went to work treating Private Casas and Staff Sergeant Wedemeyer. Meanwhile, SWT 2 and Overdrive engaged a seemingly endless number of enemy fighters who were inching closer and closer to the friendly position.

As Dustoff landed at FOB Wright, soldiers from the Forward Surgical Team (FST) swarmed the aircraft to offload Joshua Dow and begin critical care. The team bent over at the waist as they carried Dow clear of the medevac rotors, and Erdmann took off, headed back to the Watapur.

"Pale, Dustoff 2-4, over," Erdmann called Stradley.

"Send it," Stradley answered.

"Spraktes is ready with the next two patients. We are going to try and hoist all three of them out together," said Erdmann.

"Roger, we'll cover you. Overdrive, did you monitor?" Stradley asked, seeking confirmation that the Apaches were ready to suppress the enemy, as the medevac went in as well.

"Roger," replied Overdrive.

Erdmann told Spraktes that he wanted him to come out with the two patients. That struck Spraktes as strange. It was too much weight, but he assumed that Erdmann knew something he didn't. "I thought maybe the enemy was right on top of us,"[14] Spraktes later recalled. In truth Erdmann didn't want to have to risk another hoist. He wanted to get everyone out in one last hoist.

Again, Gifford lowered the cable so that it would be at ground level as they came to a hover. Spraktes was ready for the cable when it arrived. He quickly began attaching himself and both wounded men to the cable.

"I've got three enemy fighters running down the hill toward us and shooting. They are on a thirty-five-degree azimuth from my location. Can you get those guys?" Erdmann asked with a bit of urgency in his voice.

They were sitting ducks while they hovered, and it seemed that every enemy fighter in the valley was trying to shoot them down. Ryan Neal banked his Kiowa hard and took his team between the medevac and the enemy fighters. As soon as he passed the medevac, he began shooting rockets and .50-caliber. Scott St. Aubin saw the rounds impact right on the enemy. "I don't know who that was, but that's the spot," he radioed.

Staff Sergeant Gifford turned the hoist on and began to pull Spraktes and the two wounded men up, but the hoist stalled with the three men dangling about twenty-five feet off the ground. "It's stuck," Gifford told Erdmann over the radio. "We're going to have to lower them back down," he added.

For just a second Erdmann considered flying them out, hanging from the cable, and trying to sit them down at COP Honaker-Miracle, but it was just too risky. There were three of them on the cable; if it broke they would plummet to their deaths.

You've got to be kidding. Come on! Spraktes thought, once again finding himself dangling twenty-five feet above the ground with bad guys shooting at him. Twice in one hour! What are the odds? If a round hits us I wonder if it will go through all three of us? At least I won't die alone,[15] he thought.

"Lower 'em down now!" Erdmann said.

The entire time he was on the cable, Spraktes was using his rifle to shoot at enemy fighters moving toward them in the rocks. Suddenly he saw a bright flash in the rocks directly in front of him. An RPG passed just meters away.

"Shit, shit, shit," Spraktes said, knowing that if they didn't get out of the valley quickly either the men on the cable, the medevac helo itself, or both were going to be shot.

They were descending, but it wasn't fast enough for their liking. Finally, Spraktes's feet landed on solid ground, and he frantically unhooked himself from the cable. He then told Gifford to hoist the two soldiers back up. As soon as they were off the ground Spraktes emptied a magazine of ammunition into the area where the enemy were to try and get their heads down as Erdmann flew away. He wasn't waiting to get shot down. Gifford hoisted them up as they flew out of the valley.

At that moment, the complexity of the situation increased even more, if such a thing was possible. Hawg called Stradley on the radio and said that he had seen the enemy fighters who were continuously shooting at Stradley's Kiowa. He wanted to drop his bombs, but his wingman was running low on fuel, so they needed to drop the bombs right away. Captain Conlin at COP Honaker-Miracle called Stradley as well. He said that he was currently watching four enemy fighters with weapons at the mouth of the valley. He could see them through his TOW missile system sight and wanted to shoot them with the missile.

TOW stands for "tube-launched, optically tracked, wire-guided missile." The TOW has a range of approximately 3,750 meters and was designed as an anti-tank weapon, but it is very effective on hardened fighting positions such as the huge boulders in the Watapur.

Dustoff 2-4 had flown back to the mouth of the Watapur, just southwest of Honaker-Miracle. They were flying circles as they waited for Stradley to bring them back in to pick up Spraktes.

Just then Spraktes broke in on the radio.

"I've got two heat casualties down here. They won't be able to walk out. We need to hoist them out too."

"You saying we need to hoist two more out?" Erdmann asked, to make sure he understood.

"Roger that," Spraktes replied, knowing what he was asking them to do.

As the on-scene commander, Stradley took control of the situation. "Honaker-Miracle, you've got one minute to shoot that TOW missile. Break. Charlie 9-3, pop smoke in front of your location. Hawg, when you see the smoke, let me know. Once you see the smoke and know exactly where they are you can drop your bombs," he directed.

Seconds later Captain Conlin from Honaker-Miracle called, "Pale Horse, this is Honaker-Miracle, engagement complete. Four enemy fighters are no longer visible, over."

"Roger, break. Hawg, do you see the smoke Charlie 9-3 threw?" asked Stradley.

"Roger, eyes on smoke and bombs will not be a danger close to their location," confirmed Hawg.

"Okay, drop 'em," Stradley replied.

Hawg's bombs impacted with a huge explosion. Everyone in the valley felt the shockwave as it rippled across the valley. Stradley then told Dustoff to come in for the next hoist. As flight lead, Ryan Neal led the Kiowas to the mouth of the valley to meet Dustoff, and they flew inbound. John Jones and his team of Apaches traveled in with them as well. As they neared the LZ, all four aircraft lit up the ridge with suppressive fires. Thirty-millimeter, .50-caliber, and 2.75-inch rockets exploded off of rocks as they tried to force the enemy to seek cover.

Spraktes had begun to form up the remaining troops to break contact and get out of the valley. He wasn't trying to take over the patrol, but the men were clearly battle-weary and he knew they had to move soon. What he hadn't noticed was that a couple of the men were barely able to move at all. Did they get hit and I didn't notice? he wondered. He quickly evaluated them and that's when he realized that they were severely dehydrated. They began to dry-heave. They needed fluids, and they needed to cool off, but Spraktes did not want to have them remove their body armor. He thought about IVs, but decided that they would not stay in while the men continued to fight. Spraktes called Erdmann, and told him to fly to COP Honaker-Miracle to pick up water.

"Bring it on the next pass," he said.

Chief Warrant Officer 2 Scott St. Aubin, Erdmann's copilot, called the command post at Honaker-Miracle and told Captain Shaun Conlin that he needed a case of water. Conlin was the Charlie Company commander. He had used the LRT1 camera system at the COP to watch in awe as Spraktes hoisted in to help his men. He told several of his soldiers to take water out to the helicopter. Tom Gifford loaded it up and they returned to the Watapur for a low pass during which Gifford kicked the water out, along with the jungle penetrator, which would allow them to extract two or more men at a time. Emmett Spraktes ran through a hail of bullets to recover the water. He then scavenged for the bottles, which flew in all directions upon impact with the ground, and started throwing them to the soldiers.

With the water distributed to the men, Spraktes prepared the two heat casualties for the hoist. He then called Erdmann, and let him know he was ready for pickup. It seemed to take forever so he poured water on the men and tried to encourage them. He made them take small sips of water as they fought. Once again, Dustoff 2-4 came in under intense fire for the pickup. Spraktes and the remaining patrol provided cover fire as the two heat casualties were hoisted out. Spraktes worried that they would get hit on the way up, but they made it out clean.

Brandon Erdmann radioed Spraktes, "We're coming to get you."

"No. I'm walking out with these guys. I'm in good company." Spraktes did not want to leave the patrol.

"They were down five men and most of them were the age of my eldest son, William. I could see William in every one of them. I thought those boys needed me," he later told me.

"No, we're coming back to get you. We need you on board to treat these patients," Erdmann ordered.

"Hell, I can walk out with my new friends. Why risk a Black Hawk and a medevac crew?" he asked Erdmann.

"Medevac is no good without a medic," Erdmann answered. "We're coming to get you."

Once Gifford had the two heat casualties inside the helicopter Erdmann circled back around and headed back to pick up Spraktes. One final time the cable lowered. Spraktes attached himself to the cable and they began to reel him in. As Spraktes ascended he looked at the men below. They stared up at him, and he felt horrible, like he was abandoning them. He was almost ashamed to leave them, knowing that they still had to walk out of the valley. His mission was complete, he had done what he was supposed to do, but nothing about it felt good at that moment. On the way up he raised his rifle and shot several bursts into the rocks around the enemy. He felt anger—rage. Go ahead and shoot at me, he thought. Leave these boys alone.

Gifford pulled Spraktes into the Black Hawk and they flew out of the Watapur for good.[16]

Stradley's Kiowa team was out of ammunition, and Tim Harloff's team was holding at the mouth of the valley, ready to get back into the fight. Stradley gave Harloff a good battle handover, telling him exactly where Sergeant First Class Ventura's men were located and where they had shot at the enemy. After he had passed all of the information that he thought was important, and was confident that Harloff fully understood the situation, Stradley's team departed for the FARP with adrenaline still pumping through their veins.

With team after team joining the fight, the FARP had become very crowded. One of the ground units at FOB Wright had moved a large steel container onto one of the landing pads. Marzec's damaged Kiowa was shut down, still awaiting a maintenance team. Dustoff was headed to the center pad to drop off patients. Stradley's team needed to rearm and fuel up, so they squeezed in and waited for the fuelers and armament personnel.

Ryan Neal took a deep breath and began to relax for the first time that day. He actually wanted to smoke a cigarette. He was thinking about getting out when he looked over at Stradley's helicopter to find Stradley waving madly at the FARP personnel to get out of the way. He was out of the aircraft and running toward them, screaming. Ryan had no idea what could be wrong. Once the FARP soldiers were out of the way, Stradley ran back to his aircraft, and flew off without buckling up and with his armor side panels flapping in the wind. Ryan then heard someone on the radio telling everyone to clear out of the way.

Chief Warrant Officer 5 John Jones was rapidly approaching the pad Stradley had been occupying. He literally missed Stradley and Hill's Kiowa by a few yards. He hit the pad hard, bounced a little, then settled. He immediately shut the helicopter down. Meanwhile Stradley flew in a circle, then landed at another spot and ran over to the Apache, red-faced and screaming.

"You said stay put! You almost killed us all!" Stradley screamed. "Had I stayed put you'd have crashed on top of us!"

Jones, heart racing and almost in tears, said, "Thank you for moving. I couldn't see you, and I had no hydraulics. *You* saved us all," and with that he wrapped his arms around Stradley and gave him a big bear hug.

After Stradley's team had left the valley for the FARP, Jones's team had continued to fight, but on a gun run they were hit by the DShK that took Chad Marzec out of the fight earlier in the morning. Jones's hydraulics had been shot out. It was all he could do to limp the Apache back to FOB Wright, but he had to get it on the ground quickly.

As he made the turn from the Pech River Valley out into the Kunar, Jones could see the FARP and thought he saw an open pad. He transmitted over the radio for everyone to stay put because he had an emergency, and he was coming in. Stradley had heard that over the radio, so he got out and told everyone to get out of the way so Jones could put it down; however, as Jones got closer Stradley realized that he was headed for the pad Stradley was parked on. He sprinted to his Kiowa and took off right as Jones plopped down where he had been parked. In reality Jones did not see Stradley's helicopter sitting there.

Stradley smiled and hugged Jones back. "That was scarier than the fight," Stradley said with a chuckle.

After refueling, and a couple Marlboros for Ryan Neal, Stradley's team took off again, intent on returning to the fight, but before they rounded the turn to head back into the Pech they received a call on the radio. We had sent a fourth scout weapons team to the Watapur to join the fight. We also sent a Black Hawk with them. We told the new Kiowa team to begin rotating into the fight, and told Stradley to escort the Black Hawk up north to FOB Bostic, so they could pick up the Apache maintenance team and fly them back to FOB Wright in order to work on the damaged Apache. Reluctantly, Stradley told Ryan Neal to lead the way to Bostic.

Sergeant First Class Ventura's patrol was still in desperate need of help. They had been fighting for hours in the sweltering July heat. Five of their men had been evacuated, and they were running low on ammunition and water. Jack Murphy had been in contact with TF Lethal, 3rd Platoon's battalion headquarters, discussing options for how to reinforce them for over an hour. We had a Black Hawk that had originally accompanied the medevac aircraft to FOB Wright. It had been loitering most of the day at the mouth of the Pech, monitoring the fight.

"We can use that Black Hawk to fly in reinforcements," Jack told TF Lethal's command post. They agreed and began preparing men to fly into the valley.

Captain Joe McCarthy was the pilot in command of the Black Hawk, a second-generation Italian American. Joe's parents had migrated to the coal mines of Pennsylvania. They later moved to New Jersey, where Joe was born and raised. A natural athlete, he grew up with dreams of playing Major League Baseball. Joe attended Rutgers University, where he received a degree in criminal justice. On September 11, 2001, Joe had been working as a police officer and substitute teacher as he prepared to begin law school at Rutgers the following semester. After watching the events of 9/11 unfold, Joe drove to the army recruiting office and signed an enlistment contract to become an airborne ranger.

When he reported to begin his army life, the sergeant reviewing his records told Joe that he met all the qualifications to go to officer candidate school. He instructed Joe to fill out the paperwork, and within months a board convened and selected him to become an officer. Joe first went to Fort Sill, Oklahoma, for basic training, where he became the honor graduate of his class. He then traveled to Fort Benning, Georgia, for officer candidate school, where once again he was named honor graduate of his class. He was commissioned a second lieutenant in the infantry and given orders for his first duty assignment at Schofield Barracks, Hawaii. In very short order Joe was assigned as an infantry platoon leader and deployed to Zabul Province in Afghanistan, where he worked mostly in the Arghandab, Shinkay, and Atghar districts.

While on that deployment Joe kept in regular contact with a friend who was also deployed, as an army helicopter pilot. He told Joe about the branch transfer program, for which Joe decided to apply. Joe was selected to attend flight school with a follow-on assignment to the 101st Airborne Division at Fort Campbell, Kentucky.

I had been serving as the deputy brigade commander when Joe first arrived to our unit. He impressed me from the start. Colonel Lewis selected him to serve as the brigade headquarters and headquarters company commander initially, but just prior to our deployment he moved to TF Pale Horse, where he assumed command of Black Widow Company, which included all of our Black Hawk and Chinook helicopters.

Joe was a guy who had to invest a lot of energy in holding still. He wasn't the guy who crossed his legs, sat back, and enjoyed a lazy conversation; instead, Joe McCarthy rubbed his hands together as he spoke, even got up and sat back down frequently. He didn't mind hanging out and shooting the crap with you, but he'd rather throw darts while he did it. What you got from Joe McCarthy was the unvarnished, God's honest truth. I didn't always agree with Joe's take on things, but I knew he would never tell me what he thought I wanted to hear. He told me the truth as he saw it, and that wasn't the most common trait in a junior officer. Confident, fit, charismatic, and smart, Joe was a natural leader—he was exceptional.

He quickly progressed as a pilot and by July 2009 became a pilot in command. His infantry service in Afghanistan helped him to understand the needs of the infantry on the ground. Now, it was up to him to fly to FOB Blessing, deep in the Pech, pick up a ten-man infantry squad and speedball resupply, then fly them into hell to reinforce Sergeant Ventura and his men. Joe's crew included Chief Warrant Officer 2 Ray Andrel, Specialist Chuck Darbyshire, and Specialist Travis Adkins.

Joe had anticipated the need for a speedball resupply much earlier in the day, so he had told the men at FOB Wright to prepare one and have it ready when needed. They packed two body bags full of ammunition and water. Joe and his crew landed and the crew chiefs loaded the speedballs into the aircraft. Joe got out of the helicopter and ran into the command post at Wright to call Jack Murphy. Jack had already coordinated with TF Lethal, so he told Joe to fly to FOB Blessing and pick up an infantry squad.

While John Jones's Apache was shot up and unable to reenter the fight, his wingman had cycled through the FARP and was standing by, ready to get back into the fight. Jack told Joe to get with John Jones's wingman and have him escort Joe to Blessing, then into the Watapur. Jack gave Joe a grid for an LZ close to Sergeant Ventura's men that he thought might work. It would be close to the enemy, but there were not a lot of good options on the side of the ridge.

They decided to shoot artillery as they went in to try and keep the enemy's head down while Joe landed. Jack called TF Lethal and arranged for the 105-mm howitzers to prepare to shoot the planned spots in the Watapur when he called for it. He wanted them to fire "at his command," which meant that the guns would be loaded and aimed at the target. All Jack had to do was give the command to fire, and the artillerymen would pull the lanyards on the guns.

Simultaneously, Hawg would drop bombs on the locations where they thought the DShK was located. If timed perfectly the artillery and bombs would impact right in front of Joe McCarthy as he flew inbound, keeping the enemy's heads down. With speedballs loaded and a plan in place, Joe headed for Blessing.

Throughout the battle the air mission commanders had been shooting mortars from COP Honaker-Miracle, 155-mm howitzers from FOB Wright, and 105-mm howitzers from FOB Blessing. By July our air mission commanders had become very skilled at orchestrating Apaches, Kiowas, jets, artillery, and mortars into the fight simultaneously. In a fight such as the one raging in the Watapur you could not sequence fires. We kept the Kiowas low, flying underneath the gun target lines. The key was to be able to visualize multiple gun target lines—the path the artillery or mortar rounds would travel from the gun itself to the target where it would impact—so that you knew where you could fly the Apaches and jets in order to laterally offset them.

For Joe McCarthy's mission the 105's would be loaded and ready to fire from FOB Blessing. Once Joe had the reinforcement squad on his aircraft he would take off from Blessing and give the command to begin firing the howitzers. They would continue firing until he was two minutes out from landing, at which time he would call, "Cease fire," and they would stop. The idea was to force the enemy to crawl down into the rocks to seek cover, thus giving Joe a chance to get in without getting shot down.

Joe landed at FOB Blessing, and the infantry squad began loading the aircraft. The helicopter was on the ground less than a minute before the enemy responded. A mortar impacted about thirty meters off the nose of Joe's helicopter. The explosion shook everyone, but they did not detect any damage to the helicopter—miraculously.

"Get these guys on the helicopter!" Joe told Specialist Darbyshire.

"We're ready, sir," Darbyshire reported, and they took off down the Pech.

"Pale Horse TOC, Flawless 7-7, over," Joe called.

"Flawless 7-7, Pale Horse TOC, over," the radio operator replied.

"Fire the artillery, over."

"Roger," the operator replied.

Jack Murphy, who was standing by the radio operator, listened to the calls. He picked up the phone and called his counterpart at TF Lethal. "Fire!" he said.

The 105's at FOB Blessing went to work firing shell after shell up over the ridge that sat between them and the Watapur. Joe and his copilot, Ray Andrel, had agreed that Ray would fly while Joe coordinated everything on the radios.

Joe contacted Tim Harloff, whose Kiowa team was still in the Watapur at that time. Joe had already briefed Tim on the plan, so he moved his team back to the mouth of the valley to pick them up and escort them directly into the LZ. There was a very real chance that everything could go dreadfully wrong, but with the patrol pinned down and running out of ammo it was a risk everyone agreed must be taken. Specialist Darbyshire spoke over the internal radio system, "Sir, there is no way we cannot help these guys out,"[17] meaning they had to go in and risk it.

It was obvious at that point that they were committed. They were going into the fight, and they were going to land right in front of the enemy, but hearing his young crew chief say it, and acknowledge that it was the right thing to do, made Joe very proud of his team. Having been on the receiving end of aviation support as an infantryman in combat, Joe knew that army aviators risked a great deal to help their brothers on the ground, but it was a different experience now being a part of that conversation as an aviator.

As they flew down the Pech River Valley, Joe called Jack over the radio.

"Pale Horse 3, this is Flawless 7-7. Cease fire, over," he said.

"Flawless 7-7, Pale Horse 3. Roger, cease fire," Jack repeated, and called TF Lethal with the command. The artillery stopped shooting. They were two minutes out.

Ray Andrel was flying the helicopter. Charlie 9-3 marked the LZ with a smoke grenade. Ray and Joe immediately saw the billowing green smoke.

"I see the LZ," Ray said.

Suddenly, there was a flash on the ridge adjacent to them. An explosion erupted, and shock waves pierced the air in the valley. Hawg had dropped a bomb on the suspected DShK location. It was planned but still seemed to catch everyone by surprise. As they neared the LZ, Ray got a good look at where they were supposed to land.

"That LZ isn't suitable," Ray said. "It's no good. I can't get in there," he said.

The entire crew began searching frantically for a spot to land. Machine gun rounds began to impact all around the helicopter and Sergeant First Class Ventura's men. The enemy had climbed back out of their holes.

Tim Harloff came flying in, shooting the ridge with fifty-caliber. What may have been a few seconds seemed like minutes for the crew as they searched for a place to land the helicopter. Suddenly, Joe saw a spot. He took the controls from Ray and headed for it.

"I see a spot. It's going to be a one-wheel landing, but I can get it in there," he told the crew.

The infantrymen in the back, call sign "Gator 9-2," felt like sitting ducks in the back of the helicopter, which had, by this time, become the sole attention of the enemy gunfire. The enemy began chattering on their radios, "Shoot the helicopter. Shoot the helicopter!" But every time they tried to engage the Black Hawk, Harloff's Kiowa team came in with fifty-calibers and rockets.

Joe touched the left wheel down and held it steady. The squad bailed out of the helicopter, then Darbyshire and Adkins pushed the speed-balls out behind them.

"Clear!" Darbyshire announced over the radio, and Joe pulled in power and headed south.[18]

It was midafternoon. The battle had been raging for hours with very few pauses. With Gator 9-2 now on the ground, the battle slowed a bit. They distributed the ammo and water from the speedball.

The fourth Kiowa team that we had sent up to join the fight had waited for Joe to get the reinforcements on the ground. They then conducted a battle handover with Tim Harloff's team. With a fresh Kiowa team covering their movement, it was time to walk out of the Watapur Valley. Gator 9-2, along with Sergeant First Class Ventura and his men, received sporadic small-arms fire most of the way out of the valley. Rounds hit the dirt around them, they dove for cover, the Kiowas engaged the enemy, Hawg continued to drop bombs, and the Kiowas called for artillery. When the enemy stopped shooting to find cover, they'd move, until the sequence of events began all over again.

At 5:30 P.M., Charlie 9-3 and Gator 9-2 walked back into the gates at FOB Honaker-Miracle. They had first taken fire from the enemy at 9:00 A.M. They had been in Afghanistan less than a month, and for most of them, July 17 had been the longest day of their lives.

The TF Lethal and Pale Horse fight in the Watapur solidified a bond of trust between our two task forces, a trust that would endure throughout the rest of the deployment. Brian Pearl called me that night and asked what awards I planned to submit for my men. I told him I wasn't sure yet, but I was thinking air medals for valor for several of the crews, and something significant for Staff Sergeant Emmett Spraktes.

"Silver Star," he said. "And I'm putting him in for it."

"I'll do it, Brian. You've got a lot going on," I said.

"Absolutely not. He put his life on the line for my men time and time again. I am submitting it," he declared.

"Brian," I said.

"Yes, Jimmy," he replied.

"Before your boys walk into the Watapur again, please call me first," I said.

"I will," he assured me—and he did.

For over eight hours a life-and-death battle had raged against the most picturesque backdrop conceivable. When the sun rose on the Watapur that morning it had been peaceful and quiet, stunningly beautiful, then it had abruptly become hateful and ugly, terrifying. As the sun set, the only evidence of the battle was the bloodstains on the rocks, and the memories etched into our minds. I wonder if they will fade. I suppose only time will tell.

That night an exhausted group of cavalrymen sat back and took a deep breath after a long day of fighting. The Apache and medevac guys climbed up on their balcony and smoked cigars as they compared stories and laughed at each other. The Kiowa guys sat back in chairs and laughed at John Jones almost crash-landing on Stradley at the FARP.

Ryan Neal wore a T-shirt, shorts, and shower shoes. Tattoos cover almost all of his exposed skin. Ryan had added ink to his body in Italy, Greece, Florida, Kentucky, and even his buddy's basement in Maine—an event that did not impress his mother. He told a story about a small plane almost crashing on him when he was just a little boy. He'd been scared that an airplane might crash on him ever since. Maybe Jones was actually headed for him at the FARP, but Stradley had gotten in the way.

Adrenaline-raged days like the one we experienced on July 17 almost always ended in laughing and stories, men coming together to talk and tell their version of what had happened, but that was because everyone had survived. In contrast, when someone died almost no one gathered together. Everyone seemed to want to be alone, to sort things out, and to grieve in their own way. It was a sickening feeling when we lost someone. Both outcomes changed us in some distinct way. Those were experiences that would never completely leave us.

As for me, I didn't have time to take in everything that happened until later that night. As I lay in bed reflecting on the day, images of my favorite president returned to my thoughts. I recalled the qualities of the men Theodore Roosevelt had sought to fill the ranks of the 1st United States Volunteer Cavalry. In his own words he sought after men "whose veins the blood stirred with the same impulse which once sent the Vikings over the sea,"[19] men who endeavored "to show that no work could be too hard, too disagreeable, or too dangerous for them to perform, . . . they were men who had thoroughly counted the cost before entering, and who went into the regiment because they believed that this offered their best chance for seeing hard and dangerous service."[20] As I lay there, staring at the ceiling, thinking about Roosevelt's words, I saw Stradley, McCarthy, Neal, Harloff, and certainly Spraktes. I thought that while the tools of war have changed somewhat, the fighting spirit of the cavalryman remains as strong as it ever was.

While the battle in the Watapur was certainly the most significant of the week, the tempo of fighting was intense every day in Kunar Province that summer. During the week of July 12 to 18, we flew a combined total of 823 hours. We flew twenty-four medevac missions, twenty-eight air movement and resupply missions, three air assaults, and fifty-five reconnaissance and surveillance missions. We were involved in sixty-six direct-fire contacts with the enemy, there were fourteen observed surface-to-air attacks against our helicopters, and we responded to twenty indirect-fire attacks on U.S. forces on the ground. While the fighting was incredibly intense it is impressive to note the maintenance, fuel, ammunition, and staff-planning support that made all of those missions possible. I can't overstate the contributions of our support personnel. The remainder of the summer would closely mirror the events of that week.

Private Joshua Dow, Private First Class Eli Casas, and Staff Sergeant Jonathan Wedemeyer all recovered from their wounds. Sergeant First Class Ventura would later tell me that his men lived that day because of the heroic actions of TF Pale Horse.

The morning following the Watapur fight we received the following email from the command sergeant major of the soldiers in the battle.

Yesterday, in C Co's TIC [Troops in Contact], we were supported by some absolutely GREAT aircraft crews. Both rotary and fixed-wing aircraft stayed in harm's way throughout the fight, and I know several were effectively engaged by the enemy, but still fought on. The medevac crews risked their lives on a "hot" LZ to get three of my soldiers to safety, and I just wanted to thank all involved. It's reassuring for the command and for the soldiers on the ground to know when trouble starts that we can count on such fine support from the air. Please let them know we appreciate all of their efforts.
Sincerely,
Lethal 7

SUMMER

The heat and humidity made the summer fighting even more challenging. It seemed that we could not drink enough water to keep up with
what we lost under our body armor.

I watched Afghan children play cricket until they were sweaty and
hot, then jump into the Kunar River to cool off. It reminded me of
my own childhood. When I was just a little boy growing up in north
Georgia, the sun would not just shine; it bore down into our skulls,
heating our brains to unhealthy temperatures, which in retrospect may
explain a lot of things. Sweat turned the dirt on our faces to mud,
and our clothes clung like loose skin to our bodies. We didn't know
any different, had never experienced anything different, so we played
on. Shade trees did not provide a refuge like they do out west where
the heat is dry. Sweat did not drip; it drained down our shirtless tor-
sos and collected like a sponge in our underwear, where it turned Fruit
of the Looms into sandpaper that chafed our thighs with each stride,
yet we played on with no hope for refuge.

On those summer days, days when a front-yard baseball game was
more important than the World Series, since the Braves were already
out of it, we walked to my mama's little store, and she gave us each a
Push-Up. That orange sherbet was manna for the soul—a gift from
the very God that put that sun in the sky to cook our skin and turn
our sweat to salt. It made me happy, as happy as a boy could or needed
to be. Satisfied, we'd wipe our faces with the backs of our hands and
return to the game.

Like the Afghan kids, we didn't have air conditioners, so we jumped
in the Coosawattee River or took turns squirting each other with a

garden hose. I was reminded that no matter where you go, even in a war zone, children are children. What a blessing.

When we landed at our FARPs, soldiers ran out to the helicopters with an ice-cold bottle of water in each hand. It was delightful, like cool sheets on warm summer nights. We lined the dashes of our helicopters with water bottles; we dropped cases of water out the door of Kiowas to infantry patrols below, and we constantly beat the drum for our soldiers—"*drink, drink, drink,*" we told them.

The summer was filled with fight after fight, medevac after medevac. Apaches and Chinooks remained consumed with support to operations at Barg-e Matal, and the enemy in the Kamdesh Valley grew more and more emboldened. On the darkest of nights, when the complete absence of light made the deep crevasses of northern Kunar and Nuristan inexplicably uncomfortable, we flew into the cracks of the earth hoping that the eerie black veil of darkness would protect us, that the evil that lived there would not see us. Words cannot describe the utter absence of light in those deep valleys, valleys with no electricity reaching them, with no visible light other than the stars that dotted the sky like tiny holes in the floor of heaven.

Despite the heat, the danger, and the fierce pace, morale remained high across the task force. I love soldiers. They never cease to amaze me with their ability to have fun even during the toughest of times. They also provided many light moments in an otherwise stressful environment. You never know what you might see around soldiers.

I was raised to adulthood in a tribe of storytellers. It was in my blood. My people told stories for entertainment, some of which originally began as truth but over time transformed into beautiful yarns that retained only shades of the original tale. "There never was a story worth telling that didn't deserve a little embellishment," my grandfather would teach me. I learned the rudiments of tempo, tone, volume, and animation at his knee. It was an art I felt compelled to keep alive. And so I often told stories about coon hunting by lantern light, frog gigging in snake-infested ponds, and of course army stories, countless army stories. But what I found interesting over the years was that soldier stories rarely require embellishment. They stand alone as astonishing and almost unbelievable. You just can't make this stuff up.

One night I woke up around 2:00 A.M. and had to go to the latrine. Our latrine was located in a mobile trailer about twenty-five meters from my hooch. I put my headlamp on and stumbled out the door half asleep, being careful to watch for snakes. When I entered the latrine two soldiers snapped their heads in my direction to see who it was. I suspect they had chosen 2:00 A.M. in hopes that no one would walk in on them. When they saw it was me their expressions gave it away: *Great, it's the commander.*

To be honest they startled me too. One big, burly, shirtless soldier was bending over with his hands on the sink. He had a big fluffy white ring of shaving cream all over his neck and back, which was covered in a rug of hair that would have made a grizzly bear envious. The other soldier was standing behind him with a razor in his hand.

"What are you boys doing?" I asked.

Feeling a sense of responsibility, the soldier being shaved spoke up. In a humble, innocent, almost embarrassed tone he said, "Sir, my back's hairy. My dog tags get caught up in all that hair, and it hurts. I can't reach back there, so my buddy is shaving it for me."

The other soldier looked at me and shrugged his shoulders as if to say, *What are you gonna do, sir? He needed help, and I am his buddy.*

While I had caught them in a compromising position, and it was quite comical, I was actually touched by the event. I went back to my room and laid down thinking about them. Very few Americans have ever experienced anything like that, to have to rely on their buddy to do things many would consider almost intimate. It was such a quintessential soldier moment. Soldiers will do just about anything to help one another out, and that's one of the things I love most about a soldier.

I also realized that our soldiers, like me, were trying to comprehend the plight of the people we were there to help. One evening my co-pilot and I flew home from a mission in silence. For six hours we had covered a resupply mission just south of FOB Bostic. Several times during the flight he had mentioned the people and how he felt sorry for them. About halfway down the Kunar Valley he broke the silence. "They sure are poor," he said matter-of-factly.

I could tell it had been on his mind for some time. I really didn't know how to respond to that statement. I had thought about it, quite a bit, in fact. It was clear that they did not possess much materially. That's how we Americans tend to measure wealth, on a scale from nothing to more than any man ought to have, but I knew better. I grew up in the Appalachian foothills of northern Georgia. My father worked in the cotton mills most of his life, risking fingers and arms around looms every day. When I was a young boy he cleared $26 a day working an eight-hour shift. It wasn't until I was grown that I truly realized how poor we were. I could easily look to neighbors up and down the old country road we lived on and find someone who had less than we did. The thing is, we didn't consider ourselves poor. Sure, there were things we wanted and could not afford, but that was the way with everyone we knew. The fact is, we were happy, and I'm not exactly sure how that factors in on the scale of wealth.

As I thought about what my copilot said, I wondered if these seemingly poor Afghans were happy; certainly the kids appeared to be so. How do you define a man's wealth when he piles up a house from rocks he gathered on a mountain, when he sustains his family on a little grain he grows in a terraced patch of dirt, a few vegetables, and goat's milk, and on special occasions a chunk of lamb's meat?

They didn't have to worry about the Dow Jones Average or the price of beef at Kroger. Their biggest concern for generations had been which empire or neighboring country would invade their lands. Following the Soviet war their burden grew to include extremist groups who bullied them and used their country as a safe haven from which to project global terrorism. We were there to do something about that, but since they had been occupied by foreign military forces for centuries, it was easy to see how they might be distrustful, have doubts and concerns about our long-term goals in their country.

Suddenly, I felt much better. I'd seen families working together in fields, swimming in the river, kids playing cricket and cooking over an open fire. I'd seen bare-chested boys chase me, waving, or throwing rocks at me; it didn't really matter. Their brown skin stretched over bony frames that had never seen excess, never known abundance; they stood in stark contrast to most American children today. I figured those people had the one thing that truly made a family happy—love. Their lives would improve in due time. I was sure of that. The tide of literacy would eventually flood their valleys, and their lives would change, but my heart did not ache for them, because I saw families working and playing together every day—something that perhaps we, with all of our technology and modern-day conveniences, ought to pay more attention to. I looked to the east and saw beautiful snowcapped mountains, something you might see on a Christmas card. If they were deprived, it was in some ways rewarding to see people so poor living in a land so rich with beauty.

"They are poor in some ways," I told my copilot. "Rich in others."

Historically, the fighting season began to wind down in the fall, as the snows piled up in the mountains and began to breathe frosty air down into the villages. The snows had not quite begun to fall, but we had survived a long, hard fighting season and openly hoped for a lull in the action. Jack, Jillian, and I often sat in my office discussing what remained to be completed before we returned home.

"We've got less than ninety days left," I said. "We've gotta get out of Barg-e Matal."

"We'd better get out because we're setting patterns and the intelligence intercepts clearly show that the enemy gets it. We're flying over that mountain too much. We fly over it every day going back and forth. There's also a village just north of COP Keating that is supporting the fight in Barg-e Matal, and attacks on Keating and Lowell in the Kamdesh. I think they live in that village and climb up on the ridge to observe us and control attacks at Barg-e Matal and in the Kamdesh. I've got this horrible feeling in the pit of my stomach. The Kamdesh is going to be a problem," Jillian said.

"Flying over that mountain is the only option other than flying right down the valley to get up there," I said.

"I know, but the enemy is studying us. All they used to talk about were Chinooks. They wanted to shoot a Chinook down, but now we're getting a lot of intercepts in which they are talking about targeting Apaches. I think that is because they have watched us and we've set a pattern," she said.

"Well, if we can get out of there by the end of September, then we've got two new-moon phases left to close Keating, Lowell, and Fritsche. We can get it done if we prep everything ahead of time," Jack said.

"I'd really like to get out of the Korengal as well," I told him.

"I don't think that's going to happen, sir. We just don't have enough time."

"What sucks is that we have no flexibility anymore. Every airplane on the ramp is tasked out every day. We can't even take a team of

Kiowas and spend a day watching the passes into Pakistan," I said, kicking my feet up on my desk.

Jack sat on the couch in his physical training uniform. His hair was oily, giving away the fact that he hadn't showered or slept in a day.

"We had no idea how great life was when we first got here. We were full of ideas and had plenty of helicopters to go play with. Then the fighting season kicked off, then Bergdahl, then Barg-e Matal, and now we can't even get a supply convoy to Bostic without surging the entire brigade to secure it," Jack said.

"Do you think we can get out of the Kamdesh in October and November?" I asked him.

He furrowed his brow to support his confidence. "Yes, sir. I think we can."

"I don't know. Every time we go in there just to deliver mail, fuel, food, and water we get shot at. I don't know how many turns we can get in per night. If we stack ISR, lay artillery on every location from which they could shoot at us, and use Apaches, we might get three or four turns before it gets too dangerous to go back in. I just don't know," I said.

ISR is intelligence, surveillance, and reconnaissance. There are various manned and unmanned ISR platforms, which allow us to gather intelligence and watch the objective area with full-motion video. ISR is managed at the RC level, so we'd have to get CJTF-82 at Bagram to make us the priority for both months.

"Well, there will come a point during the move when we are committed, and there is no turning back. The ground guys will have to determine what that point is, but once we begin the retrograde and get enough men, weapons, and equipment out, it will be too dangerous to leave only a few guys on the ground, so we will have to finish it one way or another," he said.

"Yeah, I know."

We actually did begin to lean forward and retrograde some of the equipment from the FOBs in the Kamdesh as early as July, but we did not have permission to close the bases. Two thousand and nine was a presidential election year in Afghanistan, and President Obama was awaiting General McChrystal's initial assessment of what it would take to complete the mission in Afghanistan. We knew that President Obama would use General McChrystal's assessment to formulate his guidance for how America would proceed. No one wanted to get ahead of the president by closing a bunch of bases, which would be certain to make the headlines, nor did we want to create the perception that we were abandoning Nuristan right before the Afghan election. It was a very complex situation. We understood the political conditions, but it was extremely difficult to explain it to soldiers who were fighting for their lives day and night in an area that they saw as making no progress. If living and fighting in a small, remote outpost wasn't difficult enough, the situation was made worse by the fact that they often did not get resupplied.

Our Kiowas were constantly fighting throughout the Kunar. The actual final resupply missions—Chinooks delivering supplies to the outposts in the Kamdesh—were only one piece of the equation. Supplies were first moved to Jalalabad by air and land. We did not have the air resources available to fly supplies from Jalalabad to FOB Bostic, but even if we had, it would not have been feasible to execute aerial resupply missions from Jalalabad all the way to the Kamdesh. The problem lay with the enemy forces between COP Monti, just north of Asadabad, and FOB Bostic.

The stretch of road between COP Monti and FOB Bostic is very narrow. It hugs the mountain on the west side of the road, and the river on the east side. Our local Afghan supply truck convoys were often ambushed along the narrow stretch of road between Monti and Bostic as they attempted to make their way north.

Terrain is not neutral. Whoever holds advantageous terrain has the upper hand. In this case the terrain was ideally suited for a handful of fighters to take out an entire convoy of trucks. They would lie in cracks between rocks on the cliff that towered above the single-lane road. When the convoy drove into the enemy's ambush they simply shot the lead and trail vehicles with RPGs. This disabled the vehicles and trapped the remainder of the convoy. If someone did not immediately push the lead vehicle off the road and into the river, the enemy would begin shooting vehicle after vehicle, working from both ends of the convoy toward the center.

There wasn't enough room to turn a truck around, and rarely enough room to squeeze by a disabled vehicle on the mountain side of the road. I once watched a panicked soldier who was being shot at try and get around a disabled vehicle on the river side only to have the riverbank give way under his vehicle. I had watched thirty trucks burn on that stretch of road as armed fighters ran from vehicle to vehicle shooting them with RPGs and killing local drivers who were brave or dumb enough to remain with their trucks. It was difficult for us to assist because they attacked from positions so close to the vehicles.

I remember flying over a convoy one day when enemy fighters shot the lead vehicle. The truck was instantly transformed into a ball of flame. There was no way to get around it. The driver sat gunshot in his seat as the burning truck consumed him. The local drivers had begun the movement with good intervals between trucks. They kept about thirty meters between them as they drove, but when the lead vehicle was shot they closed the gap until they were bumper to bumper with no possible way to turn around.

They were stuck and no one knew what to do. The driver in the second vehicle was scared to try and push the burning truck off the road with his truck, and he could not get around him or turn around. So, they all just sat there. That's when I saw three men appear in front of the burning vehicle. They had rifles in their hands. I knew it was the enemy, but they were too close to the other vehicles to shoot. They quickly moved to the second truck. The driver saw them coming, but it was too late. He tried to get out of the truck and run, but they shot him before he made it to the back of the truck. I can see it like it was yesterday. He fell to the ground, and his white shirt slowly transformed to crimson red as he bled out.

Suddenly, the drivers of all the other vehicles exited their trucks and ran for their lives. The trucks sat lined up, idling with no drivers. The enemy then set all of the trucks on fire.

Jack and Jillian walked into my office one night after a convoy had been ambushed. They plopped down in chairs, slight grins on their faces, and stared at me.

"So I take it you two have colluded, and you're here to gang up on me," I said with a smile.

"No, sir," Jack said in his ever-pleasant tone. "We're just wondering what it will take before we figure out how to get supplies to Bostic without them going up like a Roman candle."

"It's the ideal spot for an ambush, and they know it," Jillian said. "They are not idiots. They know the terrain better than we do, and they know we can't do anything to stop them along that stretch of road. We have to clear the route in force," Jillian added.

"I know. I get it, but the brigade is stretched thin in every location with Barg-e Matal on the plate," I said.

"The only way to get this done is to commit a ton of resources to it. Otherwise, every convoy we send up to Bostic is going to wind up torched and in the river," Jack said. "The guys at Keating, Lowell, and Mace are running out of supplies every few nights because we can't get them to Bostic. We've got to find a way to get the convoy up there," he added.

"Well, more helicopters won't do it. I was up there last week, and I was all over the top of the convoy. They were attacked from point-blank range. Dudes with RPGs were right on the side of the road. I couldn't shoot without risking hitting our guys or the truck drivers," I said.

Jillian raised her brow and in a slightly sarcastic yet playful tone said, "Like I said, they aren't idiots."

"You'd think they've done this before. Like with the Russians," I said. "So what do we do?" I asked, and looked directly at Jillian.

She took a big gulp of air, puffed out her cheeks, and blew it out. "Well, I don't know, other than add more forces. We have to secure the route," she said.

Jillian, my intelligence all-star and intellectual nonconformist, could accurately predict what the enemy would do, but she had few ideas about countermeasures other than "secure the route on the ground." In truth I knew it was just that simple. It would take a significant amount of resources just to move supplies from Fenty to Bostic, but we couldn't come up with any other suggestions, so that's what I offered to Colonel George.

I vividly described to him how the enemy attacked the convoys. I told him everything I had seen while flying the missions. He got it, but he also understood that it would take several platoons to secure that short stretch of road, and he didn't have infantry platoons just sitting around.

I could tell that he was frustrated, but he never openly showed it. He never got angry, never lashed out at others in frustration. I knew what he was thinking. He was thinking the same thing I was. *If we had never gone to Barg-e Matal we'd be out of the Kamdesh, and we would not have this problem.* But, as my grandfather used to say, "If a frog had wings he wouldn't bump his rump when he jumped." Colonel George agreed that we had to do something, so it became a brigade operation.

We added convoy security vehicles—U.S. soldiers in gun trucks. We drove the convoys to Jalalabad during the day, then waited until dark to continue on to Bostic. We used the darkness and our night vision systems to our advantage. A large combat force picked up the resupply convoys at COP Monti. Meanwhile, soldiers occupied observation posts on the high ground above the route, while others manned checkpoints all along the route. We used two Kiowa teams to cover them, so the convoy always had coverage during their movement. We coordinated for close air support, but it was hard to use them in an attack mode because the enemy was always so close to the convoys. It took a lot of combat power away from other operations and made the resupply process go painfully slow, but we had no alternative.

While we struggled to get supplies to Bostic, and it frustrated me to no end, intelligence sources indicated a growing threat in the Kamdesh.

"Sir, they are looking for another Bari Ali event," Jillian told me. "We are intercepting a lot of communications. They constantly talk about trying to overrun an outpost."

Lieutenant Colonel Brad Brown had also been paying close attention to the threat reporting. He knew the danger to his men in the Kamdesh. He desperately wanted to add more combat forces to Lowell and Keating, but he was forced to use what men he had to try and secure the resupply convoys. In a thirty-day period Brad lost six platoon sergeants and a platoon leader, severely wounded or killed, securing the resupply convoys between COP Monti and FOB Bostic. We desperately needed out of the Kamdesh, but first we had business with Abdul Aziz.

Five years ago today forever changed our lives.

—CARRIE STEAD, 2014

GANJGAL AND SHURYAK

Jack and Jillian entered my office together. Jack spoke as they walked through the door. "Sir, they want to go after Abdul Aziz."

"Well, that's good. Can we get him?" I asked, turning my attention to Jillian.

"I doubt it, but their plan has a better chance than anything else we've tried."

"How so?" I asked.

"They are going to the back of the valley," she said.

"Nice. He'll run, but it will shake them up going in deep. Can we get in there?" I asked, turning my attention back to Jack.

"I think so. We've found an LZ near the village he stays at a lot," Jack replied.

"Not Matin or Matanga then."

"No, sir. Salam," Jillian cut in. "He comes out to Matin or Matanga for attacks but rarely stays there long. Both times we've gone after him, he's gone when we get there. He'll certainly make a run for it, but this will give him a very different look," she said.

Abdul Aziz was a Taliban subcommander who led forty to fifty fighters in the Pech River Valley. He was smart enough to spend most of his time in the back of the Shuryak Valley, where he was isolated and safe. Frequently, he and his men conducted attacks from Matin and Matanga villages near the mouth of the Shuryak, but he never remained there for very long.

We had flown all over the Shuryak on previous missions, but we had never put ground forces deep into the valley. The Shuryak is where Amahd Shah had operated. Shah, the Taliban shadow governor of the Pech District, was the target of Operation Red Wings, which was made famous in Marcus Luttrell's book and the subsequent movie, *Lone Survivor*. Shah was killed by Pakistani policemen in April 2008 for failing to stop at a checkpoint.

"Task Force Lethal wants to go into the back of the Shuryak. Then teams will move out to objectives all over the valley. Essentially, they are going to all of those small hamlets in the back of the valley to clear them and talk to the elders. If they are lucky they'll pick a few fights before it's over and maybe kill Aziz," Jack said.

I thought the mission had the potential to be very disruptive to the insurgent forces operating throughout the Shuryak, Pech, and Korengal valleys, but I suspected we'd have to fight to achieve that effect. Aziz might not personally mix it up in a fight, but I expected his men to fight while he tried to get out of the valley.

"They are calling it Operation Lethal Storm," Jack said.

The date was set for September 8. TF Lift agreed to cover our Barg-e Matal mission while our Apaches executed the air assault into the Shuryak. We briefed the mission to CJTF-82 a couple of days prior, and it was approved for execution.

Ganjgal village sits at the base of a ridge that rises east from the Kunar Valley to the Pakistan border. The village straddles a wadi, or dry wash, with half of the village sitting on the north side of the wadi and the other half of the village on the south. The wadi is only about thirty meters wide at the village. The terrain rises abruptly behind the village, and two long ridges extend to the west on either side of it. Ganjgal sits in a valley, but not a significantly deep and long valley. It's surrounded by high ground, but the valley opens up rather quickly into the Kunar. A dirt road, the only road that leads into the village, parallels the wadi. Compared to the long, deep, forested valleys like the Helgal, Korengal, or Shuryak, Ganjgal appears benign.

A day or two prior to September 8, we received an air mission request to support a key leader engagement at Ganjgal village, just a few kilometers north of FOB Joyce. Ganjgal was known as a very unfriendly village, but the elders had invited a marine embedded training team and their Afghan partners to meet with them in the village. In

accordance with Pashtunwali we were almost always safe when we were guests in a Pashtun village, so we didn't assess it to be a terribly dangerous mission. We knew our forces might get shot at as they left the village following the meeting, but nothing more.

The mission was set for September 7. We tasked a team of Kiowas to support it. The Kiowas would fly over the convoy as they drove to the village and then conduct security, looking for enemy forces in the high ground that surrounded the village, during the meeting. Once the meeting was over, the Kiowas would provide security as the marines and their partners departed the village.

Early on the morning of September 7, we were notified that the mission to Ganjgal had been bumped to the eighth because the Afghan Border Police, who were supposed to participate in the meeting, could not make it. We told them we could not support the mission on the eighth with dedicated air assets due to the large air assault in the Shuryak at that same time. Operation Lethal Storm, coupled with Barg-e Matal, would consume every helicopter in our fleet. The only helicopters not tasked for a specific mission was one team of Kiowas, which we had planned to use as a quick-reaction force should anything bad unexpectedly occur.

Our ground forces conducted key leader engagements almost every day throughout our area of operations. It was impossible to cover them all, so it was not uncommon to conduct a meeting with village leaders having no dedicated helicopter support. Fixed-wing close air support was always available, artillery was available, and we could divert Kiowas or Apaches from other missions, or launch the quick-reaction force if the situation required it. The U.S. embedded training teams that worked with the ANA and Border Police acknowledged our limitations and decided to move forward with the meeting anyway, having only artillery to cover them from FOB Joyce.

Our Apaches at Barg-e Matal had been busy all night. Liz Kimbrough, our only female Apache pilot, and Chris Wright initially killed a sniper team that was shooting at our guys in Barg-e Matal, but after they shot the sniper team they started finding groups of three to four fighters, all in the ridges.

I watched their gun tape early the next morning and saw Liz calmly identify and kill enemy fighters.

"I've got another guy in the trees. Wait, there are three. I've got a shot. Engaging," she calmly said. "I got 'em. They're dead."

We had a large air assault the next morning, but we could not take our eye off Barg-e Matal. Likewise, we planned to keep a close eye on Ganjgal.

Operation Lethal Storm began well before daylight. In the predawn darkness our pilots met in the command post for a final mission update brief. Weather was good, the enemy situation had not changed—everything was a go for the mission. Out on the flight line, crew chiefs untied rotor blades, took covers off the windscreens of the helicopters, and prepared them for the mission. They joked with one another in the quiet of the morning. It was peaceful out, and the pre-dawn, cool air was welcomed. With mission packets in their hands and flight gear draped over their shoulders the pilots scattered to their respective helicopters. Soon the silence was interrupted with the whine of turbine engines all up and down the flight line. The helicopters lined up on the runway, and we stood outside the command post to watch them disappear into the darkness. As they flew farther toward the Kunar the sound dissipated, and once again it was silent. I remember that a sliver of stingy moon hung in the western sky. It was low on the horizon, so I knew it would be dark as they conducted the insertion. They may as well have been trying to light their way with chem sticks.

I drew in a deep breath of cool air. When I was a boy there was nothing more refreshing than feeling the wind in my face during cross-country season. "Fall is coming," I told Jack. "It's almost deer season back home."

And we turned and went back into the command post.

Everything went as planned for the air assault into the Shuryak. We inserted Lieutenant Colonel Pearl's men into helicopter LZ Blue Jay, near Salam village, in the very back of the valley. They set up a tactical command post just above the village as numerous small patrols were sent out on foot to their objectives. Our helicopters woke the enemy up as we flew into the valley.

I went back to my room to catch a quick hour of sleep. Jack sent a runner to wake me just before daylight. Jack sat by the battle captain

in a folding metal chair, legs crossed. "Looks like we woke them up," Jack said as I walked in. I rubbed my face, trying to wake up myself.

"What's up?"

"The Apaches picked up a bunch of guys running out of structures as the Chinooks went in. They are engaging them now," he said.

"Did the Chinooks take any fire going in?" I asked.

"No, sir."

The Apaches killed at least ten enemy fighters before daylight. They remained over the valley for about three hours. By sunrise it was time to swap out the Apache team with the first Kiowa team of the day, but suddenly there were troops in contact across the Kunar River, at Ganjgal.

Three marines, a navy corpsman, and their Afghan partners had departed FOB Joyce well before daylight as well. An army unit from TF Chosin had established a blocking position at the mouth of the valley, and a team of scouts had moved into a position on the high ground southeast of the village. The rest of the force moved up the wadi, led by the marines. As they neared Ganjgal village enemy fighters unleashed heavy machine gun fire on them from the high ground on both sides of the valley, and from the village itself.

We monitored what was happening over the radio as best we could, but the communications were sketchy at best. We had one scout team available—the day quick-reaction force. Everything else was employed.

"Sir," the battle captain said, "it's the battle captain at TF Chosin. He's asking us to launch the quick-reaction force."

"Tell him that it's the brigade quick-reaction force. They will have to release it. Tell him to call the CHOPS [chief of operations]. We'll call them too, and ask, but he needs to call them."

"Roger, sir."

Meanwhile, about thirty minutes prior, we had launched a team of Kiowas, led by Chief Warrant Officer 2 Jerry Wood, to fly to the Shuryak Valley and relieve the Apaches that had been over the valley since the operation began. As soon as Jerry's team took over the mission in the Shuryak they made contact with the enemy.

"Gator 9-3" was the call sign of the ground force in the Shuryak.

As soon as Jerry's team took the fight, Gator 9-3 reported two men with AK-47s. The lead Kiowa was almost directly over the two men when the pilots spotted them, so they quickly pulled the pin on a smoke grenade and dropped it out the door to mark the enemy location. Gator 9-3 saw the smoke and immediately confirmed, "That's it! That's the spot. You're cleared to engage," he said.

Satisfied that the men they had seen were indeed enemy fighters and not Afghan soldiers, the lead Kiowa led the team back inbound and shot them with fifty-caliber and rockets.

"That's the same spot where the Apaches killed about a dozen guys earlier," Gator 9-3 reported. "Pale Horse, we're going to send a team down to search the bodies. Cover our movement," he said.

They wanted to see if they could gather any intelligence from the men: maps, notes, anything of use. "Roger, we'll move in closer to make sure there aren't any more enemy fighters around the field," Jerry said.

As the lead Kiowa neared the cornfield they saw a sudden flash and felt an explosion. "Crap! What was that?" one of the pilots transmitted.

"Airburst RPG," Jerry said. It had just missed their helicopter. The RPG had been shot from the treeline on the west side of the cornfield. The Kiowas immediately suppressed the wooded area with all their remaining ammunition.

"We're out of ammo," Jerry told Gator 9-3. "Hold tight and we'll run to the FARP, get more ammo and fuel, and we'll be right back."

"Roger that," Gator 9-3 responded.

Jerry Wood's team circled to the south of FOB Wright and prepared to land at the FARP into the wind. Just before they landed they received a radio call from Chosin 9-5, at FOB Joyce.

"Pale Horse, this is Chosin 9-5, over."

"This is Pale Horse, Chosin 9-5."

"Roger, we've got troops in contact at Ganjgal. We need you to move there now, over."

Jerry didn't respond immediately. He was torn. There were also troops in contact in the Shuryak, and that was his assigned mission. He realized that the decision to pull off that mission was not his to make, so he called Chosin 9-5 back.

trail aircraft glued to its lead as if by an imaginary string, is pure elegance.

Bolstered with confidence, Gator 9-3 had slowly made it up the ridge as Wood's team performed their dance and unleashed fury on the enemy.

Back at FOB Fenty, Chief Warrant Officer 2 Ryan Neal's Kiowa quick-reaction force raced to their helicopters. Ryan, who had flown flight lead for Scott Stradley in the Watapur, served as the air mission commander. They were off the ground within minutes.

Jack and I stood watching the digital map display in the command post. Every helicopter on the battlefield was depicted on the map. The global positioning system in the helicopters relayed a position update to our digital map approximately every minute, so we could watch them on the map in near real time.

Ryan Neal's team test-fired their .50-caliber machine guns as they entered the Kunar River Valley, then continued flying north. Just south of FOB Joyce, Ryan called Chosin 9-5.

"Chosin 9-5, Pale Horse, over."

Every COP and FOB in Afghanistan owned a ROZ (restricted operating zone) and some sort of indirect-fire weapon system—either mortars or artillery. The ROZ is a control measure that restricts aircraft operations when mortars or artillery are being fired in order to keep them safe. It was a safety control measure, which required every team to contact the owning unit and request the status of the ROZ before flying through it. If the guns were firing they could circumnavigate the ROZ or get permission to fly at a specific altitude and direction until they were clear. Chosin 9-5 controlled the ROZ at FOB Joyce.

"Pale Horse, Chosin 9-5. ROZ is hot, guns are hot," which meant they were firing. "Remain low, and you'll be clear. We have multiple casualties at Ganjgal. Contact Highlander 5 inbound, over."

In reality the situation was much worse than anyone had imagined. The ground forces had taken sustained machine gun fire from the north, south, and east ever since the ambush began. Ryan's team acknowledged the situation, and he prepared them for an inevitable fight.

Ryan knew that Highlander 5 was in the valley somewhere, so he called him on the radio. He wanted to know exactly where he was located. "Highlander 5" was Captain William Swenson's call sign. Will was a thirty-year-old captain from the 10th Mountain Division who was serving as an embedded trainer with the Afghan Border Police. Most of our pilots were familiar with Will, having worked with him at one time or another during the deployment.

My own introduction to Captain Will Swenson came one afternoon as I returned from a mission in the Pech. I had just filled up with fuel at FOB Wright and was preparing to relax while flying back down the Kunar to FOB Fenty when a call came over the radio: "Pale Horse, this is Chosin 9-5. We are under a rocket attack. We have a good point-of-origin grid. Prepare to copy, over."

My team took off down the Kunar, and I called Chosin 9-5 back. "Ready to copy, over."

The soldier on the radio was a young man with a drawl from Alabama, who I affectionately called "Alabama." He was the soldier who typically ran the radio net at FOB Joyce, and I enjoyed giving him a hard time about his thick Southern accent. He was a great young man with a wonderful personality. He once told me, "You talk just like me, sir." I laughed and had to agree.

Alabama gave us the grid coordinates where the rockets originated—a point of origin (POO). My lead Kiowa pilots copied down the grid, and we flew directly to that location, where we found two males who appeared to be in their twenties sitting on a hill overlooking FOB Joyce. They were not doing anything suspicious when we arrived, but they were at the exact grid Alabama had given us. There were no houses nearby, the two men were alone, and there were no sheep in sight, which led me to believe that they were most likely the guys who shot the rockets.

I called Alabama and told him what we had discovered. "Do you have a force that can come out here?" I asked him. "They are just sitting here. We can maintain contact with them until some of your guys get out here," I added.

"Gimme a minute, sir," he replied.

A couple of minutes later he returned to the radio and told me that a team would be departing Joyce in just a few minutes. He said the call sign of the officer in charge would be "Highlander 5" and gave me his radio frequency.

My lead aircraft continued to orbit over the two men while I flew back toward FOB Joyce to link up with Highlander 5 as soon as he exited the base. Within minutes four pickup trucks exited the FOB and headed our way. Two men rode up front, and the beds were filled with police forces.

"Highlander 5, this is Pale Horse 6. We have two males at the exact grid we were given for the POO. They are sitting on the ground, over."

"Roger, can you guide me up there? We'll get as close as we can and then dismount."

"Roger," I said, and flew down over the road in front of him. "Follow me," I said.

As we moved along the road I told him, "They are probably going to run when they see you. They have pretended to be innocent as we've flown around them, but once they realize you are coming to get them, I'm sure they'll run."

I had never seen U.S.—or any other coalition force—run insurgents down in the mountains before, but Highlander 5 seemed to think they could capture the men.

"We'll get them," he said.

"I don't think so," I told my copilot.

When the trucks were within sight of the two men they immediately stood up and began watching the trucks closely. They were clearly alarmed. It confirmed my suspicion that they were bad guys.

"Highlander 5, they see you. They stood up and they are watching you now. I think they are about to run."

The road took them to within about a half mile of the two men. At the base of the hill where the men now stood, Will stopped the trucks, and all the police forces dismounted.

"If you go straight up the hill to your east they are on top of it," I said.

A long line of Afghan Border Police followed him at a steady jog.

After about a quarter of a mile the line of policemen began to stretch out. Some of them stopped running altogether. They bent over at the waist with their hands on their knees and panted. Swenson led on with a couple of Afghans right on his heels. Meanwhile, the two men on the hill began to run down the back side of the hill.

"Highlander 5, they are running now. They are going down the back side, over."

"Lead," I called to my lead aircraft, "fly down in front of them. Try and stop them."

"Roger."

We swooped down at them a few times, but they ignored us. They knew they had to make a run for it. Every now and then Swenson stopped and called me on the radio to get a good direction for the men. Eventually, he could see them, and the chase sped up substantially. He and a couple of Afghans quickened the pace, and slowly they began to close the gap.

I couldn't believe what I was seeing.

The two men knew they were in trouble. They had to get away, but they began to run out of gas as well. Slowly, Will Swenson closed the gap, and finally, after about a mile of chasing, he and two policemen caught the men. Once they knew it was over they turned and put their hands in the air. Will pointed at the ground, indicating that he wanted them to lie down. Once they were on the ground his border police flex-cuffed them. They then called to some of the other Afghan policemen, who had dropped out of the chase early on and were by then smoking cigarettes. Will told them to drive to his location, so they wouldn't have to walk back with two prisoners.

"That's a first," I told an out-of-breath Will Swenson over the radio. "I've called countless quick-reaction forces out of the FOB in Iraq and Afghanistan, but I've never seen one run suspects down on foot and actually catch them."

"Well, we got these two," he said, and laughed. I was amazed and impressed.

Will Swenson didn't have to run down fleeing suspects on September 8; rather, he was running through a hailstorm of bullets up the wadi that led to Ganjgal village, dragging wounded soldiers out of death's jaws. He was being shot at from literally every direction when Ryan's team called him on the radio.

Will told him where all of the friendly soldiers were located, then told him that they were receiving a heavy volume of machine gun fire from the north, east, and south. Ryan immediately saw the vehicle patrol base at the mouth of the valley, and he found the two observation posts on either side of the wadi. He had to search harder to find Will Swenson, who was moving up the wadi, but he eventually found him. With all the friendly locations identified, it was time to begin to try and kill the enemy, turn the tide of the battle.

The largest volume of fire was from a hill to the north. Will tried to pinpoint the enemy locations for Ryan's team, but it was difficult because the team was forced to dart left and right, up and down, to avoid being shot down. Bullets popped as they passed by the helicopters. Enemy fighters shot at Will and his team until the helicopters flew near, then they turned their weapons on the helicopters. As the helicopters passed they returned their attention to Will.

Ryan was pretty sure he knew where the enemy was located on the hill. "Shoot a Willie Pete [white phosphorus] rocket right along the trees on that northern hillside," he told his flight lead.

"Roger," lead responded.

We commonly used white phosphorus rockets to get a direction to the enemy. Everyone could see the smoke, so the ground forces could give us a cardinal direction and distance from that smoke to where the enemy was located. With a white plume of smoke billowing into the air Ryan called Swenson. "Is that where they're at?"

"Roger, right there," Swenson replied, and Ryan's team circled around and flew directly at the hill.[1]

"Inbound heading zero-two-five degrees, fifty-caliber, left break," lead said.

"Roger," Ryan answered.

The lead aircraft's gun echoed across the valley with a *cack cack cack*, then he turned hard left. Ryan was right on his tail. As soon as lead was out of his line of fire, Ryan opened up with his .50-caliber machine gun. When he was about eight hundred meters from the enemy forces he turned hard and followed his lead helicopter back out. The enemy at that location was silenced, for the moment.

In the meantime, Swenson had worked his way up the wadi trying to rescue as many wounded soldiers as possible. With several men lying in the back of the truck, he was now trying to get back out of the valley so the wounded could get medical treatment. He took continuous fire as he moved back to the southwest. The enemy's machine guns sparked like lightning bugs in the green bushes all along the ridge. Everywhere Ryan's team saw a spark, they shot. While Ryan's team kept the enemy busy ducking for cover, Swenson continued to push out of the valley as fast as he could.

One of the wounded soldiers was Sergeant First Class Kenneth Westbrook, Will Swenson's battle buddy, his noncommissioned officer. Westbrook had been shot in the neck and needed to be evacuated immediately.

Unexpectedly, one of our medevac pilots transmitted over the net that he was inbound to pick up the wounded. Swenson had not made it far enough back out of the valley. Ryan came over the radio and told the medevac not to come into the valley because he thought they might get shot down. He told the medevac that the wounded were still scattered all over the valley, and there wasn't a specific point established to pick them up yet.[2]

"Hold to the west, and as soon as I can get you in safely I will," Ryan said.

As Swenson continued out of the valley, Ryan's team tried to remain to the northeast to protect his rear as he moved. They saw flashes just beyond a terrace south of Ganjgal village. Ryan's lead aircraft oriented on the muzzle flashes and opened fire. As they broke back to the southwest they saw a man lying flat on the ground. He appeared to have both an AK-47 and an RPG with him. He did not move, so initially they suspected it was an enemy fighter attempting to remain hidden.

"Hey, there's a guy lying in the prone by the wadi. Looks like he's got an AK and an RPG," lead said.

"Did he engage you?" Ryan asked.

"No. He didn't move. I can't tell if he's lying still because he thinks we didn't see him or if he's dead."

"I'm going to move back in to take a look," lead said.

"Be careful, and don't get too slow."

"Roger, my left-seater is going to keep his M4 on him."

Chief Warrant Officers Kris Bassett and Jimmy O'Neal flew as Ryan's team lead. While Kris flew the aircraft, Jimmy O'Neal removed his M4 rifle from the dash, where it was secured, and oriented it on the man. As they got closer they noticed a red spot on his back, and a large pool of dark red blood that ran from his belly into the wash below.

"He's dead," Bassett said.

"Holy shit! There are bodies everywhere. Look at all these wounded and dead!" Bassett said.

It was like those auto stereograms that you stare at to try and see a three-dimensional picture. At first you see only a bunch of colored dots until you stare at it without focusing, then suddenly an image jumps out at you. The pilots had not noticed all the bodies until suddenly they clearly saw the image—there were men lying everywhere. Some were wounded and could not move, others cowered in fear, perhaps out of ammunition, and yet many more would never move again.

Swenson linked up with a team of men that had moved forward into the wadi. It was safe enough to bring the medevac in to evacuate the wounded at that point. Swenson pulled an orange VS-17 signaling panel out of his pack and began waving it to show the medevac pilot where he was and where he wanted him to land.

The medevac landed on a terrace at the end of the valley. Westbrook had to be boosted up over a rock terrace wall onto the next level. He collapsed on the upper level, but the flight medic and Swenson helped him up and to the helicopter. Westbrook sat down on the floor of the helicopter, growing weak from the loss of blood, and completely exhausted. Swenson and Westbrook had been battle buddies, two men partnered with Afghans in a remote and very dangerous location. They had grown close, had depended on one another in ways only a combat soldier can understand. Swenson leaned in over him and kissed him on the head. The medic laid him down and closed the door. It was the last time Will Swenson would see Kenneth Westbrook.

"Clear," the crew chief called out, and the medevac departed the valley for FOB Wright.

Once again, Will Swenson planned to travel back into the valley toward Ganjgal to try and evacuate more wounded. As Swenson prepared to return to the valley, the medevac made the short flight to FOB Wright and delivered the wounded to the forward surgical team. The medevac pilot then called the Pale Horse command post and requested Apache support.

I was standing by the radio in the command post when they called. I could hear frustration in the pilot's voice, so I called Ryan.

"Do you need an Apache team?" I asked. It wasn't normal for the

medevac to call and ask for support, but he was demanding help in
the form of an Apache team. Ryan called the medevac pilot and they
had a heated exchange over the radio. It was a very emotional time
for every man involved, and what happened afterward remains a point
of extreme contention to this day. Only Ryan Neal and the medevac
pilot knew exactly what they were thinking and why they made the
decisions they made. To say that they differed in opinion as to what
was required in the fight that day would be an understatement. Their
recollections differ significantly enough that it would be unfair to
write exactly what each man said to the other.

Ryan called me back on the radio. "Dustoff called and asked. Sir,
there are wounded all up and down the valley on the terraces. They
have been able to move some of them back, but we can't fly a medevac
into the valley yet. It will get shot down. There isn't anyone to load
the casualties, so if they landed they'd be on the ground a long time
trying to go recover casualties and load them on the bird themselves,"
he said.

He was convinced that we had to collect the wounded and move
them back out to the mouth of the valley, where the medevac could
land safely. He also believed that adding the Apaches to the mix would
congest the airspace and create a more dangerous situation. "Pedro
has already tried to land and had to take off immediately because they
took so much fire," he told me.[3]

Pedro was the air force combat search-and-rescue helicopter that
often helped us out with medevac missions.

I felt uneasy. It wasn't common for medevac pilots to make a request for a team of Apaches. The medevac pilots had worked more
with the Apaches than with the Kiowas. Our medevac crews literally
lived with our Apache crews. They shared the same company command post. They had become a tight-knit team. I knew that the
medevac crew wanted to get into the valley and do whatever they
could to get the wounded out. I knew they hated to have to wait. I
admired their courage and I trusted their judgment, but I understood
what Ryan had told me and I was committed to trusting my air mission commanders. What I didn't realize, until later, was that emotions
were very high and tempers were raging in the valley. The medevac
team felt that Ryan Neal was being selfish, that pride was preventing
him from calling for Apache support.[4]

I trusted Ryan as an air mission commander. He was a very strong pilot and leader, but I also knew that we already had an Apache team moving north in the Kunar. They were tasked to go to FOB Bostic and remain on standby in case the men at Barg-e Matal were attacked.

"Call the Apaches. Tell them to check in with Ryan in the Ganjgal. See if they can help out," I told the battle captain.

Ryan did not resist when the Apaches arrived. He told them to remain at six thousand feet and above, and his team would remain below six thousand feet. He then began shooting rockets at enemy locations, so the Apache pilots would know where they had been engaging enemy forces. In a matter of minutes Ryan expended all of his ammunition and turned the fight over to the Apache team. He and his team returned to FOB Wright to get more fuel and ammunition.

As Ryan approached FOB Wright for refuel, Jerry Wood's Kiowa team was getting ready to depart out of the FARP. They had supported Gator 9-3's move to the top of the ridge, and then it had quieted down a bit. They had flown to the FARP and were going to head back to Fenty after that. Mike Woodhouse's team was on the way to take over the fight in the Shuryak.

Jerry's team had been flying for almost six hours. Ryan explained the situation in Ganjgal to Jerry and asked, "Can you guys go to Ganjgal? Help the Apaches out until we rearm and refuel, then we'll be back."

"Yeah, we'll head there now," Jerry said, but he didn't feel like he had a good handle on what was really going on at Ganjgal.

Ryan had bombarded him with so much information so quickly; it was hard to keep it all straight. Ganjgal was a complex situation. It seemed chaotic. He knew it would take time to sort out where everyone was located before it would be safe to start shooting. It was particularly difficult to keep up with where the Afghans were located, and it sounded like they were scattered all over the valley.

Regardless, Jerry departed FOB Wright with his team and headed south for Ganjgal. He checked in with both Pale Horse and Chosin to tell both that he was taking his team to Ganjgal to help out. As Jerry's team rounded the slight curve in the river he saw two Pedro helicopters flying circles at the mouth of the valley, waiting to go in. They were flying about fifty feet off the deck. Over the valley he saw two Apaches at about six thousand feet. *We have to squeeze in there and fight,* Jerry thought to himself.

Yosarian Silano, one of the pilots in Jerry's lead Kiowa, called the ground force. He got Marine Corporal Dakota Meyer on the radio. The radio was very difficult to hear. It sounded to him like their frequency was being jammed, but he knew it wasn't. Silano spoke with Meyer and was told that they were missing four men. They needed the Kiowas to find them.

"They should be in Ganjgal," someone he didn't recognize transmitted over the radio. "Look for a VS-17 panel," they told him.

Silano, a former marine himself, swooped in low and fast. This situation seemed more personal than most. He had been pissed off for hours. Silano felt that they could and should have left the Shuryak to assist at Ganjgal hours prior. He was glad finally to be where he thought he should be.

They flew up and down the valley right over the ground, searching for the three marines and the navy corpsman. They weren't really concerned with the enemy at that point. They just wanted to find the missing men. Jerry flew about one hundred feet higher than Silano, covering him as he searched. The situation was as Jerry had suspected: chaotic. Their communications with Dakota Meyer and Will Swenson were spotty at best, but Silano was able to make out what they were saying most of the time. Swenson and Meyer were headed back into the valley in pickup trucks.

Silano dove and flared and darted left and right as quickly as he could to keep from being shot down, but he had to stay low to the ground in order to see men that might be hiding. There were bodies lying all over the terraces, and as quickly as Silano could point them out Meyer would run and drag them to the truck. Slowly, they moved farther and farther into the valley. They were getting close to the village.

After about thirty minutes Ryan Neal called Jerry. "We're departing the FARP now. We'll be there in five minutes for a battle handover," he said, ready to take over the fight again.

Ryan's team had been in there fighting all morning so they had the best situational awareness. Jerry agreed, but when he called Silano to tell him to climb back up and fly to the south so Ryan's team could take over, Yosarian said, "No."

He'd found something and needed to take a closer look. He circled and came to a hover over a group of men lying in a trench.

What he saw horrified him.

Silano had found the missing men. The four men had tried to patch up each other's wounds, as they fought an insurmountable enemy force. Bandages lay scattered around them on the ground. It was an emotional moment for Silano as he confirmed that he had found the four missing Americans and an Afghan. They were the bodies of Marine First Lieutenant Michael Johnson, Gunnery Sergeant Edwin Johnson, Staff Sergeant Aaron Kenefick, Navy Corpsman 3rd Class James Layton, and an Afghan interpreter.

Jerry told Silano to hand it over to Ryan's lead aircraft. Reluctantly, he did so. "We're going back to FOB Wright to get gas, and then we're done," he said.

They had been fighting in two valleys, two totally different battles, for almost seven hours. Their mission was complete. Emotions flared in the cockpits again. No one wanted to leave with wounded and dead soldiers still littering the battlefield, but Jerry was not comfortable with all of the helicopters buzzing around in such a confined space. The Apaches were up high, Ryan's team was right over the valley, and Pedro continued to circle at the mouth of the valley.

FOB Wright was incredibly busy with the medevac, their escort, and the Kiowas rotating in and out of the Shuryak fight.

"We're going home!"[5] he told his team. Not a word was said throughout the flight back to FOB Fenty.

Ryan's team continued to cover Swenson and Meyer as they evacuated another truckload of wounded and dead out of the valley. Ganjgal had literally become death valley.

Meanwhile, back at FOB Fenty, the fourth team of Kiowas had launched. Their mission, initially, was to support Lethal Storm in the Shuryak, but with the situation at Ganjgal being what it was, I decided to have them go there first. The team consisted of my task force safety officer, Chief Warrant Officer 4 Patrick Benson, and Chief Warrant Officer 3 Adam Stead. They flew flight lead for Mike Woodhouse and Chief Warrant Officer 2 Ray Illman. The team flew directly to Ganjgal and checked in with Ryan.

He was ready for relief since his team needed to get to the FARP for gas. Ryan quickly brought them up to speed on what was going on at that time, but said that the guys on the ground were already preparing to move back to FOB Joyce. Swenson and Meyer had made it out of the valley with the dead and wounded, the medevac had picked up those that were urgent, and the rest were in their trucks. For the most part the fight at Ganjgal was over.

Mike's team flew around the valley for a few minutes but soon decided to go to FOB Wright and top off with fuel, then continue to the Shuryak.

"Head to Wright. We'll top off with gas and then head to the Shuryak," he told Adam, but before they could get there they got a call informing them that Gator 9-3 was in contact again, so they decided to head directly to the Shuryak.

As they entered the Shuryak Valley, Patrick checked in. "Gator 9-3, Pale Horse; we've got fourteen rockets and six hundred rounds of fifty-caliber. One-hour station time, over."

"Pale Horse, we're taking fire from the cornfield and hill across the valley from us."

It was the same location where most of the fighting had occurred throughout the morning, but Mike's team had not been there all morning, so they were trying to figure out exactly where the cornfield was located. Patrick went back and forth over the radio with Gator 9-3, while Adam flew in circles searching for the cornfield. Finally, Mike, who had listened to the entire conversation over the radio, figured out where the enemy was located.

Mike was flying in the left seat, and you can't fire the weapon systems from the left seat in a Kiowa, so he told Ray Illman to shoot "right there," and pointed.

"Where?" Ray asked.

Mike took the flight controls from Ray and lined up the helicopter, then said, "Shoot a rocket, now!" Ray pulled the trigger.

The rocket hit in the edge of the field. Mike then gave the controls back to Ray, and at the same time told Patrick, "Ask Gator 9-3 if the rocket was in the location he was talking about."

"Yes! Right there," came the reply.

Adam had to fly in an arch to line up for the shot, but before he could shoot, Gator 9-3 told him that they were going to shoot artillery. "We know where you want us to shoot now. You don't need artillery," Adam said.

"Pale Horse, move back out of the valley. We are going to shoot artillery."

"Gator 9-3, Pale Horse. Which guns are you going to shoot, over?"

"We're using the 155s at FOB Wright, over."

Patrick quickly visualized the gun-to-target line. They could remain in the middle of the valley and not get hit. "Roger, we can still operate in the valley and remain clear of the gun–target line, over. We'll be out of the way," he said.

"Negative, Pale Horse, move clear of the valley."

Patrick relayed to Mike, "They want us to move out of the valley."

"Roger. Looks like a good time to go get gas to me. Tell them we are going to get gas. We'll be back in a few minutes. Maybe they'll be finished with the artillery by then," Mike said.

"Gator 9-3, Pale Horse, we're going to FOB Wright for gas. We'll be right back." And they departed.

Before they made it to FOB Wright, back at FOB Fenty, we received a medevac request from Gator 9-3. One of their soldiers had rolled his ankle in the rocks; another soldier had become severely dehydrated. Both were unable to continue the mission, leaving us only one option: they would have to be hoisted out of the valley by our medevac helicopter. It was a risky mission. The medevac pilots would have to hover the aircraft completely still above the trees in broad daylight in an area where our men had been fighting since two hours before daylight. Unlike Spraktes's hoist in the Watapur, this hoist would be down into trees. It was not a good situation at all, but our options were limited. I called Mike Woodhouse. "Mike, top off with gas, and then link up with the medevac bird. Escort them into the Shuryak. They have two injured soldiers. They'll have to be hoisted out."

"Okay. No problem, sir," he replied in his usual upbeat tone.

The pilot-in-command of the medevac was Chief Warrant Officer 4 Gary Heine. The medic who would descend into the trees on a cable was Sergeant Nate Whorton. Mike linked up with Gary at FOB Wright, and as soon as they finished filling up with gas they departed for the Shuryak. It was going to be a long descent, a seventy-foot hoist down into the trees on a tiny cable.

As flight lead, Adam and Patrick would provide close security of the medevac. Mike and Ray would move farther out and provide an outer ring of security.

As soon as they entered the valley Nate Whorton leaned out of the door, put all of his weight on the cable, and began to descend below the helicopter. As they neared the spot, Gary began to slow the helicopter down with Whorton dangling fifty-plus feet below the aircraft. Once over the injured soldiers, Gary came to a hover and Whorton descended the last twenty feet or so down into the trees. Gary then flew away. He planned to hold at the mouth of the valley until Whorton was ready. Whorton wanted to hoist both of the patients out together, get them into the helicopter, then he'd come out last.

With Whorton on the ground, Gator 9-3 said that the enemy knew what we were doing. The anxiety increased in every cockpit.

"Tell him to work fast," Gator 9-3 urged.

"Send fighters to the helicopter. Hurry! Shoot them down. They have wounded. Shoot the helicopter," the Taliban leader told his men.

Whorton worked quickly. He attached the injured soldiers to the cable and called Gary on his radio. "Come get them," he said.

The crew chief lowered the cable as Gary flew to the extraction point. The cable hit the ground, and Whorton hooked the two soldiers onto the jungle penetrator.

"You need to hurry. They see you, and they are coming," Gator 9-3 said in a clearly concerned tone.

Gary held the Black Hawk steady as the crew chief pulled the two men into the helicopter. Once they were in he made a circle, and the cable was lowered one more time.

Adam and Patrick nervously searched for enemy fighters moving toward the medevac, but it was difficult to see down into the trees. The report was credible; it was exactly what the enemy would do. It was only a matter of time before the firefight began. The anticipation was painful.

As soon as the cable reached Sergeant Whorton, he was on it. Mike Woodhouse was relieved. He knew that Gary would fly out of the valley with Whorton hanging below the aircraft. He'd reel him in on the fly, being careful not to drag him into anything, of course.

Meanwhile, the enemy fighters who had moved into a position

under the helicopter made it just in time. They opened fire on the vulnerable Black Hawk. Bullets hit the nose of the aircraft, yet Gary held his position under fire.

"We're hit," Gary transmitted over the radio, but he held the hover with Whorton still below the treetops.

Adam banked his Kiowa around the medevac and searched for the enemy fighters. Mike was behind and above Adam, covering him. Suddenly, "the nose of Adam and Patrick's Kiowa pitched up, and rolled right, and they began to fall,"[6] Mike later told me.

Then Patrick transmitted over the radio, "We've been hit. I've been hit. Oh God, Adam is dead!" he said, and the helicopter continued to fall.

Mike thought Patrick was going to crash into the ridge. The helicopter was upright but continued to fall in a right-hand turn. Instantly, Mike began to try and figure out where they were going to impact the earth. He searched for a place to land so he could run to try and help them after they crashed.

Inside the helicopter, Patrick had quickly grabbed the controls and leveled the altitude of the aircraft, yet it continued to descend toward the valley floor. He pulled up on the collective control to stop the descent, but it wouldn't budge. He pulled harder, but it was stuck; something was blocking it.

Both the pilot and copilot have collective controls that are mechanically attached to one another, so Patrick looked over at Adam's collective to see if something was blocking it. He saw that Adam's hand was still on the collective, so when he tried to pull up it would not move. He quickly reached over and took Adam's hand off of the controls and pulled in power. The helicopter stopped falling and leveled out. Mike Woodhouse let out a big sigh of relief.

Two bullets had entered the aircraft between Patrick's feet. One had exploded his leg. The other bullet cut a groove through the center console of the aircraft before striking Adam behind the left ear. The bullet passed through his brain and came to rest against his skull on the right side of his head.

Despite his leg being shattered, Patrick was in control and flying the helicopter. His mind was going a thousand miles per hour. Suddenly, Mike Slebodnik popped into his mind. He could see Mike's face. It terrified him to think he might die in the Shuryak Valley. *I don't want* to die. We lost Mike like this, but I don't want to die in this valley,[7] he thought.

Random images flashed in his mind. He saw himself as a prisoner of war. He didn't want to be captured, but he knew that the valley was swarming with enemy forces. If he landed he would almost certainly be captured. He was in the same valley Marcus Luttrell had been held in. Knowing he had to focus, Patrick cleared his mind and concentrated on what he had to do. If we're going to get out of this alive, it's up to me, he thought. But Patrick was going into shock.

"Patrick. Are you okay?" Mike asked over the radio.

"I've been hit in the leg. Adam is dead, and there is blood everywhere," he said.

"Okay, you are doing great. Is the aircraft flyable?" Mike asked.

"I don't know. I don't want to die," he said.

"You're doing fine," Mike reassured him. "There is an open spot on the hill to your right. The medevac can land and pick you up," he said.

"I want to get out of the valley," Patrick replied. "I can't see. There is blood everywhere."

Patrick literally could not see through his and Adam's blood, which now covered the windscreen and dash. "You're almost to COP Able Main. It's coming up on your right," Mike told him.

"Where is it? I can't see it," he said, squinting, straining to see.

"It's to your front right," Mike said, with clear concern in his voice. He knew Patrick was going into shock. He was losing blood fast. His life hung like a thread.

He began to descend, and Mike began to feel hope for the first time. He thought, Patrick is going to do it. He's going to get on the ground safely.

"Adam is talking! He's alive!" Patrick said in an excited voice.

Mike thought it was a good sign. "Great. Just land it on the pad. The medevac will follow you in," he said.

Mike had called COP Able Main and told them they were coming in. He informed them that two of the pilots had been shot. As Patrick landed, about a dozen men swarmed the helicopter. Patrick had chopped the throttle, and the turbine engine was winding down, but the rotors were still turning when the men ran to the helicopter. They pulled Patrick and Adam out, put them on stretchers, and ran to their aid station.

The medevac followed them in. As soon as they touched down Sergeant Whorton ran to the aid station to help assess them. Mike and his copilot Ray Illman saw a tiny area just big enough for a Kiowa to land. They squeezed in, and Mike was just beginning to get out when they received a radio call: "The enemy saw you land. They are coming to attack."

Ray asked Mike, "Do you want me to sit here and wait?"

"No. Take off and orbit. If they attack, hammer them. I'll call you when I'm ready to be picked up," he said, and Ray took off.

Mike went to Adam and Patrick's helicopter to see how badly it was damaged. The windscreen and all of the instruments were covered in blood. There were pools of dark, thick blood on the floor on both sides of the aircraft. He checked to see if any limits were exceeded, but didn't see anything wrong. He moved around to Patrick's side and he saw the bullet hole. The bullet hadn't hit anything vital, other than Patrick and Adam. He saw something dark pooling up under the helicopter. He assumed that one of the fluid lines had been cut so he checked all of the fluid levels—they were normal. He then got down under the helicopter and traced the liquid back to its source. It was coming from the drain hole at Patrick's feet. Closer inspection revealed that it was Patrick's blood, draining from the floor and pooling under the aircraft.

Suddenly, Sergeant Whorton exploded out of the aid station. He and several other men carried stretchers to the medevac. As they loaded Adam and Patrick, Mike called Ray to come get him. Ray landed and they took off with the medevac. As they departed Ray looked over at Mike. "It's lonely up there all alone," he said. Mike managed a chuckle.

They landed at FOB Wright, where a forward surgical team was located. Mike called me and asked to fly Patrick and Adam's helicopter back. We needed to get it out of Able Main quickly or the enemy would target it. Chief Warrant Officer 3 Scott White was already at FOB Wright. He was a maintenance test pilot, so I told him to split the crews.

"You fly with Scott, and Ray can fly with Captain Speace," I told Mike.

"How are Adam and Patrick?" I asked. It was the first time I had been able to talk to anyone directly.

"Patrick will be fine. He's got a long road ahead, but he'll be okay. Adam doesn't look good. He was conscious, so I'm hopeful, but everyone was very concerned. A gunshot wound to the head. The helicopter was a mess. They lost a lot of blood."

"Well, all we can do is pray for them now. They're in good hands, but we need to get Adam up to Bagram. Okay, I'll talk to you when you get here. Good job today."

"Thanks, sir."

I hung up with Mike and realized that I had a knot in my stomach. I knew Adam's brain would start swelling from the trauma. They'd have to cut part of his skull away to let it swell. That's where the danger would come in. I thought about what a horrific injury he had, and how the surgery itself would be almost as risky.

September 8 was a warm sunny day in Clarksville, Tennessee. Carrie Stead took her son, Cohen, to day care, then went to work. "I was at work, sitting at my desk, checking email and eating breakfast like I did every morning,"[8] she told me.

"At 7:45 A.M. Lisa Harloff called. She asked if I could meet her at my house." Lisa was Tim Harloff's, the A Troop commander's, wife. Tim was Adam's troop commander, and he was home on midtour leave. Lisa served as a point of contact for the troop, so Carrie assumed something had happened in Afghanistan. Lisa was responsible for keeping a group of spouses within the troop informed of events, and to pass on information about the troop. "I immediately thought that someone had been injured, and she was calling me to start the call down to notify the spouses of what had happened,"[9] Carrie said.

Carrie drove home to find Lisa and Tim Harloff at her house. She let them in, and within minutes the phone rang. It was the Department of the Army with official notification that Adam had been injured. You never know how people will respond when they receive such information. I have found over the years that you are foolish to try to predict how even soldiers themselves will respond to the injury or death of their friends and loved ones. I have seen strong people become completely inconsolable upon hearing bad news. Other soldiers, whom I thought might have tremendous difficulty dealing with the death of close friends, were strong and handled it incredibly well. I had no idea how Carrie would handle it, but she was absolutely amazing. I don't know if it was due to her medical background, but she was calm and controlled throughout.

My wife, Lisa, arrived shortly after Carrie was notified. "She knew why I was there. She had already been notified. She did not cry at all. She was a health care provider, which must have helped her to some degree, but still, she was so composed," Lisa said.

"What do you know? How bad is he hurt?" she asked my wife as soon as she walked in.

"I don't know how badly, just that he is hurt," Lisa said.

"That question just seemed to hang in the air, 'how bad?'" My wife later told me. "It was painful not knowing, waiting for the phone to ring, yet scared of it ringing. So many thoughts run through your head in situations like that—pity, sadness, worry—and then you suddenly think how grateful you are that it's not you, and you feel horribly guilty for even having such a thought."

"He must be alive because I got a phone call and not a visit," Carrie said.

"Cohen was just a baby. He was so cute, and I could see how much she loved Adam. It made me sick to my stomach," Lisa said.

I admit that I broke army protocol when Adam was shot. I knew that Tim Harloff was on midtour leave, and I knew how close their families were, so I called Tim and told him to be there when Carrie was notified. Because Adam was injured and not killed, I knew she would receive a phone call versus a personal visit, so I didn't want her to be alone when she received that call. I would not have done it had I not known all of them so well, but I chose to do it in that situation. I told my wife to go to her house immediately as well.

Carrie called her family and Adam's family to notify them. Many of them dropped what they were doing and headed for Clarksville to be with her. She called her good friend Bree Folk, Chief Warrant Officer 2 Chuck Folk's wife, to come and be with her as well. Once Bree was there, and it was clear that Carrie was strong and going to handle the situation well, my wife, Lisa, and the Harloffs left.

"Bree and I tried to go on with the day, just waiting for more updates and a phone call. We went to pick up Cohen from day care and Bree's son from preschool. We had lunch and just waited for more information."[10]

Carrie received numerous phone calls from the Department of the Army that day, providing her updates. Initially, she was told that Adam had been *grazed* by a bullet. Later she was told that the bullet was still in his head. It was scary not knowing exactly how he was doing, not being there with him, but the most alarming call came late that afternoon.

"I remember exactly where I was standing in my house when the lady told me, 'death was imminent within seventy-two hours.' I was in the hallway on the second floor leaning on the banister. Right after I hung up the phone my parents walked through the door, and the first thing I said to my mother was, 'What does "imminent" mean?' I obviously knew the meaning of the word; however, I just wanted someone to tell me it didn't mean what I knew it did."[11]

Back at FOB Fenty, we had planned an air assault to go back into Ganjgal and clear the village of any remaining enemy. It's hard to imagine a busier day, a day in which almost every decision we made was critical. Scott and Mike flew Patrick and Adam's helicopter back to Fenty. When Scott landed I went out to see the helicopter, to try and understand how one, single bullet could do so much damage. I don't remember what Scott said as I leaned into the cockpit to take a look, but all these years later I still remember the smell of the thick, baking blood. The memory of the seat cushions like sponges soaked in their blood, and roasting in the heat, almost steaming, makes me sick to my stomach today. I asked Scott to have the guys clean it up and repair the damage.

Jack briefed me on the air assault plan in our conference room. They had selected landing zones on the northeastern ridge above Ganjgal. We'd fly our Special Forces brothers, and their Afghan commando partners, in with two Chinooks. Apaches would escort them, then remain on station as they cleared the village. We'd find any enemy forces left behind. I conferred with Colonel George, and he approved the plan.

We got word that the surgeon was ready to move Adam to Bagram and Patrick to FOB Fenty. Our medevac guys loved Patrick. He hung out and smoked cigars with them a lot, so they all wanted to go get him, to bring him home. A TF Lift medevac bird flew from Bagram to FOB Wright to transport Adam back to Bagram, and our guys went and picked Patrick up. I went out to meet Patrick as the medevac landed.

The medevac guys who weren't on duty at the time were all standing by to meet him, a big crowd. I stood in the back and waited. As soon as the door opened they jammed a cigar in his mouth. Patrick, high on morphine, was all smiles. His leg was wrapped up and his pants had been cut off. I worked my way forward and asked him how he was doing. "I'm great, sir," he said with a huge, drugged smile on his face, and I knew he would be okay.

My heart ached for Adam.

That night we conducted the air assault into the high ground above Ganjgal. There were a few stragglers that had not yet moved back into Pakistan. When the assault went in, they made a run for it, and our Apaches killed them. The Afghan commandos cleared the village that night, and the battle at Ganjgal was over.

Adam spent two days at Bagram. Leah Shubin, the TF Thunder headquarters and headquarters company commander, was close friends with Adam and Carrie. She remained in the hospital the entire time Adam was there. She routinely called Carrie with updates. On September 10, Adam was transported to Landstuhl Regional Medical Center in Germany, and on Friday, September 11, Adam was moved from Landstuhl to the National Naval Medical Center (NNMC) at Bethesda, Maryland, where Carrie and her family were reunited with him.

Amazingly, Adam began to recover. No one would have bet that he would recover from a bullet through his brain, but Adam wasn't just anyone. He spent months at Bethesda and underwent numerous surgeries, but with each passing day he grew stronger. Later, he was transported to the James A. Haley VA Medical Center in Tampa, Florida, and then to Emory University in Atlanta. In April 2010, Adam required one final surgery. His neurosurgeon wanted to remove the bullet from Adam's head, so he returned to Bethesda and underwent surgery on April 21.

Following surgery he returned to Emory, where he continued rehab through August. In August 2010, eleven months after being shot, Adam returned to Fort Campbell, Kentucky. He was later promoted to Chief Warrant Officer 3, and in October 2011 he retired, two years after being shot. Adam still suffers from prosopagnosia, a condition that inhibits his ability to recognize faces, but otherwise he is doing great. Adam emailed me in the spring of 2013 and he said, "They are giving me a driver's license, sir. I can only drive in the daytime and in my neighborhood, but I'm driving."

Tears poured down my face as I read his words.

Adam, Carrie, and Cohen now live in Charlotte, North Carolina, where Adam works at Bank of America, and Carrie works part-time as a pediatric home-health physical therapist. At 7:33 A.M. EST, on March 10, 2014, an eight-pound, five-ounce boy named Elijah Keith Stead came screaming into this world, bringing even more life and love into a family that already knew a lot about both.

Sergeant First Class Kenneth Westbrook died of complications from his wounds on October 7, 2009, at Walter Reed Army Medical Center. He was posthumously awarded the Silver Star.

Both Captain William Swenson and Corporal Dakota Meyer received the Medal of Honor for their gallantry in battle at Ganjgal.

Chief Warrant Officer 4 Patrick Benson recovered from his gunshot wound. Patrick was awarded the Distinguished Flying Cross for his heroic actions in saving his and Adam's life after being shot. Patrick retired in 2011.

GETTING OUT OF NURISTAN

I landed back at Fenty at 3:30 A.M. It had only been two days since the battles at Ganjgal village and in the Shuryak Valley, yet it seemed as though the fighting had gone on forever. By this time there was a significant fight somewhere every day. That night a recovery team was ambushed as they tried to tow a truck to FOB Bostic. They were just north of OP Bari Ali when they were ambushed.

I was exhausted after it was all over, but it had perhaps taken more of an emotional toll than anything else. I threw my flight gear in my office and walked over to the command post to talk to Jack. I entered the building through Jillian's and Staff Sergeant Karvaski's office. When I opened the door I saw Jillian sitting at her desk, staring at the computer screen. She was rolling a lock of her hair with her left thumb and forefinger. "What are you doing?" I asked.

"I'm looking at all the pilot debriefs from today and bouncing it off other collection assets," she said.

She read my face. She could tell I was irritated. "How many ended up getting shot?" she asked. Like everyone else in the TOC, she had heard that several of the 3-61 Cavalry guys had been shot, but you only get bits and pieces trying to follow the battles on the radio. It's hard to tell what really happened until you talk to the folks that were actually there.

"Four," I said. "It was horrible! We lost a lieutenant, and two NCOs and a specialist were shot in the legs. The three of them should be okay."

I continued through her workspace. She followed me to Jack's office.

"Hey, sir. Not a good night," Jack said, as I walked in and sat down. "No doubt."

"It sounded like they went up the ridge after the enemy. It was hard to keep up with exactly what was happening, other than the part about the wounded guys that you couldn't get to until dark. What happened?" he asked.

"They got hammered trying to recover that truck with the ammo," I said.

The night prior, on September 9, we had sent a resupply convoy from FOB Fenty to FOB Bostic. We actually didn't get hit during the resupply mission, but later, just north of OP Bari Ali, an Afghan Jingle truck broke down. The truck had fifty 155-mm artillery rounds in it, rounds they desperately needed at FOB Bostic. Lieutenant Colonel Brad Brown sent a recovery team out the next day to tow the truck to Bostic. They were ambushed as they tried to conduct the recovery operation. Apparently, the enemy knew we would come back for the truck.

"The Apache team at FOB Bostic immediately launched to support them," I told them. "They had been fighting for a long time, and then they were sent to escort a medevac to Barg-e Matal, then came back and fought more in the draw. It was a busy day for the medevac and the Apache team. When I heard them on the radio I took my Kiowa team up there as well. The ground guys were already up the draw, pinned down when I got there, and the platoon leader, Lieutenant Tyler Parten, had been shot."

"How did they get up that draw?" Jack asked.

"C Troop drove down with some Afghan soldiers to recover the truck. When they got there they were ambushed immediately. You know the steep draw directly across the road from COP Pirtle-King, the one called Zangerbosha?" I asked.

"Yes, sir," Jack replied.

"That is right across the river from the Saw Valley," Jillian interjected, recalling the recent events in that area that put the Saw and Helgal prominently on the map as two more hellish places to add to the growing list.

"Yes, it is," I confirmed. "Well, about twenty to thirty men attacked them with AK-47s and PKMs from that draw." The AK-47 was the standard Soviet rifle carried by most insurgents. The PKM is a 7.62-mm machine gun with a rapid rate of fire.

"That draw forces the road to make a sharp curve, and the road is really narrow right there. That's where the truck was broken down, and it was in the middle of the kill zone, so when the shooting started the Afghan truck driver got out and ran. The truck then blocked the road," I continued.

"So they were stuck," Jack said, shaking his head.

"Yes. The Afghan soldiers were in a mix of HMMWVs and Ford Ranger pickups. The soldiers in the Ranger jumped out as soon as the shooting started, but they were right in the middle of the kill zone. Several of them just fell dead in the road. Sergeant First Class Stephen Laroque and his medic, Specialist Aamed Noormohamed, ran into the kill zone to pull the wounded Afghans out and both of them were shot in the legs."

Sergeant Laroque and Specialist Noormohamed never hesitated. It didn't matter that they were risking their lives for Afghans versus Americans. Soldiers were injured and they needed help. That was all that mattered. So, without wavering they ran into gunfire and pulled them to safety, and got shot doing it.

"Were you there when the ambush started?" Jillian asked.

"No. We were still down by Asadabad. Brad Brown sent some military police with a ten-ton wrecker, and he sent Lieutenant Tyler Parten's platoon as well. The Apache team covered them. They had just come back from being up at OP Mace, in the Kamdesh."

"That is tough terrain to fight in," Jack said, his normally placid features twisting into a grimace as he recalled the area. "They must have been attacked from straight above them."

"Well, their plan was to have Tyler's platoon dismount on the north side of the draw and walk up that ridge. The platoon from C Troop would go up the south side of the draw. Once they got up the ridge and quieted the enemy, the military police would evacuate the wounded and recover the vehicle out of the kill zone.

"Tyler had led his platoon up the ridge. They actually got a good ways up there, but got caught in an open area and he was shot. Tyler had been killed instantly, and Sergeant Jonathan Russ was wounded. I had shown up right as they were hit.

"Then they were in a fix. Their lieutenant was dead, and they needed to get Sergeant Russ down the mountain," I said.

"How bad was Sergeant Russ?" Jillian asked.

"He was shot through the hamstring. They put a tourniquet on him, but they had a worse problem. There was a sniper in the village up above them. They used the huge rocks for cover, but every time one of them so much as peeked out they got shot at, and he barely missed them each time. He had them pinned down."

"What happed to your lead Kiowa?" Jack asked.

"Right after we got there we shot everything we had at the base of the village, just in front of it, to try and suppress the enemy. Once we were out of ammo, we headed to the FARP at Bostic, but on the way there my wingman said he had tail rotor chips. They would not burn off, so he shut down, and I went back single ship."

There are several chip lights on the engine, transmission, and tail rotor of a helicopter. Chip detectors are simple magnets that pick up pieces of metal in the fluid lines. If it's a tiny, microscopic piece of metal the chip detector burns it off. If you get multiple chips it means you have a lot of metal in your fluids, so you need to land and have the aircraft inspected by maintenance personnel. If the piece of metal is big then it won't burn off, and you have to shut down and get the aircraft inspected. They serve as an indicator that the engine or transmission could be eating itself and are never taken lightly.

I continued describing the battle to Jack and Jillian. "The Apaches and I shot everything we had, all our ammunition, several times, but the ground force was stuck on the side of that mountain. Every time they tried to move, the sniper was on them. I knew he was in one of the houses, but I couldn't figure out which one. It sucked! Obviously, I couldn't level the village, and I had no idea where he was hiding. I flew in fast and close several times trying to draw his fire so I could figure out where he was, but I couldn't find him."

"That village is straight up that draw too, so he could see the guys on the ground perfectly below them," Jack said.

"Yep. So I thought maybe we could build a smokescreen with Willie Pete. I told the NCO on the radio that I was going to get seven white phosphorus rockets and that when I came back he needed to be ready to move. I told him I'd shoot them in front of the village, and when the smoke built up he could try and get back down the mountain. He agreed."

"Were they shooting artillery from Bostic?" Jillian asked.

"Yeah, but mostly above the village. Just behind it. I flew back to Bostic and got seven rockets. When I returned I told the NCO to get ready. He got back to me in a few seconds and said that they were ready. I flew right at that village. I wanted to shoot the rockets as close to the houses as I could."

"Didn't you think the sniper would shoot you?" Jillian asked.

"Yes," I said. "I figured he would shoot at us, coming straight at them like that, but we had to mass the rockets right in front of the village. I kept waiting to hear the popping of his bullets, but I never heard them. Several times the ground guys said that the enemy was shooting at us, but they never hit us. Anyway, I shot the entire pod of rockets right at the doorsteps and told the NCO, 'Go!'

"It built a pretty good wall of smoke, but he called me on the radio within a minute or two and said, 'It's no good. They are too heavy to move in these rocks. We can't carry them out.' "

I then explained that I had flown back to Bostic, and while my co-pilot got fuel and more rockets, I went inside the command post. Sergeant Whorton was there.

Sergeant Whorton was our flight medic. He was the same flight medic who had hoisted into the Shuryak two days prior when Adam and Patrick were shot. He had already picked up patients under fire at OP Pirtle-King and Barg-e Matal.

"He was itching to go in," I told Jack and Jillian. "He wanted to hoist into the draw and get them out right then. I pulled him aside and told him that if we tried to hoist him in during daylight the medevac would almost certainly get shot down, and he'd probably be killed. There was no way we could get in until dark."

It was going to be a very dark night. There was no moon, so as soon as it got dark I knew it would be pitch black up there. The mountains in northern Kunar and Nuristan had almost no ambient light.

He didn't like it. He didn't say it, but I could read it in his body language and in the expression on his face. He wanted to go then, but I didn't believe there was any way to pull it off without getting that medevac shot down, so we waited until dark.

"Did they recover the 155-mm rounds? What happened to that Jingle truck?" Jack asked.

"While we were fighting up the draw," I explained, "trying to get the platoons down the mountain, the military police picked up the wounded from the original ambush, and then they pushed that friggin' truck into the Kunar River!"

"With all the artillery rounds on it?" Jack asked.

"Yes! They badly needed those rounds at Bostic, and they pushed them into the river. I just about broke down and cried. The truck kind of flipped as it rolled in, and some of the rounds spilled out, but the river snatched that truck and pulled it under. It was getting dark, and they had a hard time finding it. I flew up and down the river right on the water and finally found a corner of the bed sticking up out of the water. I shined a laser pointer on it, so they could find it. They picked up as many rounds as they could find on the bank."

"When did Sergeant Whorton go in?" Jack asked.

"As soon as it was dark," I explained, "I flew back to the FARP and walked over to talk to Gary Heine face-to-face. He was flying the medevac bird."

Gary Heine was the pilot who had flown Sergeant Whorton in the Shuryak when Adam and Patrick were shot only two days prior. I explained to him everything that had gone on and where the casualties were located. After I finished talking to Gary Heine they cranked and took off. The Apaches covered the medevac as they went in, and I hung back behind them. They had a better sight than me with just my goggles, so I figured I'd watch where they shot, and I'd pound it when they broke off.

At first it was extremely dark because the moon had not risen above the mountain, but by the time we were ready to go in, it was up and it was bright out, so bright we could have flown without our night vision goggles. We were worried because the enemy was going to be able to see the wounded men. The draw was so steep that the helicopter would be very close to the mountain. Since Sergeant Whorton would be hanging one hundred feet below the helicopter, the bird would actually be closer to eye level with the village. I didn't like it, but it had to be done.

On the first approach they took small-arms fire and an RPG. Gary broke off and came back around again with Sergeant Whorton hanging from the cable. The second time, Gary put him in, and then he moved back out over the valley while Sergeant Whorton prepared Lieutenant Parten to be hoisted out.

After taking fire the first time I was really worried. I knew the enemy was smart enough to know that he was going to come back and pick them up, and I knew he had to make two trips. Sergeant Whorton called over the radio and said he was ready, so Gary went back in, this time taking fire immediately. He broke off and circled back around. The second time, they shot an RPG at him. The Apaches pounded the side of the ridge with thirty-millimeter and rockets. Gary came back around a third time and was able to get Lieutenant Parten's body on the hoist. They pulled him up, then had to go back again to pick up Sergeant Whorton.

"Holy crap, sir," Jack exclaimed as I related the harrowing series of events.

"Yeah, I know," I said. "Gary got back in and picked the other two up. He flew them all to FOB Bostic. In the meantime we covered the ground guys as they moved back down the mountain. They made it down pretty quickly without casualties."[1]

"That medevac crew has had a rough couple of days," Jillian said.

I agreed. "You're not kidding. They had the Shuryak two days ago, and today they did three medevacs under fire including the hoist, and they did one to Barg-e Matal," I said. "It wasn't long before the surgeon wanted Gary to fly the wounded from Bostic to FOB Fenty, so the Apaches escorted them back. My wingman had his Kiowa back up by then so we covered the ground guys until they were back inside the wire at Bostic. I made it back at three A.M.

"So what's the plan on Barg-e Matal? Did you guys finish planning?" I asked Jack, changing the subject.

Jack shook his head. "We will keep chipping away this month. If all goes well we'll have it done by the end of the month. Every time we take a load in, we bring out TF Chosin soldiers."

"How many turns will it take to winterize the Afghans with supplies?" I asked.

"Fifty-one," he told me. "We'll get it done, and then we can turn our focus to Keating and Lowell."

I could hardly believe it. "Man, that's a lot of turns. We've got to maximize every night. If the enemy isn't affecting us then we have to keep turning and get this done as quickly as possible," I said.

"We will, sir."

"But the enemy *is* going to affect us sooner or later," Jillian broke in. "They are watching all these turns. It's just a matter of time before they try to shoot a Chinook or Apache down. We have to fly over that ridge, the BK pass, on every turn, so it's predictable."

"I know, but there aren't many alternatives. The Chinooks have to wait on the Apaches to get over that pass as it is. It's either over the top or through the Kamdesh, up the gut, and that is a shoot-down waiting to happen.

"We've just got to pay attention to the enemy. If their discussions get credible, if we think they are in position and will shoot at us, then we stop the turns. If not, then we keep on going—situation-based turns," I said.

Both of them just looked at me and neither spoke. They knew we had to get it done, but it was painful to watch the turns every night, praying they wouldn't get shot down. I knew most of all. Most nights I would lie in my bed, half in and out of sleep, praying, until I heard the sound of Chinook rotors coming back in. It was painful to endure.

"When can we start bringing stuff out of Keating?" I asked.

"As soon as we get a new-moon cycle in October—middle of the month," Jack said.

"Okay, so we finish up Barg-e Matal this month, close Keating in October, and close Lowell in November."

"Yes, sir."

"I assume you've gone over all of this with Mountain Warrior, and they are good with it, right?"

"Yes, sir."

"Okay, good. I'm heading to bed," I said.

"See you in the morning, sir," Jack said.

I took my pistol from my body armor, holstered it on my side, and left the office. I used the back door to get to my living quarters. As I turned onto the walkway, just outside the berm of Hesco barriers, I saw Doc McCriskin. He was walking in the dark with his head down. "Hey, Brendan," I said.

Brendan mumbled something I could not understand. "Brendan," I said, as I stopped and looked back at him.

"Oh, hey, sir. Sorry about that."

"Are you okay?" I asked.

"Yes, sir. I'm fine," he said, but I wasn't convinced.

"You seem like you're not. What's on your mind?" I asked.

"Well, honestly, sir, I've been better," he confessed. "I had a rough one the other night."

I leaned against the wall of Hescos. "Tell me about it."

As our flight surgeon, Brendan McCriskin remained on medevac call all the time. He chose which missions he actually went on based on the incident, how bad the trauma was, and if it was a U.S. casualty or not. Otherwise, a flight medic went on the mission as the sole provider.

Late one evening, just after dark, we received a medevac request for several Afghan soldiers. They had been traveling on a dirt road south of Jalalabad when they struck an IED. The damage to their small pickup truck was devastating. The report said that one soldier had lost both legs and the other was severely burned. Brendan took the mission.

When the helicopter landed at the site Brendan got off and helped carry the patients to the aircraft. The burn victim was loaded first. His skin was melted and he was nonresponsive. The man who'd lost his legs was placed beside him. They laid him down flat on the floor of the Black Hawk and placed both of his legs below him as if they were still attached to his body. He was screaming out in pain and asking Brendan to help him. "His screams were a good sign," Brendan said. "The fact that he felt pain and could yell was a very encouraging sign."

The other man, however, concerned him. The burn victim was not responsive, yet he had vital signs. Brendan began to work on him. He wanted to look him over carefully to ensure that something wasn't missed on the initial examination in the field. A small pin light taped to his helmet helped Brendan to see in the dark cabin of the Black Hawk. He cut the man's clothes and looked over his body to try and determine the extent of his injuries. The smell of sweat and dirt mixed with blood and burned flesh was horrid.

The other man kept asking about his legs. It was apparent that he did not realize that they had been blown off. His fellow soldiers had applied tourniquets to both legs, so he felt the pressure, and when he looked down he could see his legs and boots, but could not move them. He continued to yell out, so Brendan decided to sedate him more so he could focus his attention on the other patient. He turned to prepare drugs for him, and when he did, the burn patient suddenly sat up and grabbed him by his shirt. He pulled Brendan in close to his badly burned face and said, in a feeble, raspy voice, "Help me. Please, help me."

It was an eerie moment. The image of that man's face was indelibly burned into Brendan's memory. He managed to get both patients back to FOB Fenty alive. Both made it into surgery alive, but both later passed. They realized that the burn victim had suffered internal injuries, so it was necessary to open him up to determine the extent of the injuries. As soon as they opened his chest cavity he bled out. The blood had been contained inside his chest. There was nothing they could have done.

Doc McCriskin's emotions had not been extracted at medical school. He cared. He cared that two Afghan men whom he did not know had died despite his best efforts to save them. The things he saw—that all of our medics saw—are things no one should have to witness, yet once you see them, it's hard to erase the images. Brendan McCriskin's dreams had transformed into nightmares.

One dream began with his medevac helicopter landing in the Watapur Valley. As it neared touchdown they experienced a brownout. A brown-out is a huge cloud of dust created by the rotors. It engulfs the helicopter as it nears the ground, and it's almost impossible to see through when landing. In his dream Brendan's medevac hit the ground hard, harder than expected, due to the pilot's inability to see the ground clearly.

The flight medic, Sergeant Marc Dragony, a massive, baldheaded man who had played tight end at Brigham Young University, leapt from the aircraft to try to find the wounded. Brendan started to follow him off the helicopter, but Dragony turned and yelled over the turbine engines, telling him to remain on the aircraft. Just as Brendan climbed back aboard soldiers appeared out of the thick dust carrying their buddies. They threw seven or eight wounded soldiers onto the aircraft. The casualties were piled up on top of one another, forcing Brendan to try frantically to sort through them so he could treat the most urgent first. The stress began to build.

Outside the helicopter the dust cloud never dissipated, which was strange. Brown-outs usually cleared once the aircraft was on the ground, but this time it remained, a thick, churning, brown whirlwind. The American soldiers disappeared back into the cloud and within seconds enemy fighters emerged. They walked out of the dust like ghosts and began spraying the helicopter with bullets. Brendan grabbed his machine gun and tried to shoot back, but his rifle jammed. He attempted to clear the jam, but it jammed again. Bullets were hitting his patients and there was nothing he could do to protect them. Suddenly, the pilot pulled in power and began to fly away. *"No!"* Doc screamed. "Dragony is still on the ground!" But it was too late, and he jolted awake, scared to return to sleep.

Most of us had one recurring dream—Brendan had two.

Brendan's second dream, the one that haunted his sleep most frequently, was of a nighttime medevac mission to the Korengal Outpost. A child, no more than a year old, had been hit with shrapnel in a blast. Brendan's mission was to pick the child up at the Korengal Outpost and provide en-route care as they transferred the child to Bagram Airbase. For some reason he didn't have a flight medic with him on the mission. The pilots landed, and Brendan went inside the aid station to assess the child before transporting him to the helicopter.

The injured child was tiny, a pitiful sight. Brendan checked the IV and the endotracheal tube in his throat. He appeared to be as stable as could be expected, so Brendan transported him to the helicopter and they departed.

Due to the enemy threat in the Korengal and Pech valleys, we always kept the lights off in the helicopter. Brendan used a small pin light, taped to his helmet, to provide just enough light to work on his patient. He was giving the child some medications to keep him sedated when he noticed the child's oxygen saturation level decreasing. His oxygen level had been in the high nineties when they departed. It then dropped into the eighties, then seventies.

Usually, when this happened, it meant that the oxygen tank was running out, or that the ventilator had stopped working. Both of those things were easy fixes, so Brendan didn't panic. He quickly checked to ensure that everything was working properly—it was.

Working alone, crouched over his patient, with a pin light in his teeth, Brendan decided to bag the child to see if that would help. He glanced at the monitor displaying the child's oxygen saturation: sixty, then fifty and dropping. He put a bag over the child's mouth and nose to provide more oxygen—no improvement. He searched for the Broselow bag, a pediatric resuscitation kit. Everything was organized on the medevac helicopter so that the medical provider could quickly access what they needed, yet at that point in Doc's dream, time slowed down. No matter how hard he tried, he could not move fast enough, as in those childhood dreams when you wanted to run but couldn't. Menial tasks became incredibly difficult. He checked the vent tube again, and it appeared to be in the right place. Everything seemed okay, yet the child's oxygen saturation level continued to drop. Fully understanding that there was no way he would be able to put it back in again, Brendan decided to pull the vent tube. He thought the child's lungs must have collapsed. He could stick a needle through the child's ribs and into his lung, but he'd never seen a child that young decompressed with a needle. He tried an oxygen bag once again with no improvement. The stress began to mount. He didn't want to lose the child.

"We've got to get to Asadabad," Brendan told the pilot.

"We're ten minutes away," came the reply.

That was too long. The child would certainly have brain damage, that is, if he lived. The last option was to make an incision in the child's throat to try and restore the airway. He would have to do it alone, on a child, in the dark, on a helicopter. He knew it wasn't a smart procedure on a child that small, but he felt helpless, hopeless. He made the incision, but he didn't find the soft spot he was looking for in the child's throat. He struggled to see clearly. The child's throat turned dark with blood. Suddenly his oxygen saturation hit zero and his heart stopped beating. Brendan sat bolt upright in bed, drenched in sweat. His heart was racing, and all he could think was that he had killed a child.

It was so real, so vivid. He was there, in the helicopter. The sights, the sounds, the feel, were so realistic. When he awoke he was relieved that he hadn't actually killed a child, but somehow felt guilty "for lying in a clean bed, with air-conditioning, while there were probably young medics struggling through just such a mission, somewhere in the world"[2] at that very minute.

Professional counselors say that the underlying emotions associated with these types of nightmares are guilt and a sense of helplessness or inadequacy. Brendan McCriskin did not disagree, but I think he more poignantly described it as, "subconscious scars that I am certain pale in comparison to those sustained by the injured guys we picked up."[3] On the surface that seemed to help Brendan, to think that it had to be worse for those he tried to help, but the reality is that Brendan and countless others have suffered in varying degrees from wounds not visible on the surface. War is in no way natural, and thus its effects are devastating. War wounds all of its participants to some degree.

My hope was that I had, in some small way, helped Brendan just by listening. I told him that we were all feeling the effects of the war. The stress of combat does not know rank, age, sex, or socioeconomic background. It affects us all. If it didn't I'd be even more concerned. Brendan shook my hand and continued to his room.

The rest of September we focused on Barg-e Matal winterization and retrograde, all the while struggling with a very effective sniper positioned in the mountains above. He killed or wounded Afghan and American soldiers literally every couple of days, which forced us to fly a medevac, escorted by Apaches up there and back, thus patterning ourselves more and more with each trip.

Jillian produced a superb targeting packet to narrow the search down for the sniper team. Jack then used Jillian's product to make a list of targets—target areas of interest (TAI). We told the Apache pilots that they were free to shoot into those areas to deny the terrain to the enemy (terrain denial fires) as the Chinooks flew into the valley to land. Furthermore, when TF Chosin reported sniper fire our Apaches immediately knew where to begin looking for the enemy. We ended up killing multiple sniper teams. Her analysis was spot-on.

With each successive trip to Barg-e Matal we brought out TF Chosin soldiers and equipment. By late September, almost unnoticed, we were finally out of Barg-e Matal. Our complete focus then turned to the Kamdesh. We had only October and November left before our mission was over, and we still had to figure out a way to get out of COPs Keating and Lowell.

Hell has laid an egg and it hatched right here.

—ATLANTIAN DURING THE CIVIL WAR

COP KEATING

The first call that came in to the TOC on October 3, 2009, was a medevac request for wounded soldiers at COP Keating, in the Kamdesh River Valley. By listening to the urgency of the radio calls we quickly deduced that the men at Keating were receiving much more than typical, daily enemy contact. This appeared to be a significant firefight with multiple casualties. Due to the historical threat in that area and ongoing enemy contact, the medevac mission required an Apache escort.

"Alert the QRF," Jack said. "I'm going to get Lieutenant Colonel Blackmon."

The Apache QRF team consisted of Chief Warrant Officer 3 Ross Lewallen, who served as the air mission commander, and Chief Warrant Officer 2 Chad Bardwell, who flew as Ross's front-seater/gunner. Ross and Chad's wingmen were Chief Warrant Officer 3 Randy Huff and Chief Warrant Officer 2 Chris Wright. Having fought countless times in the Kamdesh and supporting operations at Barg-e Matal, all four men were very familiar with the terrain around COP Keating. Ross and his team had just sat down for an early breakfast when their handheld alert radio went off. Ross had a spoonful of biscuits and gravy in his hand when the call came.

"Let's go," Ross said.

They quickly put their food away and ran for the command post.

I was awakened by a knock at my door. "Yeah," I yelled as the door opened and Jack Murphy stuck his head in, momentarily blinding me with a focused light beam from his Petzl headlamp.

"Sir, we've got a big fight at Keating. It looks like the enemy is trying to overrun the COP and the weather is crap up there," he said.

I squinted and shielded my eyes with my hand. "I'll be right there," I said as I got up and began pulling my shorts on.

When I arrived at the TOC, the battle captain had just finished briefing the crews, and they were preparing to run out to the helicopters. I grabbed Ross before he left.

"What route do you plan to use?" I asked him.

"I don't want to fly through the Kamdesh Valley," he said. "The enemy will expect us to come that way. They'll either hide in the rocks or they might have an aerial ambush set up waiting on us to respond. If that's the case they'll wear us out in that valley."

"So what do you think? Loop around to the north?" I asked.

"I think so. We'll circle around to the west. We might surprise them that way."

"Okay, sounds good. Good luck," I said as he jogged out the door to his Apache.

"Have the medevac follow them up the Kunar until they start turning west then just keep going to Bostic. Tell them to hold at Bostic until Ross calls for them to go to Keating," I told the battle captain.

"Roger, sir."

COP Keating sat in the bottom of a fishbowl. It was dominated by high terrain on every side. In order for the medevac—or any other helicopter, for that matter—to land they would have to fly slowly, then vertically descend to the tiny postage-stamp landing zone on the edge of the river.

The Apaches launched right at 6:00 A.M. When they reached the Pech River Valley they climbed up over the ridge north of the Watapur Valley. As they flew by the Pitigal Valley they called 3rd Squadron, 61st Cavalry at FOB Bostic to get an update on the situation. Lieutenant Colonel Brad Brown, the squadron commander, spoke with Ross.

"The perimeter has been breached. They have fired their final protective fires," he said, which is their last line of defense. "You can expect to see enemy fighters intermixed with our guys on the outpost."

The enemy was inside the wire.

"Let's go. Push it," Ross told his lead Apache.

The crews pulled every ounce of power they had to get there as quickly as possible.

The medevac departed right on the heels of the Apaches with our flight surgeon, Captain Brendan McCriskin, on board. We never flew a single aircraft unless it was an emergency. We always flew in teams of two, so the medevac required a chase ship. Warren Brown, who had earned his cavalry spurs at Bari Ali, and Chief Warrant Officer 2 Ray Andrel flew a Black Hawk to chase the medevac that morning. When they arrived at FOB Bostic, Warren climbed up high and began to orbit around the FOB so that he could relay communications between Ross's team in the Kamdesh and our TOC back at Jalalabad. Line-of-sight radios were useless in the mountainous terrain. Even satellite communication was spotty down in the deep valleys, but we had good satellite communications with Warren, so we were able to remain abreast of what was happening. 3-61 Cavalry prepared a five-man team, which they wanted Warren to fly into COP Keating as soon as possible.

As the Apaches approached the valley, Chad Bardwell tried repeatedly to raise the men at COP Keating over the radio, but only silence answered him. What he didn't know was that the generators were shot up, so their radios didn't work. Finally, they flew within sight of the COP.

"Ahh, shit, it's burning," Chad said. "Black Knight X-Ray, Weapon 1-6," he called. His and Ross's call sign was "Weapon 1-6."

"Weapon 1-6, Black Knight X-Ray." It was Lieutenant Andrew Bundermann, a platoon leader in Black Knight Troop, answering him on a handheld radio.

"Black Knight X-Ray, Weapon 1-6, you've got two weapons aircraft overhead at this time. Requesting ROZ and gun status, and a situation update," Chad said.

If it weren't for the machine gun fire rattling in the background Chad would have thought he had the wrong guy on the radio. The calm voice was out of place, considering the destruction Chad saw ahead. "Guns cold, anyone outside the wire is hostile. We are down to about two or three buildings. We have enemy inside the wire, over," Bundermann said. Under the thermal system in the Apache, COP Keating was a glowing white blob with a black tail that streamed into the sky.

"Roger, I copy—anyone outside the wire is enemy and you are down to two or three buildings," Chad answered.

"Roger."

"Find out what buildings they are in," Ross told Chad.

At that time twenty to thirty enemy fighters ran down the mountain on a switchback trail and onto the road that traversed the valley floor. They were going to try and assault the outpost through the front gate.

"Black Knight, we need to know what building you are in," Chad said.

"Roger, we are in the TOC. Can you recognize the ECP [entry control point] from where you are?"

"Negative." Due to the fire and smoke it was impossible to tell what was what inside the outpost. It appeared as though the entire COP was burning down.

"Hey, we are not shooting inside the friggin' COP. It's too close," Ross told the other pilots.

"Hey! What are those dudes doing? There's a bunch of dudes running around." Ross saw the men scrambling down the switchback trail with rifles in their hands. Like a long line of ants on a summer picnic, they filed down the trail and into the road, glowing white under the thermal sighting system.

"Black Knight, we've got about twenty personnel running down the hill. Understand we are cleared to engage?" Chad asked to be sure.

"You are clear to engage," Bundermann said.

"Confirm they don't have ANA [Afghan National Army] outside the wire," Ross told Chad.

"Confirm there are no ANA outside the wire?" Chad asked Bundermann.

"Negative, we have no ANA outside the wire," Bundermann answered.

"I've got visual," Chris Wright said, now using a more excited voice. The pilots had finally found enemy forces, and they were eager to turn the tide of the battle, to start killing those who had attacked our brothers on the ground.

"My video is out in the back. What do you need me to do, brother?" Ross asked Chad. His ability to see what Chad was looking at through the sight was gone. He'd have to take directions by voice.

"Come down and left a little bit," Chad said.

"Are you guys shooting yet?" Bundermann asked, clearly eager to hear that they were killing the enemy.

Bundermann wasn't the only one eager to hear the Apaches shooting. "The Apaches could not get to us quick enough," Sergeant Clint Romesha later told me. "The Apache was the best weapon to have in those mountains," he said. "When they showed up, you knew everything was going to be okay."[1]

"Lazing," Chad said, indicating that he was lazing the enemy to store a range in his system in order to compute a firing solution for the gun.

Suddenly, the 30-mm cannon echoed across the valley, and enemy fighters received the force of it all. Chad shot five- to fifteen-round bursts as they flew straight at the enemy.

"I've got a shot, call clear," Chris said. He was in the trail aircraft but had a good shot at the enemy already.

"If you've got the shot and you can shoot past me, then take it."

After Chris's first burst the enemy dove off the side of the road by the river. They tried to seek cover in the bushes and trees between the road and the water, but that provided no refuge. The 30-mm rounds impacted all around them, exploding trees six inches in diameter. Shrapnel flew through the air, cutting through trees and flesh alike. After the first gun run, between Chad and Chris, only two fighters remained alive. Chris saw them and killed both on the second gun run. All that remained, looking under the thermal, were hot spots, the only evidence of men who moments before had planned to kill our men at COP Keating.

They had prevented what would have almost certainly been a final enemy assault to overrun the outpost. They had stopped the immediate threat, but the fight was far from over. They began searching the ridges, looking for groups of fighters. Ross felt in his gut that there were DShK teams somewhere, seeking the perfect shot. Jillian had told them that there were teams set up to shoot aircraft down and something told him she was right. They were out there and he needed to find them.

Slowly, they began to find and kill enemy fighters in groups of two to three. This lasted for over an hour, before they needed to leave the valley for more fuel and ammunition. It made all four men sick to their stomach to have to leave. They had no idea how many fighters still remained, but they knew there were a significant number of enemy forces still fighting. After an hour they had engaged so many groups of fighters that they could not accurately recount where they had shot. "They were everywhere!" Ross would later tell me. The ridges were literally crawling with enemy fighters. As they departed, promising they would "be right back," Black Knight X-Ray updated the casualty count to eleven.

"No!" Sergeant Romesha shouted when he saw the Apaches leaving the valley. "My heart sank when I saw them flying away," he later told me. "It seemed like they had only just arrived."[2]

Back at FOB Fenty I realized that it was going to be a very long day of fighting. I called Colonel Lewis.

"Sir, it's Jimmy."

"Hey, Jimmy. I just got a battle update from my guys in the command post, but tell me how you're seeing it."

"All I know is that the perimeter is breached and they are holed up in a couple of buildings. I got Ross Lewallen on the radio as he was going back into Bostic for gas after their first turn. He said they have eleven casualties, but he also said the mountains are crawling with enemy."

"How many do you think?"

"He said probably two hundred attacked them."

"Wow. That's not good, not good at all. What do you need? How can we help you out?" he asked.

"I need another Apache team for sure. I may need more later. We'll just have to see how it plays out. I suspect we'll reinforce with more ground forces, but we're not there yet."

"Okay, I'll have Rob Dickerson send you an Apache team. I'll tell them to check in with your guys before flying in there, and we'll stand by to help with more when you know what you need."

"Thanks, sir."

"Okay, update me as often as you can."

"Roger, sir." I hung up the phone and walked back to the TOC.

While Chad Bardwell sat in the FARP filling the Apache up with gas and ammunition, Ross ran inside the 3-61 Cavalry TOC and called me on a secure phone. "Hey, sir, this is bad. The ridges are full of enemy and if we try and get that medevac in it'll get shot down," he said.

"Okay, well, you are the air mission commander, so kill the enemy, and as soon as you can get it in, do it," I told him.

I had always believed that we had to train our air mission commanders, invest a lot of time in them before we deployed, and then, most important, we had to trust them. If we were making tactical decisions from the TOC then we had failed in training our mission commanders before we ever deployed. Ross and his team had the best situational awareness of anyone on the battlefield. I knew he wanted the medevac to go in as badly as anyone, but he also knew that if we got it shot down we would make an already difficult situation much worse. I trusted his judgment and knew he would make the right calls. "Okay, sir, I need to get back out there. I'll call you on the next turn," he said, and we hung up.

Meanwhile, I launched another single Apache flown by Chief Warrant Officer 2 Gary Wingert and Captain Matt Kaplan to go join the fight.

Warren Brown, who had been orbiting since arriving at FOB Bostic, landed and went inside the 3-61 TOC to call us. Jack spoke with him. "Work with those guys to refine a plan to air-assault reinforcements into Fritsche," Jack told him. "The hills around Fritsche are covered with enemy so pick spots we can get into and out of as fast as possible," Jack added.

"Roger that, sir," Warren answered and began scouring maps for good landing zones.

Ross strapped himself back into his Apache and briefed his team on the plan. They had to destroy the DShKs and as many enemy fighters as possible so it would be safe enough to fly the medevac into Keating. Facing a DShK, potentially multiple DShKs, you'd think they were terrified. They had no idea where the guns were set up, but they were certain that they were there. But, they weren't scared. All they could think about was how the men on COP Keating must feel. They knew that if we didn't get a medevac in soon, more of the men on Keating might die. That sense of urgency to help their brothers on the ground drove them beyond fear for themselves. They had a DShK to destroy.

Chad checked in with Black Knight as soon as they entered the valley.

"Black Knight X-Ray, this is Weapon 1-6, situation report, over."

"Weapon 1-6, Black Knight X-Ray, we're taking a large volume of machine gun fire, DShKs and RPGs, from the mosque adjacent to the COP."

Chad put their sight on the mosque and could see muzzle flashes sparking in window and door openings all over the building. Both crews prepared to shoot Hellfire missiles at the building.

"Black Knight X-Ray, Weapon 1-6, we see the mosque and see the enemy fire. We're inbound with Hellfire missiles."

"Roger."

Flying lead, Chad shot first, but his missile didn't fire, so he broke off the engagement. Chris prepared to put a missile into the mosque. Just as he squeezed the trigger to shoot the missile, Randy Huff transmitted over the team internal radio, "We're hit."

Their electrical system had shut down in their Apache. They had no idea how bad the damage really was or how many bullets had actually hit the helicopter, but they knew systems were shutting down. Ross quickly spun his aircraft back around and oriented on the mosque to give Chad another shot. This time the Hellfire worked, and the explosion silenced the enemy inside for good, but not before they too were hit. Ross saw the large-caliber flashes and recognized them. It was most certainly a DShK.

The DShK was set up somewhere on the ridge between OP Fritsche and COP Keating. Ross realized that the gun was incapable of shooting directly at the men on COP Keating from that position. They did not have line of sight from their position. He wondered if it had been set up specifically to ambush helicopters, which would have to pass directly in front of it to land at COP Keating. He knew that the enemy would expect us to rush to the fight with our helicopters. The enemy also knew that we would fly our medevac helicopters in to evacuate the wounded. The DShK was set up in a perfect position to shoot a medevac on approach to Keating. Our helicopters could withstand a few rounds of small-caliber machine gun fire, but the 12.7-mm rounds fired at a high rate of fire from a DShK was a completely different matter. If the enemy caught us slowing down on approach to the outpost they could easily chew a helicopter up with that gun. It had to be destroyed in order to get the medevac into Keating, but first Ross had an immediate issue to deal with. He and Chad had completely lost their hydraulics and Randy and Chris had an electrical failure in their helicopter. The team had to get out of the valley to see how badly their aircraft were damaged. They left Black Knight with a promise to return and headed for FOB Bostic.

The crews landed at the FARP and shut down just as the team of Apaches from TF Eagle Lift was arriving—call sign "Overdrive." Ross explained the situation to the Overdrive crews.

"Don't get below six thousand feet or that DShK will eat your lunch, and try not to fly directly over the valley," he warned them.

With that in mind, the Overdrive team departed FOB Bostic and entered the battle while Ross ran inside the TOC and called me on a secure phone to explain the situation.

"Sir, the DShK is set up for an air ambush. They knew we'd come and they were prepared. They're counting on us flying in to get our wounded out. We've got to kill those guys," he explained.

"Okay, that makes sense. How bad is Keating?" I asked.

"Sir, it's burning down. The buildings are on fire. They are holed up in the command post and I think their aid station. Most of them are wounded and it looks like several are dead. We got there just in time. You know that switchback trail that comes down the mountain from Fritsche to Keating?"

"Yeah."

"There was a line of them running down that trail to the road when we got there."

"Did you kill them?"

"Yes, sir, we got them all. Then we just started finding guys here and there and killing them. Then they had us shoot the mosque, which was filled with bad guys, and that's when we got shot."

"Okay, John Jones is on the way. Hopefully he can patch your airplanes up. Did the Overdrive team make it up there?"

"Yeah. They just launched to go up there. I told them where the DShK was, so hopefully they'll kill it. I don't think we can fly our airplanes back into the valley, but Gary Wingert just landed in an Apache, so we can take his and John's and go back," he said.

Gary Wingert and John Jones were both maintenance test pilots, so they could try and fix the shot-up Apaches and get them back into the fight.

"Okay, let John and Gary try and patch the airplanes up, and if you guys are comfortable with them, if they will fly safely and the weapons systems will work, then go back in, or you can fly the aircraft they flew up there. We have to get that medevac in as soon as possible. Good work, Ross."

"Thanks, sir. I'll get back with you when we know something."

"Okay. Sounds good."

Ross ran back out to his helicopter and asked the first soldier he saw for a cleaning rod, a long metal rod used for cleaning the barrel of machine guns. He took it over to his Apache and ran it through the hole that the DShK round had made in the helicopter. He knew exactly where he was when he got shot, so by determining the angle in which the bullet entered the helicopter he could visualize pretty darn close where the DShK was located. He told Randy, Chris, and Chad where he thought the DShK was set up. "We've got to get back out there. How bad is the damage?" Ross asked, meaning the damage to their two helicopters.

Both would require some repairs. Gary Wingert had already begun working on the hydraulics line that was damaged on Ross and Chad's helicopter. Just then they heard the sound of rotors coming from the north. It was the Overdrive flight.

They haven't been gone long enough to have fought very much, thought Ross apprehensively. Why on earth are they already coming back?

As the Overdrive crews landed, it was immediately apparent that their lead aircraft had taken significant battle damage. Ross could see the holes in it.

"It was that damned DShK!" he said out loud.

John Jones, who famously almost crash-landed on Scott Stradley after being shot up in the Watapur, approached from the south and landed. Ross ran to his aircraft and asked if they could take it back into the fight while he tried to fix the ones that were shot up. "Sure," John said. "I'll get to work fixing these. Hopefully, I can get them back in the battle," he added.

John took a close look at all of the battle damage, then went into the command post and called me. He gave me an assessment and a list of parts he needed. We gathered everything he needed and flew them to FOB Bostic, along with an avionics technician and an electrician. Meanwhile, Ross, Chad, Randy, and Chris got in John and Gary's Apaches and launched back into the fight.

The weather had been deteriorating all morning, but now thunderstorms were nearing and the sky grew dark over the Kamdesh. Our fear was that the weather would force the crews out of the mountains altogether. Time was not on our side. Ross and his team realized that they had to work fast. "We've got to find that DShK and kill it," Ross reiterated to the team.

He told Randy and Chris to cover him as he and Chad began descending into the valley, all the while being careful not to get too close. They had to entice the DShK crew to fire on them so they could pinpoint their location. Within minutes the DShK team took the bait. They began shooting at Ross and Chad, and due to the darkening skies, Ross was able to see the muzzle flashes clearly. He immediately turned inbound.

"I see you, asshole," he said. "We've got 'em. Cover us," he told Randy and Chris.

"Roger," Randy replied.

Ross planned to shoot them with rockets, which could be done from the backseat. Chad had not seen the muzzle flashes so he continued to scan the ridge trying to find them. Ross opened fire with a salvo of rockets, but Chad suddenly saw tracers coming at them from a different spot. Big tracers! He took control of the gun, so as soon as Ross stopped firing rockets Chad engaged another DShK with thirty-millimeter. As Ross was shooting rockets he had noticed his wingman out of the corner of his eye, creeping up on him and engaging the enemy as well. Ross thought, *He's not covering me, and what is he shooting at?*

There were three DShKs set up on the ridge. The enemy wanted to make certain that they shot a helicopter down, and they certainly would have, if Ross and his crew had not found them. Randy and Chris had observed the second DShK and feared it would shoot Ross and Chad down, so they shot it. The enemy had set up all three weapons behind a fighting position that was made out of rocks stacked up in a half-moon shape. As Ross suspected, they had been positioned to cover the approach path to COP Keating. Now all three guns were silenced and their crews dead, and just in time. The weather closed in on the valley quickly. They had to get back to FOB Bostic. Everything had seemed like a racing blur so far. The team had been fighting for five and a half hours, yet it had happened so fast they had lost track of time.

The thunderstorms lasted for a couple of hours. Waiting was terribly painful for all of us. Everyone wanted to get back into the valley. There were wounded soldiers at Keating, men who desperately needed our help, yet there was nothing we could do but wait. It was a gut-wrenching couple of hours, but we used the time to move forces up to FOB Bostic.

While the weather was bad in the Kamdesh, it was suitable to fly in the Kunar, so we began moving soldiers from Mark O'Donnell's TF Chosin to FOB Bostic. I spoke with both Colonel George and Colonel Lewis about how we might get them into Keating once the weather permitted. I wanted to use Black Hawks versus Chinooks because we could get in and out more quickly in Black Hawks. We could carry more soldiers in a Chinook, but it was a huge, slow target, and it would take longer in the landing zone to unload. We would have to make more turns in Black Hawks, but we could come in fast and unload very quickly. If we tried to take troops directly into COP Keating we could only land one helicopter at a time, and Ross had insisted that there were more DShKs in the area, so that was too much risk. The LZ at Fritsche was large enough for three Black Hawks to land simultaneously. Based on the number of soldiers we needed to get to Fritsche, it would take five turns of three Black Hawks.

Captain Justin Sax commanded headquarters and headquarters company. Mark O'Donnell had given him three platoons and treated him just like another infantry company. Justin's company had only recently returned from Barg-e Matal, where they had spent a month fighting and training Afghans. Mark O'Donnell chose Justin to lead the rescue effort at Keating. The son of a Wyoming game warden, Justin had cut his teeth in the Rocky Mountains. Having grown up in Cody, at the eastern entrance to Yellowstone National Forest, Justin had a deep knowledge of the wild country.

This was his second deployment to Afghanistan with the 10th Mountain Division. Prior to his first deployment he had taken his platoon to Cody, so his father could teach them the ways of the Old West. He trained them how to lash supplies to donkeys, and most important, how to move in rugged terrain at high altitudes. Army life had come naturally to Justin. He graduated first in his ROTC class at the University of Wyoming and was designated a distinguished military graduate. Justin loved Wyoming. He really didn't want to leave, but he knew in his heart that someday he'd return for good. Justin Sax quite simply joined the army looking for a physical and intellectual challenge. The problems he faced in Afghanistan certainly met his expectations.

We picked up two of Justin's platoons, one at FOB Joyce and one at COP Monti, and flew them to FOB Bostic in order to prepare for the rescue operation. Lieutenant Jake Miraldi and Lieutenant Jake Kerr were the platoon leaders.

Once at Bostic, we loaded Jake Miraldi's men on the Black Hawks and waited for a break in the weather. Justin Sax was in the first flight with Miraldi's crew. At Fenty we watched the weather radar closely, praying for an opportunity to go. At Bostic, Warren Brown paced around his helicopter watching the sky. Finally, he called me. "I think we can get them in, sir. Worst case, we launch and have to turn back," he said.

I had already spoken to Colonel George and he said to get them in as soon as we could. "Okay, Warren. Go get it done," I told him.

The options to approach the LZs at OP Fritsche were very limited. The terrain and the winds that accompanied the storm dictated that we approach using a relatively open area on top of the ridge. The pilots flew as fast as they could, trying to reduce their exposure time. As soon as they hit the ridge south of COP Lowell they began taking fire. They weren't even halfway up the valley, and the enemy was already shooting at them. The door gunners, Specialist Mick and Specialist Hatfield, suppressed the areas where they saw muzzle flashes. Everywhere the Apaches saw Mick and Hatfield shooting, they shot thirty-millimeter and rockets. The first two Black Hawks landed simultaneously. The third one sat down as the first two departed. Twenty-one soldiers were inserted on the first turn.

The terrain forced them to fly an egress route that almost mirrored the route they had used to fly in, but empty and much lighter, they could fly faster and more radically. They returned to FOB Bostic and loaded twenty-seven more soldiers on board, along with two speed-ball resupply bags filled with ammunition and water.

While the Black Hawks returned to pick up the second load of troopers, Sax debated whether to go ahead and begin down the mountain or wait for the rest of his men. Ultimately, he decided to take some of the men from OP Fritsche with him and begin the long descent down the mountain to COP Keating. We expected it to take them at least two hours to get to Keating. It was a long, painful wait monitoring their progress from the command post, but nothing like waiting for help to arrive in COP Keating itself.

The men on Keating knew that help was on the way, but it would take time for that help to get there. That's what scared them most. They didn't know how much time they truly had. Private First Class Stephan Mace had been shot multiple times early that morning. He had lost a lot of blood, and they had been giving him body-to-body, live blood transfusions to keep him alive. They weren't sure how much longer he could hold on.

On the second turn the Black Hawks took heavy small-arms fire for the last three miles into Fritsche. Apaches engaged enemy fighters as the Black Hawks made it in and out once again, but as they departed after the second turn, the clouds closed in fast and sealed the passes behind them.

Warren's team landed their Black Hawks at Bostic and shut down. He went to the TOC and called me. "Sir, the weather moved in as we were leaving after the second turn. We can't get back in right now."

"When do you think you might be able to go back in?" I asked.

"Talking to the air force weatherman, it looks like we might have a window in about an hour."

At that point I wanted to move forward, go to Bostic personally, a natural reaction for a commander at such times, I suppose, but I had to be honest with myself. I was needed in my command post. I was in the best position to determine what assets we needed or would need in the next twenty-four hours and to coordinate for those assets. If I went forward I would limit my ability to communicate and coordinate while in a helicopter. In fact, I would most likely have less situational awareness in a Kiowa, and I would not fly a Kiowa to Keating. I had a team of Kiowas forward already, and they had called multiple times asking to go to Keating and help.

Chief Warrant Officer 2 Jeffrey Keown, a former infantry noncommissioned officer in the 82nd Airborne Division, was the air mission commander. Jeff had been in combat as an infantryman on previous deployments. An airborne ranger with a combat infantryman's badge, he wanted to go to Keating as soon as it started, and he was more than pissed off at me for saying no.

The Apaches had been shot to pieces in the valley. I was amazed at how much damage they took and yet still flew out, but the Apache is a dual-engine airplane. The Kiowa is the army's only remaining single-engine helicopter. The Kiowa could not handle the damage the Apaches had taken, and if one of them was shot down it would take the entire brigade to get it out. It was a very difficult decision, but if I let the teams go I would have been not only risking their lives, but the lives of countless ground soldiers who would have had to go and get them if anything bad happened.

These thoughts kept running through my mind, and I realized that if I were forward in a Kiowa I would not be able to think decisions through. I was where I needed to be—in my command post, weighing risks, coordinating for resources, and trying to forecast the next tactical move.

Warren called back after the hour passed. "Sir, I think we can get in," he said.

"Okay, go!"

Turn three was on its way. Each turn, we received more and more enemy fire. It was clear that the enemy knew that we were putting soldiers into OP Fritsche, so they began scrambling up the ridge from COP Keating to try and hit us on the way in. All three Black Hawks landed simultaneously on the third turn, but as the lead aircraft was departing they were called back. A mortarman had left the base plate to his mortar on the aircraft. Lead quickly circled and came right back into the LZ, dropped the base plate, and rejoined the flight.

The Black Hawks loaded thirty more soldiers for the fourth turn. This time all three chalks got in without taking direct fire. On the way out Warren Brown saw four enemy fighters running toward a boulder to seek cover. He gave his door gunner, Specialist Mick, the direction and distance to the enemy, and Mick immediately saw them. The enemy, realizing they would not make it to the boulder, turned and started to shoot at the helicopter, but Mick beat them to it. He hit three of them on the opening burst with his M240 machine gun, and the Apaches took over from there.

The number of enemy fighters on top of the mountain seemed to continue to increase, so while the final group of thirty soldiers loaded the Black Hawks, the pilots discussed how they might get over the highest point on the ridge in order to fly a different route to Fritsche. The Apaches were not sure if they had the power to get up and over the ridge.

Fully loaded, four Black Hawks and two Apaches launched on the fifth and final turn. It was getting dark, we'd been fighting since dawn, and wounded men had been hanging on for medical help a long time. The Black Hawks departed Bostic and immediately began climbing. They were nearing the summit when the Apaches called on the radio, "We don't have the power to get over the ridge. We can't make it over."

So, Warren Brown returned to the original route, and just as they made it to the ridgeline, enemy fighters shot at the lead Apache with an RPG and machine guns. The Apaches returned fire and the Black Hawk door gunners opened up with their machine guns. For the final time, they fought their way back into the LZ.

By that time in the fight, in command posts all over Regional Command–East, soldiers huddled around radios and stared at digital maps, trying to keep up with what was happening. Eleven men were reported wounded, six killed.

Meanwhile, Justin Sax had made his way down the mountain. He and his men made sporadic contact during their descent, killed a couple of enemy fighters, but made no significant contact, and they took no casualties on the way down. They walked into a destroyed outpost and linked up with the survivors. The commander of Black Knight troop, Captain Stoney Portis, had flown into Fritsche with Sax. "I'll establish security. You take care of your men," Sax told Portis, who agreed.

The remainder of Sax's men had been delayed by weather but were now on their way down the mountain. Sax had chosen not to use the trail for fear of an enemy ambush. They had blazed a trail of their own, much as he had done in his formative years in Wyoming.

With Sax and his lead elements having cleared the route on the way down, the follow-on forces were able to move much faster as they descended.

Meanwhile, back at FOB Bostic our flight surgeon, Captain Brendan McCriskin, was a nervous wreck. His day had begun when the original medevac request had come into our command post at daylight that morning. He had run to the TOC to receive a quick mission brief, then flew to FOB Bostic, only to be told that it was too dangerous to go in. But with Justin Sax's men on the ground at Keating and darkness quickly swallowing the valley, it was finally time to go and get the wounded.

The medevac crew had been on edge all day, pacing around the pad at Bostic, hanging on every word of every radio transmission, hoping, praying, to get approval to launch. Once it came they were like a race horse out of the starting gates. They exploded off of the helo pad and flew the guts out of the Black Hawk to get there. Brendan expected a full load of wounded men to be hefted onto the aircraft when they arrived, but that wasn't the case. As the helicopter touched down on the tiny island LZ, three soldiers were loaded onto the aircraft— one American and two Afghans. The two Afghans were stable. The flight medic attended to them, while Brendan focused on the young man whose status he had been monitoring throughout the day over the radio. His patient was Private First Class Stephan Mace.

Mace had been shot several times through the abdomen early in the morning. Shrapnel from RPG blasts had badly damaged his legs. Throughout the day the men on COP Keating had given him blood from their own bodies to keep him alive. When Mace was placed into the helicopter he had an oxygen mask over his mouth and nose, a tourniquet on his left leg and two on his right thigh, a pressure dressing was wrapped tightly around his belly, and an IV lay on his chest. "His PA and medic had done everything they possibly could, and they had done it well," Brendan later recalled.

Later, reliving vivid, painful memories, memories that had not faded with time, Brendan stared into space and told me the story. "Working with a pin light in the dark, I hooked up our cardiac monitor, replaced his IV bags, which were nearly empty, and put him on our oxygen tank. His was empty. I checked his tourniquets to ensure that they were tight, and then he looked up at me, and spoke."

"I'm not in pain, Doc," he said. Mace had been given all of the appropriate antibiotics, every fluid available at Keating, and finally morphine, which had washed the pain away.

As they flew out of the dark valley that had literally been hell on earth throughout the day, Mace looked up at Brendan McCriskin and smiled. In the darkest hour of Stephan Mace's young life Brendan McCriskin must have seemed like an angel of mercy flown in to rescue him. "I'm not in any pain," he said again through a thin smile.

Suddenly, his vitals registered on the monitor beside Brendan. Red numbers glowed in the dark indicating the strength of life left within him. "His heart rate was in the 160s, and his blood pressure so low that I would not have believed it in almost any other patient. He was in hemorrhagic shock," Brendan said. He had lost so much blood that his cells were dying due to lack of oxygen.

Despite shock, an elevated heart rate, and low blood pressure, Mace remained conscious throughout the flight. He answered every question Brendan asked him about his wounds, "but what he needed was far beyond anything I had to offer in flight," Brendan recalled. As Brendan relived those memories, five years later, he was distant, as if he were there, seeing it all again in dramatic detail.

Stephan Mace needed more blood and a surgeon to stop the bleeding in his belly. The surgeon at FOB Bostic was Dr. Brad Zagol, a West Point graduate and general surgeon. He was "as good as any I'd seen," Brendan later said.

The medevac landed on the pad at FOB Bostic, the same pad they had sat on all day, waiting to go. A team of medics rushed the helicopter, grabbed the litters, and hustled off toward the aid station. Brendan stumbled out of the helicopter and chased after them. He caught up to them in the trauma bay, where Brad began examining Mace. Brendan told Brad everything he had learned about Mace's wounds in the short time he'd examined him in flight. As the medical team prepared Mace for anesthesia, he pushed the mask aside and asked Brendan, "How are the other guys doing? Have they been medevaced, Doc?"

Brendan knew the real answer but told him, "They are hanging in there, but they are worried about you."

Mace smiled again. "Tell them I'm okay. I'm doing fine."

Brendan took Stephan Mace's hand in his. "I'm almost done over here. My tour is almost over, and I'm going home soon," he told him. "Do you want to meet up when we get back to the States?" he asked. "I'll buy you a beer. What kind of beer do you like?"

Mace seemed ashamed to answer. "Coors Light," he said, as if Brendan might not approve.

With that, the anesthesia kicked in and Stephan Mace slowly closed his eyes. Having done all he could do and needing to return to Keating, Brendan ran to the helicopter and launched back into the blackness of the night.

An hour later Brendan landed back at FOB Bostic with another helicopter full of wounded but stable soldiers. He ran from the aircraft to the aid station, "expecting to pick up Stephan for transport to Bagram."

It had been twelve hours from the time Mace was shot to the time that he entered surgery. Brendan thought he had a reasonable chance of making it, but as he blew through the doors he saw Dr. Brad Zagol leaning in a doorway across the room, drenched in sweat, tears running down his cheeks. "He looked devastated and exhausted," Brendan recalled.

Stephan Mace had coded during surgery. There was too much damage to his bowel. Brad had opened his chest and tried to force his heart to beat again with his own hands. "I felt as if I had been kicked in the stomach. I tried to think of something to say to Brad, something that would console him, but I had nothing. Stephan was the eighth American to die at Keating that day," he later said, almost in shock from the pain of the memory.

"He had his name, 'MACE,' tattooed across his belly. I'll never forget his name as long as I live, having seen it written in ink on his stomach, overlying the wound that killed him," Brendan later told me.[3]

In the days that followed we closed Keating and Fritsche. We hauled out everything that wasn't destroyed with Chinooks, then air force bombers went to work. When they finished it was unrecognizable. There was nothing left but an imprint in the earth where an outpost once stood, and memories, powerful memories that will survive a lifetime in the minds of a handful of soldiers—survivors.

We inserted an Afghan special purpose force that went village to village searching for those responsible for the attacks at Keating and Fritsche. It was estimated that two hundred to three hundred enemy fighters attacked Keating on October 8. A large majority of them never saw another Afghan sunrise.

Eight American soldiers were killed and twenty-seven were wounded at Keating. Eight Afghan soldiers and two Afghan security guards were also wounded. Staff Sergeant Justin T. Gallegos of Tucson, Arizona; Specialist Christopher Griffin of Kincheloe, Michigan; Private First Class Kevin C. Thomson of Reno, Nevada; Specialist Michael P. Scusa of Villas, New Jersey; Sergeant Vernon W. Martin of Savannah, Georgia; Specialist Stephan L. Mace of Lovettsville, Virginia; Sergeant Joshua J. Kirk of South Portland, Maine; and Sergeant Joshua M. Hardt of Applegate, California, fell in battle that day. They were lost but will never be forgotten.

We didn't ask permission to close Lowell—we assumed it was a given—so we immediately began planning.

COP LOWELL

While the battle at Keating was over, it seemed as though it was never-ending. From the time Ross Lewallen launched with his team of Apaches to support COP Keating until the Kamdesh was completely closed it seemed like one long, strung-out fight. The lift crews didn't have much to say to me. They just seemed to walk around with their heads down, dreading what was inevitably coming.

Everyone knew what was next, but no one spoke about it. No one wanted to think about it. We had to go back in. We had to close COP Lowell. Our original plan was to close Keating, Fritsche, and Lowell. The attack took care of Fritsche and Keating, but Lowell remained and everyone knew it would not be easy. COP Lowell was the largest outpost in the Kamdesh Valley. It would take us at least five or six days of all-night turns to close it. It would be an incredibly danger-ous operation. We would make turn after turn only a few kilometers from Keating, but it had to be done.

Colonel George told me to plan for the next red-illumination cycle, so we began preparing. One of my Chinook instructor pilots, Chief Warrant Officer 2 Mike Maggio, had been an infantryman in a Path-finder unit before he became a pilot. Pathfinders are infantrymen with unique, specialized skills, one of which is sling-load operations. We expected to have to rig several nonstandard slings, so we sent Mike forward to take a look at all the slings and ensure that they were rigged properly and ready for operations to begin.

Once we began making turns with our Chinooks we wanted to fly to Lowell, hook up a load, and depart immediately, with no delays.

Mike spent four days at Lowell, then returned, angry. "Mike is pissed off," Jack told me.

"Why?"

"They plan to bring *everything* out of Lowell, including weight sets, shower trailers, everything," he said. "That is why it's going to take forty-seven turns to get it all out. He's got the Chinook guys worked up. They are all on edge because of Keating. You're going to have to go talk to them."

"Okay. Tell Joe McCarthy to get them all together. Whenever it's best for them. I'll go talk to them." Joe commanded both the Black Hawks and Chinooks.

"Okay," he said.

Talking to Joe's men was one of the more challenging things I had to do in command. It wasn't that they were scared to go. Certainly, there was a degree of fear, particularly after Keating, but that wasn't the primary issue. They were willing to go in, but they didn't want to risk their lives for gym equipment and shower trailers. They were fine with going to get the soldiers but not the equipment.

Initially, I struggled with it myself, so I went to see Colonel George. Mike had brought a list of all the loads back from Lowell. It was an itemized list of the composition of each load. I showed the list to Colonel George and explained my dilemma.

"Jimmy, these guys have been living in that valley all year," he told me. "They get attacked every day; we haven't been able to get them mail or supplies. Now we are going to move them out of the valley. They will be happy just getting out of the Kamdesh, but they are going to have to live in the Kunar, build a new home, and we have nothing to give them. Their life support systems are at Lowell, and if we don't bring it all out then they will have nothing."

"I get it, sir; I've just got to help my guys understand it. With each load they bring out, they are literally asking if each load is worth their life. They hook up a shower unit and they ask, 'So is this shower unit worth risking my life?'"

He smiled at me, knowing that I would figure it out. I walked back to my headquarters trying to find the words to say. I sensed that there was more to the decision than Colonel George had shared with me. My gut told me that he had been directed to remove everything from Lowell so that it could not be used against us as propaganda. I recalled Major General Schloesser telling us to bury every piece of the Chinook that was shot down in the Korengal Valley. He feared that the enemy would use it against us, and ultimately he had been right. If we left equipment at Lowell on the heels of the very deadly battle at Keating, the enemy could, perhaps credibly, say that they had run us out of the Kamdesh Valley. I sensed that Colonel George had been told to remove every piece of equipment on the outpost, so being the leader he was, he did not pin the decision on his higher headquarters. He owned it.

I went to Jack's office to talk to him about what Colonel George and I had discussed. When I walked through the door I could tell he was frustrated about something. The small tuft of jet black hair on his head was sticking straight up, as if he'd been rubbing his head in frustration.

"What's up?" I asked.

"Joe," he said, referring to Joe McCarthy. "You just missed him. He's all pissed off about the plan as well. He understands why we have to go in, but he doesn't like the number of turns we've planned each night. He'll be fine—I told him we're working on ways to mitigate the risk—but he was hot when he was in here."

"I'm not worried about Joe. It's his Chinook crews I'm worried about. I've got to go talk to them."

Later that evening, Joe came to my office and we walked down to his troop area together. When I walked through the door the first sergeant called the room to attention. They all stood and I told them to "carry on." They sat down and their eyes went straight to the floor. Most of them didn't even want to look at me. I knew it was because they knew what I was going to tell them.

I explained that the men at COP Lowell had been there fighting for their lives ever since they arrived in Afghanistan. "They can't walk out. They'd never make it out of the Kamdesh. We've got to go get them, and *we are going to get them*. I know you're pissed about their life support and gym equipment, but here's the deal. They won't have anything in Kunar. Everything they have is at Lowell, and we can't get life support up to Bostic. You've seen what happens to the logistics convoys we try to push up to Bostic. They get blown up and burned. We have to bring what's at Lowell out," I said.

"Sir," one of them spoke up. "That's a lot of turns, and you know the enemy will try and shoot us down."

"Yes, it's forty-seven total turns, and we want to do as much of it as possible during the red-illumination cycle, so you're right, it's a lot of turns each night. We are working on some options to mitigate it. Lieutenant Wisniewski is producing a product like she did for Barg-e Matal. Her team is working to try and determine where the enemy will try and engage us. We'll have the Apaches shoot those locations as we go in. Also, we are going to request pre-assault fires. It will take General McChrystal to approve it, but I think he will after Keating. We are going to ask to drop bombs on those grids and shoot artillery at them right in front of you as you fly in. We'll have full-motion video on the area for hours before you fly in. If anyone is in there we'll see them and kill them. We'll listen to the enemy and make a decision after each turn if it's safe enough to go back in. Once we feel that the enemy might be in place and ready to shoot at you, we'll stop. That will be our last turn for the night," I told them.

I don't know how I expected them to react, but my little speech didn't seem to move them either way. They would certainly go, but they were not happy about it. I guess it was good enough. It had to be.

On the afternoon of October 13, Chief Warrant Officer 2 Mike Maggio walked into the TOC to see what his crew's mission would be that night. He stopped by the planner's desk first and saw that he was to fly twelve turns between COP Lowell and FOB Bostic. He was pissed.

"Are you kidding? Twelve turns!" he said to Jack Murphy as he walked into Jack's office. "This is bullshit! You're going to get us killed."

In his ever-calm manner Jack said, "Mike, we've been through this. Lieutenant Colonel Blackmon has made the decision. He spoke with Colonel George and we've reduced the list some, but the turns have to be made. You will have a huge stack of enablers above you. If the enemy gets active we'll stop making turns."

"We're going to get shot down," he said.

"We've got close air support, Apaches, bombers, and artillery. We have permission to shoot pre-assault fires. That's unobserved fires, Mike."

"I know what it is, sir. Still . . ."

"We've never been able to do that. We'll hit all the likely spots the enemy would be, shoot right in front of you as you go in."

Mike walked out, still upset. He went back to his troop area and briefed his crew.

Jillian had developed the same terrain-analysis products that she had created for Barg-e Matal. General. McChrystal gave us permission to drop bombs and shoot artillery on those historical enemy positions right in front of the Chinooks as they went in. We would listen to the enemy. If it sounded like they were in position to shoot at our helicopters, we'd stop for the night.

It was a very tough time as a commander. I could empathize. I understood the troops' position, but it had to be done, and we were going to do it. We were still fighting every few nights to get resupply convoys from FOB Fenty up to FOB Bostic. I flew the escort missions every few nights myself, and we fought to try and get the crews through almost every mission. They had no idea how hard I was praying for their safety.

Mike's copilot was Chief Warrant Officer 2 Tom Young. In the back of the aircraft he had Sergeant Mike Pettit, who manned the back ramp, Sergeant Ryan Rybolt, who manned the cabin door on the right side of the Chinook, and Specialist Carlos Hernandez, who served as a door gunner on the left side of the aircraft.

A team of Apaches flanked them on either side as they flew over Bostic and continued north toward COP Lowell. As they entered the Kamdesh Valley they saw explosions ahead of them—artillery and bombs dropped from jets overhead. In the TOC, Jack and I sat glued to the digital map. Jillian's analyst on duty watched the computer screen for SIGINT traffic. The Apaches flanked them all the way in. Tom Young flew the helicopter and Mike called out their altitude and airspeed during the approach to Lowell. It was dark in the Kamdesh, but for the crew it wasn't dark enough. Still, it gave them some degree of comfort knowing that the enemy would have a difficult time seeing them.

On the first turn, they landed and picked up twenty-seven soldiers. They flew them to Bostic, where they dropped them off, and prepared for turn number two. It was comforting to get that first turn in with no enemy contact. In fact, it had been very quiet. We watched the UAV feed in our TOC. Everything seemed calm. And it remained so on the second, third, fourth, and fifth turns. It seemed as though the night would go very smoothly. It certainly had thus far.

"One more turn and we're halfway done for the night," I told Jack.

"Let's just hope it remains this smooth," he said.

On the sixth turn Tom was on the controls again. Mike called out their altitude and airspeed. At two minutes out from landing, the Apaches fired a burst of thirty-millimeter into historical fighting positions. At one minute out Mike made the radio call to the men at Lowell.

"Apache X-Ray, this is Flex 6-3, one minute out, over," he called to let the sling-load teams in the pickup zone know that he was one minute out. They were going to pick up two slings of equipment.

"Roger."

Tom began his descent and slowed the aircraft. "One hundred, fifty feet, forty knots, point-four miles out," Mike called out.

Specialist Hernandez leaned out of the left gunner's hatch to scan the area below the helicopter. Through the monochromatic green night vision googles he could see pretty well. At first, he didn't see anything suspicious, then suddenly he saw "a bright flash, almost as if someone had taken a picture with a flash inside a dark theater during a movie,"[1] he said.

A shockwave went through the Chinook, and the whole helicopter pitched forward. The concussion momentarily dazed Mike Maggio, but he quickly recovered and grabbed the controls. "I have the controls," he told Tom, but there had been an electrical failure, so Tom could not hear him. They were both flying the aircraft at that point.

Specialist Hernandez was thrown backward, into the center of the Chinook. His world went from green to black, so he knew that his night vision goggles had been ripped off of his head. He could not feel anything below his waist. He could move his hands, so he immediately found his goggles and put them back on.

"Left gunner is hit! Left gunner is hit!" Specialist Hernandez said, but no one could hear him. "All I could hear was the sound of the engines and the blades popping," he later told me.

Mike looked at Tom, who was staring at him. The controls were stiff and smoke was quickly filling the cockpit. Mike could see the LZ at Lowell to his front. With him and Tom both on the controls they continued the descent toward the LZ.

Specialist Hernandez tried to get up, but it was as though his legs were not there. He was burning, but there were no flames.

"I looked around the inside of the bird. I saw Sergeant Rybolt frantically strapping himself down, securing himself with a seatbelt. I looked for the flight engineer, in the back of the bird, but I could not find him. I prayed that he had not been thrown out of the aircraft, that he was strapped to a seat. I knew what was coming, and I feared the worst. I could hear the engines screaming. I had heard that sound before during heavy sling-load operations. I knew the engines were straining. We were about to crash. I felt helpless lying there. I grabbed what I could to hold on to and waited for it."[2]

Mike and Tom planted the Chinook in the LZ. The aircraft was stable on the ground, but smoke began to build fast. Mike opened his window to try and clear it out of the cockpit. Because they had no power they had no idea what was going on in the back of the helicopter.

Mike pointed out the door. "Get the hell out!" he screamed to Tom, who could not hear him over the engines.

"Cut the engines," Tom yelled back, but Mike had been trying to cut the engines since they landed. The systems were not responding. The blades were still turning and the big turbine engines continued to churn at full RPM.

"Get out!" Mike yelled again and pointed to the back of the helicopter.

Tom crawled between their seats, jumped over Specialist Hernandez without seeing him, and headed out the back. With the engines still at full throttle, Mike followed. As soon as he hopped into the crew area he saw Specialist Hernandez lying on the floor.

Rybolt and Pettit ran to Hernandez, whose foot was barely attached to his leg. Hernandez looked at Rybolt and motioned to get his attention. Then he pointed to his tourniquet. Rybolt grabbed the tourniquet that was attached to Hernandez's gear and slipped it over his leg. "Two inches below the knee," Pettit yelled over the engines.

"What?" Rybolt couldn't hear him.

"Two inches below his knee. Put the tourniquet two inches below his knee!"

"Okay."

Then Pettit leaned down over Hernandez's head. "Are you in any pain?" he screamed.

Hernandez wasn't in any pain, but "he was pasty white and clearly going into shock," Pettit later told me.

Meanwhile, Mike had run off the back ramp, screaming, "Medic! We need a medic!"

The first person he saw was Sergeant First Class Wood, our Pathfinder senior noncommissioned officer. We had sent him to Lowell with a few of his men just before the mission began to assist with the loads. Sergeant First Class Wood turned and ran to get a medic. Mike realized that the engines still had not stopped, so he went back onto the aircraft and cut the fuel to the engines using the emergency system. Within a few seconds the fuel-starved engines began to slow, and eventually stopped.

Back at FOB Fenty my heart stopped beating for a moment. The first report was from the Apaches. "Flex 6-3 is hit. They are going down."

Then the call came: "They are down in the LZ at Lowell. It was an RPG." That report gave me some level of comfort. At least they were inside the security of the COP. The medevac, which was stationed at FOB Bostic for the mission, immediately launched.

After everything was under control Mike Maggio called our TOC, and I spoke with him. "Hernandez is hit, sir. We got shot down. He's hurt."

"Mike, is anyone else hurt? Are you okay?" I asked.

"I'm okay. Hernandez, his leg, he's hurt." Mike was clearly in shock. As he spoke it was difficult to hear him due to the fifty-caliber in the background firing away. I am not sure what they were shooting at, but they were certainly letting it rip. The Apaches had seen the RPG when it was fired and had immediately shot the gunner.

"Mike, how bad is Hernandez?" I asked.

"His leg. They put a tourniquet on his leg. He's going to lose his leg."

"Okay, how bad is the aircraft? Will it fly?"

"We were hit by an RPG. I don't know. No. It hit us right in the gunners' hatch. It exploded inside the aircraft. We didn't have cockpit readings. The multifunctional displays had power, but they were blank." I could almost feel him shaking through the phone.

"Okay, Mike, I need you to stay near the phone. I'll call you back." And I hung up.

Colonel Lewis was standing by in his TOC. He had been tracking the mission just like everyone else. He was giving me time to figure it all out, but he wanted a report as soon as possible. I called him. "Sir, it's Jimmy."

"Jimmy, what's the damage?"

"Hernandez, the left door gunner, was hit. Sounds like an RPG came right in his hatch on short final. They were just about to land."

"Is he the only one hurt?"

"Yes, sir, but Mike, and I'm sure the others, are pretty shook up."

"I imagine so. How bad is the helicopter?"

"Well, it's hard to tell. They flew it in and landed it, so it had power. The engines seem to work, but the electrical systems may be shot. I am going to need a very good maintenance guy to take a look at it. We've got to get that airplane out before daylight or every enemy fighter within a hundred miles will converge on it and our guys will get hammered at daylight."

All year we had listened to the enemy talk about shooting down an aircraft. We knew that the enemy fighter who shot Flex 6-4 down in the Korengal in January was generously rewarded by Taliban leadership. Shooting a helicopter down would give them an information operation victory. If Flex 6-3 was sitting at COP Lowell once it was daylight, the enemy would surge forces to destroy it and film it. Just like Flex 6-4, we'd see the aircraft being destroyed later on Al Jazeera.

"Okay, let me call Rob Dickerson; maybe Rob Devlin can take a look at it. I'll call you back."

"Roger, sir." I hung up. Chief Warrant Officer 4 Rob Devlin was a maintenance examiner in Task Force Lift. He was a very experienced Chinook maintenance test pilot. If anyone could get it cranked and flying, it was Rob.

I called COP Lowell on the secure phone. I knew it was not going to be a pleasant conversation. Mike Maggio answered.

"Mike, Lieutenant Colonel Blackmon."

"Yes, sir." He still sounded shaken up, but much calmer than the first time I spoke to him.

"Mike, I need you and the crew to remain there. We're going to fly a maintenance guy up there in a Black Hawk, and he'll need you guys to crew the bird with him when he flies it out."

"Sir, we've got a medevac about to land and pick us up. It's here to get us! We just got shot down." If there was an ounce of his fiber that wasn't infuriated at me for sending him in to haul out all of that equipment, then it was surely infuriated now.

"Mike, we have to get that bird out of there or it will become the biggest target in Afghanistan by daybreak. I think we are going to send Rob Devlin up there. He will call you and ask you what's working on the aircraft and what's not, so he'll know what tools and parts to bring with him."

"Okay, sir," he said with no emotion at all. I knew he and his crew had been pushed to the limit, and I knew that I was asking a lot of them, but I also knew that Mike Maggio would ultimately make it happen.

"Mike, you did a great job; now I need you to hang in there."

Rob Devlin called Mike and asked him questions about what systems worked and what didn't work. When he was satisfied he said, "I'll see you in a few hours," and hung up.

Devlin packed all the tools and equipment he thought he would need, loaded everything onto a Black Hawk at Bagram, and departed for COP Lowell. Several hours after Flex 6-3 had been shot down by an RPG, Rob Devlin began trying to wire it back together, at least well enough to start the engines. "If we bypass the electrical compartment and get power to the PDP, then we've got a shot at starting the auxiliary power unit and getting the engines going," he had told Mike on the phone, which made me nervous, but not nearly as nervous as the thought of a Chinook sitting on the LZ at COP Lowell once it was daylight.

After about three hours of work, Rob was able to rewire the electrical system to connect the battery directly to the essential battery buss and start the auxiliary power unit, which was all he needed to start the engines. He walked to the command post and called me. "Sir, we've got one good electrical system, and most of the systems we'll need to fly it."

"Can you safely fly it out, Rob?" I asked. "Just tell me straight up."

"Well, I don't want to die, so I'd tell you if I didn't think I could.

The bottom line is, I think I can crank it, and if I can get both engines up to one hundred percent, then, yes. It will fly. I don't know if we'll be able to talk to one another, and we'll be missing some flight systems, but I can fly it out."

"Okay, let's do it," I said.

Mike gathered up his crew. He joined Rob Devlin in the cockpit, and Tom Young rode in back with the crew. Rob cranked it, and got both engines online and up to one hundred percent RPM. The intercom system did not work so the crew could not talk to one another. The only person who could talk on a radio outside the aircraft, to an FOB or another helicopter, was Mike. Rob and Mike agreed to a series of hand-and-arm signals, and notes passed back and forth, to communicate. They used hand-and-arm signals to communicate with the men in the back of the aircraft as well.

The Apaches circled overhead, waiting to escort them back to Asadabad, where another Chinook would meet them and accompany them the rest of the way to FOB Fenty. After handing them off to the other Chinook, the Apaches would return to COP Lowell and provide security for the men there.

Slowly, Rob pulled in power and brought the Chinook to a hover. The flight controls seemed to be working properly, so he took off. They had committed at that point. The Apaches fell in behind him, and they were on their way. They climbed up over the mountain, and the Chinook seemed to be doing great. Once they crested the mountain they began to descend down the backside toward the Kunar. As they descended the men in the back noticed that the aircraft began to vibrate badly. Suddenly, the floor of the helicopter began to shift like it was coming apart.

Tom Young ran to the cabin and screamed, "Stop descending so fast. The floor is shifting!"

Devlin had been descending at about one thousand feet per minute, so he pulled in some power and reduced the descent to five hundred feet per minute. "That's better," Tom yelled and gave a thumbs-up.

Everyone in the TOC was on the verge of an anxiety attack for the fifty minutes it took them to fly to FOB Fenty. Finally, I heard the familiar sound of rotor blades beating the air, a wonderful sound. I exhaled and felt instant relief. They landed safely at home. We were out of that fix, but we still had a significant problem at Lowell. We had to finish closing it. We were past the point of no return. We had to get back on the horse immediately.

Suddenly, a lesson learned long ago flashed into my mind. The mountain phase of Ranger school is conducted just outside Dahlonega, Georgia, primarily in the steep mountains of the Chattahoochee National Forest. Because I grew up hunting and camping in that area, and because I attended North Georgia College, my Ranger buddies asked me to lead their patrols. I knew where almost all of the objectives were located.

By the time we reached mountain phase, in November, we had completed the Ranger assessment phase, patrolled at Fort Benning, Georgia, and had walked countless miles in the deserts of New Mexico. I had begun the course weighing 185 pounds. By the time the parachute canopy opened over my head and my knees were in the breeze over Wimpy Airfield in rural northern Georgia, I weighed 158 pounds. We had begun the course with 352 men. We had added a few men who were recycled—men who'd failed to meet the standards and were required to repeat the phase—to our numbers at each phase, but of those original 352, fifty-three men remained. Each one of us was exhausted and starving.

One frigid December night a young Ranger student from 3rd Ranger Battalion crawled up beside me in the perimeter.

"Blackmon," he whispered. "Will you walk point on my patrol?"

This young Ranger had been put in charge of our patrol, and he needed a "Go" to move on to jungle phase. He was asking me to make sure we made it to the object without getting lost, and just as important, on time. We had not slept more than four hours in three days. It had rained for days and the creeks were up. The temperature was in the mid-twenties, so the Ranger instructors (RI) had a choice. If they stopped us then they had to let us build warming fires, otherwise they had to keep walking us to ensure no one got hypothermia. To our dismay, they sadistically chose to keep walking us. Also, they could not put us in the creeks. We had to find crossing points. Some nights we walked several kilometers out of the way to find a log across the creeks to cross. The men had hit a wall.

"Sure. Give me the map and the grid," I said.

He handed me the map, and lying beside each other under a canopy of mountain laurel, we threw a poncho over our heads. I pulled out a red-lens flashlight and plotted the grid to our objective.

"Dude. This is going to suck," I told him. "We've gotta get to three forks, and to get there we're gonna have to climb a monster mountain."

"Can you get us there?" he asked.

I smiled at him. "I know that place well. I've used it as a base camp for hunting trips many times. My parents camped there when I was just a kid. Yes, I can get us there, but the hard part is going to be getting the guys over that mountain. We need to leave as quickly as we can. As soon as the RIs will let us begin movement we need to go. Put the support squad up front. They will be the slowest with their heavy machine guns. We'll go as fast as they can move."

"Okay. Thanks, man," he said and smiled.

"No problem," I said and smiled back, feeling good to be able to help.

I plotted a course and we moved out quietly, slipping through the forest. It was not overly difficult to navigate in the mountains. I used terrain association mostly. If I were in a valley or on a ridge I'd use my pace count to measure the distance, but primarily I just looked at the terrain features on the map, and even in the dark I could figure out where to go. I stopped the patrol at the base of the mountain and the patrol leader came forward. "What's up?" he asked, praying I wasn't lost.

"This is it. From here we've got a long climb, then it's downhill to the objective. Tell the guys to stay tight and just keep walking," I said.

"Okay," he said, then passed the word to "keep it tight" as we climbed.

We walked uphill for what seemed like hours, then the complaints began to emerge. Initially, they were random complaints. I could hear the whispers behind me. The machine gunners were suffering under a much heavier load than everyone else. "Let's take a break," they said. "We need to take a knee for a few minutes."

At first I acted like I didn't hear them, but soon a chorus emerged behind me. They were begging me to stop and take a break. About two-thirds of the way up the mountain I gave the hand-and-arm signal to halt, and I took a knee.

Within seconds a Ranger instructor came scrambling up the mountain. He pushed Rangers out of his way to get to the front of the patrol. When he got to me he was breathing pretty heavily. He put his hand on my shoulder and then spit a big stream of black tobacco. "What are you doing, Ranger?" he asked.

"Rest halt, Sergeant," I said. "The men need a break."

"Ranger, don't ever stop before you crest the mountain. If you stop now it will take an hour to get them moving again. It's all in their heads. They'll want to quit. Now get this patrol moving. Push them to the top and then you can conduct a rest halt," he said, and walked away.

"Roger, Sergeant," I said.

It had been seventeen years since I had learned that lesson, but it was so clear to me at that moment, it was like I'd experienced it the day prior. We've got to get back in the saddle, I thought. We can't stop now. I told Jack, "Call COP Lowell and figure out what loads are left. We've got to go right back in there tomorrow night."

I knew if I gave them a few days to think about how close they'd come to death it would be almost impossible to get them back in the saddle. I could not let them stop before we crested the mountain, so Jack, Jillian, the planners, and I began working the plan. I called Colonel George, Jack called Colonel George's chief of operations, and Jillian went to work trying to figure out exactly where the RPG was shot from and how to counter such threats the following night.

As a leader, I failed four of my men that night. Mike, Tom, Sergeant Rybolt, and Sergeant Pettit landed and returned to their company area. In my mind, they were not physically injured, so I focused my attention on what we were going to do next. The mission was important, vitally important, but I should have stopped what I was doing and gone to see how they were doing.

Mike would later say, "It was the biggest disappointment in my fifteen years of service. Not a single person in the command, other than the executive officer, who wanted to make sure we had all of our equipment, was there when we landed at FOB Fenty. I felt like the unit had abandoned us."

Those words rightfully stung. I realized that everyone responds to traumatic events in very different ways. I knew they were not physically hurt, and I had a mission to plan. I didn't really think about it.

In fact, I expected Mike to come busting through the door to tell everyone how he had pulled it off, but I was wrong.

In hindsight, I made a terrible mistake. The only way to know how a soldier is feeling, how he is coping, is to ask, to spend time talking to him. I should have known that. Throughout our deployment I had seen soldiers surprise me with their reaction to trauma and death. Men that I thought would handle death stoically broke down and needed consoling. Others, whom I thought would have a difficult time, never wavered. They just kept soldiering on. A soldier's reaction to death is unpredictable, so leaders should always be prepared for the worst. Mike does not harbor ill feelings, but he and his crew have my apologies. I failed them that night, and I promised it would never happen again.

Over the following three nights we closed COP Lowell. The enemy did not interfere with our operation again. Finally, with a month left in our deployment, the Kamdesh was closed.

(Note: Specialist Juan Carlos Hernandez lost his right leg from the knee down. When we returned to Fort Campbell in December, he was already walking with a prosthetic and planning a ski trip.)

For war was not just a military campaign but also a parable. There were lessons of camaraderie and duty and inscrutable fate. There were lessons of honor and courage, of compassion and sacrifice. And then there was the saddest lesson, to be learned again and again in the coming weeks as they fought across Sicily, and in the coming months as they fought their way back toward a world at peace: that war is corrupting, that it corrodes the soul and tarnishes the spirit, that even the excellent and the superior can be defiled, and that no heart would remain unstained.

—RICK ATKINSON, *THE DAY OF BATTLE*

BITTERSWEET GOODBYE

By November our replacements had begun to flow into Fenty in earnest. Our sister squadron, 3-17 Cavalry, had arrived to replace us. We began the same relief-in-place process that we had conducted with 2-17 Cavalry a year prior. Slowly, our soldiers began to board helicopters and airplanes, headed for home. In Chinooks, Black Hawks, and C-130s, they trickled out until at last only I, Command Sergeant Major Eric Thom, Jack, Jillian, and Mike Woodhouse remained. With five days until the official transfer of authority, 3-17 Cavalry had the reins. Our services were needed only for occasional advice; otherwise we remained out of their way. I felt "in the way" at a place where I had never felt more ownership.

I knew what was coming, and I was left to assume that Jack, Sergeant Major Thom, and Mike did as well, but we never spoke of it—the anxiety of leaving. Some days it felt like I was sleepwalking. It's a hard thing to leave a life of deep routine, particularly when you've poured your heart and soul into a mission as we had. The mission in N2KL had become as much a part of us as our army life in general. It *was* our life. I felt guilty for wanting to stay, ashamed of not being excited to go home, but I didn't want to give it up. I missed my family, wanted to be with them so badly, but leaving felt terribly wrong. I also knew that the bonds that we had formed over an emotional year would be cleanly severed upon return to Fort Campbell. Within ninety days we would all go our separate ways, begin the next chapter in our army lives. Such is the life of a soldier.

It was Jillian's first deployment. She didn't know what to expect, and so she suffered, perhaps the most, from the whirlwind of emotions. "3-17 Cavalry just needed the space to settle into their mission. I was no longer needed, and it was torturous to be there and not feel like I was doing anything,"[1] she said.

Jillian wrote in her journal as she struggled to make sense of it all:

> At mealtime we would trudge to the dining facility and exchange uncomfortable remarks about the not-so-distant past. Those conversations made me think about how such a year of compact action and experiences would unjustly be condensed in a typical history book sentence (e.g. ". . . and in the charge X number of lives were lost, but the battle was won"). The more global headlines would certainly talk about Afghan elections, or perhaps the closing of the outposts in the Kamdesh, or the failures and losses in the Korengal Valley. Then I wondered, did I do enough to help? Did my being here matter? This was important to me, having left my first child behind with her grandparents—I should have a good reason to leave a child; if not, then I failed as a parent and as a soldier.[2]

The day finally arrived. Command Sergeant Major Thom and I cased the 7th Squadron, 17th Cavalry Regimental colors, I gave Colonel Randy George a big hug, and we boarded a Black Hawk for Bagram. It was a beautifully bright, sunny day. I felt a multitude of conflicting emotions as I watched FOB Fenty disappear into the distance.

> Jillian wrote:
> When we donned all of our gear for our final flight out of Jalalabad, I realized that I didn't want to leave. Didn't anyone know the war was still going on? I should be here! I looked across the helicopter at Lt. Col. Blackmon. He looked up from viewing the airfield and looked at me, too. I swear he could see the tears in my eyes, and he understood them. I looked away, not embarrassed at all, just wanting to keep

thinking. I somehow didn't let those tears fall. I certainly would have let them, but I was still somewhat numb. I still felt like I, as an individual, was too insignificant to make this personal. I watched the airfield shrink from my sight.[3]

I once heard a man say that the business of life is the accumulation of memories. I quite agree with that poignant statement. In Afghanistan we accumulated memories by the score, memories that we would cherish for the rest of our lives, as well as painful memories that would haunt our minds for years to come. My fondest memories were not of battles won, or missions accomplished, but rather, memories of the soldiers.

I believe that it is the soldiers that matter most, each and every one of them, and I believe that will always be the case. The implements of killing, the technology, will continue to evolve, as they have since Cain slew Abel, but war will always be a human endeavor. I tried to get the most out of our soldiers, to encourage them to think critically, and perhaps most important, I tried to create a climate of trust and respect. Our overarching mission was to maximize our collective potential in support of the ground forces. I hope, I believe, we accomplished that mission.

Writing it all down has been bittersweet. It felt good to put an extraordinary year of our lives on paper, to live it again in some small way. But some days, as I wrote, I felt the wind go right out of my lungs and a pain begin to well up in my chest, and I would miss it. I'd miss it with every fiber of my being and I'd want to keep on living it, somehow go back. I hope I captured that feeling for my soldiers as well. It's gone—that year and those experiences are forever gone—but I hope my soldiers can hold on to these words and feel it again, if only for a speck of time.

Today, our army is the most highly trained and capable force the world has ever known. We are incredibly flexible and adaptive, a result of empowering junior leaders to solve problems and make decisions at the lowest level. We have exploited new technologies at an unprecedented pace. The resident technology at the battalion level in 2009 was commensurate with that of a division in 2003. We successfully learned to exploit both the technology and the skills of our soldiers to accomplish a multitude of missions for over a decade of war. Furthermore, we learned, grew, and became more and more capable with each deployment to Iraq and Afghanistan.

I don't know what the future will hold. I don't know what technologies will emerge in the coming decades, but I do know that at the end of the day we will have to trust in the American soldier, for he will carry freedom's torch. He will defend what we hold most dear.

I did not write this book to try and etch a tiny footnote in history about something I did. I wrote it to ensure that a handful of America's sons and daughters, whose history would have otherwise been ignored, are remembered. At the writing of this book our combat mission in Afghanistan had just ended, after thirteen years of war. America's longest war will not soon be forgotten, but the men and women who fought it will fade with time to nothing more than serial numbers on a roster pressed between pages, if we allow it. The story I have told demonstrates that this war was fought by everyday Americans, men and women from Anytown, USA. They came from wealthy and poor families alike. Their mothers and fathers were doctors, lawyers, mechanics, and mill workers. They had PhDs and GEDs. They were black, white, Hispanic, Native American, Asian, Samoan, and Latino.

They were all extraordinary.

AFTERWORD

In 2010, Task Force Pale Horse became the first unit in history to win both the Ellis D. Parker Aviation Unit of the Year award and the Army Aviation Association of America (AAAA) Combat Unit of the Year award in the same year. For the battle in the Watapur Valley, Task Force Pale Horse was awarded the Valorous Unit Award. Chief Warrant Officer 3 Scott Stradley was selected as the AAAA Aviator of the Year, Chief Warrant Officer 3 Brian Lackey was selected as the Army Aviation Trainer of the Year, and the Dustoff 2-4 hoist mission in the Watapur Valley won the Air/Sea Rescue of the Year Award. Captain Joe McCarthy won the Aubry "Red" Newman leadership award, and Staff Sergeant Joebob Parker won the AAAA Avionics Award. Captain Brendan McCriskin won the AAAA Aviation Medicine Award, and Staff Sergeant Emmett Spraktes was selected as the Army Aviation DUSTOFF Flight Medic of the Year. Chief Warrant Officer 4 Patrick Benson won the Order of Daedalians Valor Award for his actions after being shot in the Shuryak Valley.

Lieutenant Colonel Jimmy Blackmon relinquished command in May 2010. He subsequently attended the National War College in Washington, DC, where he earned a master's degree in national policy and strategic studies. In December 2011 he was promoted to colonel, and in May 2012, he assumed command of the 159th Combat Aviation Brigade (Task Force Thunder). He deployed the brigade back to eastern Afghanistan in January 2014.

In 2010, Major Jack Murphy was assigned as an observer controller at the National Training Center in California. Jack was promoted to lieutenant colonel, and in the summer of 2013 he assumed command of 2nd Squadron, 17th Cavalry Regiment.

Captain Jillian Wisniewski moved to Fort Rucker, Alabama, where she taught intelligence at the aviation captain's career course. In 2013 she began work on a master's degree in engineering and management at MIT. Her husband Isaac attended Harvard. Both teach at the United States Military Academy at West Point.

Captain Joe McCarthy was selected as a Joint Chiefs of Staff intern. Joe earned a master's degree in public policy management at Georgetown University. Joe then served as the military assistant to Secretary of Defense Robert Gates and later Secretary Leon Panetta. Following his fellowship, Joe returned to the 159th Combat Aviation Brigade, where he served as Colonel Blackmon's brigade operations officer and later executive officer.

Chief Warrant Officer Adam Stead slowly recovered from his gunshot wound to the head. It was a long and challenging road for Adam, but he was strong and determined. Words fall short in describing the love and devotion of Carrie Stead. Carrie patiently nursed her husband back to health over several extremely challenging years. She is truly the model army spouse. Adam medically retired from the army in October 2011. After his retirement, Adam, Carrie, and their son Cohen moved to Charlotte, North Carolina. In March 2014, Adam and Carried welcomed a new baby boy into their family, Eli Stead.

After multiple surgeries Chief Warrant Officer 4 Patrick Benson recovered from his gunshot wound. He retired in Clarksville, Tennessee.

Specialist Christopher McKaig, who survived against all odds at Wanat, has continued to rise through the noncommissioned officer ranks. At the writing of this book he served as a staff sergeant in the Pathfinder Company in 159th Combat Aviation Brigade.

Specialist Juan Carlos Hernandez lost his foot in the Kamdesh Valley, but that did not slow him down. Carlos is the GP of Ride 2 Recovery, an organization that helps wounded warriors recover from their combat injuries through cycling.

Colonel Ron Lewis was promoted to brigadier general. He returned to Afghanistan as the deputy commanding general for support, 101st Airborne Division (Air Assault). Following that assignment he was promoted to major general and assigned as the public affairs officer

of the United States Army. In July 2015 he was promoted to lieutenant general and assigned as the senior military assistant to the
secretary of defense, Ashton Carter.

Following command, Colonel Randy George served on the Coun-
cil on Foreign Relations. Following that assignment he served as the
executive officer to the vice chief of staff of the army and later executive officer to the commanding general, U.S. Central Command. In
2014, he was promoted to brigadier general and assigned as the deputy commanding general of the 4th Infantry Division, Fort Carson,
Colorado.

I owe a special thanks to numerous people who made this book
possible. First and foremost I want to thank the men and women of
Task Force Pale Horse who were willing to dig through their jour-
nals and patiently endure literally hundreds of emails as I tried to
get the story right. Their willingness to relive some challenging and
oftentimes very emotional memories made the story truly authentic. There were also several people whose sage advice I relied upon.
General (Ret.) Richard "Commander" Cody, our thirty-first vice
chief of staff of the army and one of the most influential aviators in
history, read the entire manuscript. I thank you for your counsel and
mentorship.

Stuart Jones read the entire manuscript and gave wonderful advice
and suggestions as I wrote. His optimism kept me motivated to continue writing with enthusiasm. Author, editor, and friend Renea Winchester gave wonderful insights and encouragement, but perhaps most
important, she urged me to "go big." She saw incredible promise in
the book and convinced me to find an agent who would have the same
enthusiasm. Fortunately, I found that man. My agent, Roger Williams,
fell in love with the story from the start. Thank you for making a
dream come true, Roger.

I owe a lifelong debt of gratitude to the English Department at Cal-
houn High School. Dr. Bob Linn, Ms. Gail Satterfield, Mrs. Pat Leming,
and the late Mr. Ken Proctor were an inspiration to me as a young
man. They lit a literary spark in me that took many years to ignite, but
eventually it evolved into an inextinguishable flame. I am so very thank-
ful that they never gave up. I graduated high school in 1987, but they
have remained my biggest supporters. Thank you for making a difference in the lives of countless young men and women over the years.

Finally, I want to thank my wife, Lisa. From the day we met in January 1988, I have loved you more than you can imagine. By marrying me you committed your life to the army, to your nation, yet you never received a paycheck and your sacrifices almost always went unnoticed. Countless times I've heard baseball parents say, "I don't know how you do it. I know I certainly could not."

Your ever-supportive reply: "This is our life. This is what we do."

ENDNOTES

Preface
1. As with numerous place-names in Afghanistan, Kunar is also spelled Konar. For the purpose of the book I will use Kunar throughout.
2. Nathan Longworth, email to author, May 13, 2013.
3. Gary Parsons, interview with author, May 17, 2013.
4. Ernest Hemingway, *A Farewell to Arms* (New York: Scribner, 2012).

Surrounded by Talent
1. General Order 5 in its entirety read:
   "The 101st Airborne Division, which was activated on August 16, 1942, at Camp Claiborne, Louisiana, has no history, but a rendezvous with destiny. Like the early American pioneers whose invincible courage was the foundation stone of this nation, we have broken with the past and its traditions in order to establish our claim to the future.
   "Due to the nature of our armament and the tactics in which we shall perfect ourselves, we shall be called upon to carry out operations of far-reaching military importance and we shall habitually go into action when the need is immediate and extreme. Let me call your attention to the fact that our badge is the great American eagle. This is a fitting emblem for a division that will crush its enemies by falling upon them like a thunderbolt from the skies.
   "The history we shall make, the record of high achievement we hope to write in the annals of the American Army and the American people, depends wholly and completely on the men of this division. Each individual, each officer and each enlisted man, must therefore regard himself as a necessary part of a complex and powerful instrument for the overcoming of the enemies of the nation. Each, in his own job, must realize that he is not only a means, but an indispensable means for obtaining the goal of victory. It is, therefore, not too much to say that the future itself, in whose molding we expect to have our share, is in the hands of the soldiers of the 101st Airborne Division." Lee, W.C., *General Order 5* (Camp Claiborne, LA)

Pre-Deployment Site Survey
1. The TOC serves as the battalion's primary command and control hub (information management center), assisting the battalion commander in synchronizing operations. It is the location in the battalion where the majority of planning, staff coordination, plan execution, receiving/disseminating information, and monitoring of key events occur. Since writing this book the term "TOC" has been replaced by "command post."
2. Lester W. Grau, ed. *The Bear Went Over the Mountain: Soviet Combat Tactics in Afghanistan* (Washington, DC: National Defense University Press, 1996).
3. *Ibid.,* 177.

Wanat
1. "Wanat: Combat Action in Afghanistan, 2008." (Ft. Leavenworth, KS: Combat Studies Institute Press, 2010), 45.
2. The events that took place at Wanat came from my notes, taken in the TF Out Front TOC and countless days spent talking with Chris McKaig.

A Cavalry State of Mind
1. A guidon is a small flag. The guidon is carried by a select solider who is always located with the commander. Wherever the commander is, so goes the guidon. The guidon is used to rally the troopers in battle. It represents their unity. Different colors represent the different branches of service. The cavalry guidon is red and white.

Counterinsurgency
1. Thomas H. Johnson and M. Chris Mason. "No Sign until the Burst of Fire: Understanding the Pakistan-Afghanistan Frontier." *International Security*, Vol. 32, 61. 2008
2. *Ibid.,* 59.
3. G. R. Gleig. *Sale's Brigade in Afghanistan, with an account of the Seizure and Defense of Jellalabad.* (London: John Murray, Albermarle Street, 1846), 5.
4. *Ibid.,* 11.
5. Johnson and Mason. "No Sign until the Burst of Fire: Understanding the Pakistan-Afghanistan Frontier," 59.

Korengal—Learning the Hard Way
1. Matthew D. McNeal, email to author, February 26, 2013.
2. Kendall Clarke, in discussion with author, April 24, 2013.

Cowboys and Indians
1. The information about Jillian Wisniewski was gathered between 2008 and 2015, but I conducted a formal interview via email on April 20, 2014.

2. The information about Jay Karvaski's life and experiences was gathered over several years, although a formal interview occurred on April 20, 2014. Jay Karvaski and I served together for over five years. He was my intelligence noncommissioned officer in charge of TF Pale Horse, and he was my brigade noncommissioned officer of charge when I commanded TF Thunder. We spent two years together in RC-East.

Bari Ali

1. Azad Ebrahimzadeh, email to author, June 6, 2014.
2. Russell Klika, email to author, May 18, 2014.
3. *Ibid.*
4. *Ibid.*
5. Azad Ebrahimzadeh, telephone interview with the author, March 20, 2014.
6. Klika, email, May 18, 2014.

Mountain Warrior

1. Rodney Dycus, email to author, April 17, 2014.

The Plan Begins to Unravel

1. It is a great tradition in the 3rd Armored Cavalry Regiment to memorize the history of the regiment. A tribute to General Scott's words is used in the regimental accolade. When the regiment forms up, the regimental commander posts himself at the front of the formation and yells to the regiment, "Prepare for the regimental accolade."
   The troopers reply, "Prepare to sound off," in unison.
   Commander: "Brave Rifles."
   Troopers: "Veterans."
   Commander: "Blood and steel."
   Troopers: "AI-EE-YAH!"
2. Greg Jaffe, "Gen. McChrystal, New Afghanistan Commander, Will Review Troop Placements," *The Washington Post,* June 16, 2009.
3. Mark O'Donnell, email to author, May 2, 2014.
4. *Ibid.*
5. *Ibid.*
6. Michael Harrison, "Operation Mountain Fire: The Assault of Barg-e Matal" (unpublished manuscript, July 12, 2010), Microsoft Word file.
7. Mark O'Donnell, email to author, May 3, 2014.
8. Harrison, "Operation Mountain Fire: The Assault of Barg-e Matal."
9. O'Donnell, email to author, May 2, 2014.
10. O'Donnell, email to author, May 3, 2014.
11. *Ibid.*
12. *Ibid.*
13. Michael Harrison, email to author, June 5, 2014.
14. Chad B, multiple emails and discussions with the author throughout the

spring of 2013; Michael Harrison, "Operation Mountain Fire: The Assault of Barg-e Matal."

The Watapur

1. Roosevelt, Theodore, *The Rough Riders*. (New York: The Library of America, 2004), 18.
2. Note on sources: This chapter was written based on my own personal recollections, notes, sworn statements of participants, and multiple interviews and emails with those involved.
3. Charles L. Folk, email to author, February 22, 2013.
4. Chad Marzec, email to author, April 24, 2013.
5. Asadabad was approximately an eight-minute flight from the Watapur Valley. Asadabad, also FOB Wright, was our FARP and central hub for everything in the Kunar and Pech. We had four arming and refueling points established on large cement pads. Abad was also home to a forward surgical team.
6. Chad Marzec, email to author, April 24, 2013. Chad Marzec would later be shot through the ankle in an almost identical situation in the Watapur. He was evacuated from Afghanistan to later fully recover and continue service.
7. Scott Hill, Scott Stradley, emails to the author, May 2–3, 2014.
8. "A DART is comprised of select personnel who perform assessment, repairs, and recovery of downed aircraft. This team is equipped, trained, and rehearsed to accomplish aircraft recovery in various environments and conditions." Field Manual (FM) 3-04.513/Aircraft Recovery Operations. (Washington, DC: Headquarters, Department of the Army, 21 July, 2008), 1–2.
9. Sergeant First Class Ventura wanted the Kiowas to conduct Close Combat Attacks (CCA). "CCA is defined as a coordinated attack by Army aircraft against targets that are in close proximity to friendly forces. During CCA, the ARC/SWT engages enemy units with direct fires that impact near friendly forces. Targets may range from tens of meters to a few thousand meters from friendly forces." Field Manual (FM) 3-04.126, Attack Reconnaissance Helicopter Operations (Washington, DC: Headquarters, Department of the Army, 16 February, 2007), 3–59.
10. SSG Emmett William Spraktes with Victoria M. Newman, *Selfish Prayer: How California National Guard DUSTOFF Changed the Face of Army Medevac amid Chaos, Carnage and Politics of War*. (North Charleston, SC: CreateSpace Independent Publishing Platform), 2013.
11. Emmett Spraktes, email to author, June 11, 2014.
12. Spraktes with Newman, *Selfish Prayer*, 200.
13. Spraktes, email to author, June 11, 2014.
14. *Ibid.*
15. *Ibid.*

16. The account of Emmett Spraktes's actions on the ground and the entire Dustoff 2-4 crew came from multiple sources: Scott H. Stradley, sworn statement, July 18, 2009; Ryan E. Neal, sworn statement, July 19, 2009; Brandon Erdmann, "Watapur Recollections," email to the author, February 27, 2013; multiple emails and telephone conversations with Emmett Spraktes, Brian Pearl, and Henriques Ventura.
17. Joseph McCarthy, email to author, February 24, 2013; Jean-Jacques Murphy, in discussion with the author, March 12, 2013.
18. The account of the speedball resupply was taken from my field notes and multiple emails and telephone conversations with Jean-Jacques Murphy, Joseph McCarthy, and Raymond Andrel.
19. Roosevelt, *The Rough Riders*, 18.
20. *Ibid.,* 19–20.

Ganjgal and Shuryak
1. The conversation between Ryan Neal's team and Will Swenson came from Ryan's statement immediately following the battle and my interviews with him.
2. *Ibid.*
3. *Ibid.*
4. The medevac pilot-in-command shared this with me and other pilots after the battle.
5. Jerry Wood, email to author, March 31, 2014.
6. Michael Woodhouse, in conversation with the author.
7. Patrick Benson, email to author, March 21, 2014.
8. Carrie Stead, email to author, May 23, 2014.
9. *Ibid.*
10. *Ibid.*
11. *Ibid.*

Getting Out of Nuristan
1. Colonel Brad Brown was very helpful in recalling the specifics of this battle. We corresponded via email numerous times to ensure the accuracy of the event.
2. Brendan McCriskin, email to author, March 28, 2014.
3. *Ibid.*

COP Keating
1. Clint Romesha, telephone conversation with author, April 1, 2015.
2. *Ibid.*
3. Brendan McCriskin, email to author, April 18, 2014.

COP Lowell
1. Juan Carlos Hernandez, email to author, June 4, 2014.
2. *Ibid.*

Bittersweet Goodbye
1. Jillian Wisniewski, email to author, May 29, 2014.
2. *Ibid.*
3. *Ibid.*

INDEX